THE NEW SOCIAL CONTRACT
ESSAYS ON GAUTHIER

THE NEW SOCIAL CONTRACT

ESSAYS ON GAUTHIER

Edited by

Ellen Frankel Paul, Fred D. Miller Jr, Jeffrey Paul and John Ahrens

BASIL BLACKWELL

for the
Social Philosophy and Policy Center
Bowling Green State University

Typeset in 10 on 12 pt Ehrhardt
by Columns of Reading
Printed in Great Britain by Whitstable Litho, Kent.

Contents

GILBERT HARMAN   Rationality in Agreement: A   1
Commentary on Gauthier's
Morals by Agreement

KURT BAIER   Rationality, Value and   17
Preference

JAMES S. FISHKIN   Bargaining, Justice, and   46
Justification: Towards
Reconstruction

RUSSELL HARDIN   Bargaining for Justice   65

JAMES M. BUCHANAN   The Gauthier Enterprise   75

EDWARD F. McCLENNEN   Constrained Maximization and   95
Resolute Choice

CHRISTOPHER W. MORRIS   The Relation between   119
Self-Interest and Justice in
Contractarian Ethics

LAURENCE THOMAS   Rationality and Affectivity: The   154
Metaphysics of the Moral Self

DAVID GAUTHIER   Morality, Rational Choice, and   173
Semantic Representation: A
Reply to My Critics

INTRODUCTION

The idea that individuals are bound together in society by a contract – real, implied, or hypothetical – is one that can be traced at least as far back in the Western philosophical tradition as the writings of Plato. However, most contemporary versions of social contract theory can be traced either to John Locke or to Thomas Hobbes. Lockean and Hobbesian versions of social contract theory have at least one significant feature in common: civil society is grounded in an appeal to a hypothetical "state of nature." That is, civil society, which is characterized by the existence of positive laws and determinate procedures for the enforcement of these laws, is thought by both Locke and Hobbes to be justified and shaped by the recognition on the part of all rational persons that it is an improvement over the rigors of the state of nature. However, Locke and Hobbes differ radically on the question of just what the social contract accomplishes.

According to Locke, human beings, even in the state of nature, are bound by the Law of Nature. Prior to the rise of civil society, it is equally the responsibility of all persons to enforce this Law. But this is ineffective at worst and inefficient at best; and, thus, it is in the interest of all individuals to relinquish their right to identify and enforce the Law of Nature to a set of mutually acceptable institutions, i.e., to civil government. The social contract, then, is a device for justifying enforcement by government of *preexisting* moral principles.

Hobbes, on the other hand, argues that persons in the state of nature are not bound by duties to others. Rather, they need only to consider their own interests. Thus, says Hobbes, life in the state of nature is "nasty, poor, solitary, brutish, and short." It is so for two reasons: first, no person is so superior to others that he can hope to have much success in the pursuit of his interest in the face of universal opposition; and second, the absence of effective restraints on individual pursuit of self-interest precludes the enjoyment of the fruits of cooperative activity. The rigors of the state of nature thus encourage rational individuals to accept some principles of morality, i.e., some constraints on individual pursuit of self-interest. The social contract thus becomes a device for deriving these principles, as well as justifying the institutions to enforce them.

The most influential version of social contract theory in recent years is that of John Rawls's *A Theory of Justice*. The parties to Rawls's hypothetical contract are construed as self-interested individuals whose primary concern is to agree upon a set of principles for the governance of social interaction. David Gauthier, in *Morals by Agreement*, also construes the social contract as a device for deriving moral principles. However, Gauthier's construal of the social contract is different from Rawls's in three important ways. First, Gauthier's contract is an agreement between real and distinct people, whereas Rawls's is not. Rawls strips the parties to the hypothetical social contract of all knowledge of their unique characteristics and interests, and of their social status. Gauthier utilizes what he thinks is a more general contractarian methodology: the content of the social contract is a set of moral principles that would be accepted by rational individuals who know who they are, what they want, and where they stand in society.

Second, Gauthier is concerned primarily with the derivation of moral principles and only secondarily with the derivation of political principles. Gauthier argues that his principles are not merely those that someone would choose *if* he were called on to formulate the basic principles that would govern his society. Rather, he claims to show "why an individual, reasoning from non-moral premises, would accept the constraints of morality on his choices." And it is the acceptance of these moral principles, of *voluntary* constraints on the pursuit of one's own interests, that give shape to the institutions of civil society.

Third, Gauthier claims to generate substantive concepts that are more explicit and more specific than those derived by Rawls: (1) the concept of a morally free zone, within which the constraints of morality would have no place; (2) the principle of maximin relative benefit (or minimax relative concession), according to which the greatest concession one should make, measured as a proportion of the bargainer's stake, is as small as possible; (3) constrained maximization, by which a person is disposed to comply with mutually advantageous constraints; and (4) a proviso prohibiting bettering one's own position through interaction which worsens another's position.

Hence, Gauthier's view represents a significant departure from recent versions of social contract theory and, Gauthier claims, a significant advance. The essays in this volume provide a critical assessment of Gauthier's methodology and of a number of the substantive arguments that he makes.

Gilbert Harman, in "Rationality in Agreement: A Commentary on Gauthier's *Morals by Agreement*," is highly skeptical of Gauthier's attempt to ground his moral theory. He concludes that Gauthier is successful in showing that it can be rational to cooperate in ideal circumstances like one time only Prisoner's Dilemmas. But he deploys numerous counterexamples to show that Gauthier does not demonstrate, even for ideal cases, that rational bargainers will reach an agreement in accordance with the principle of minimax relative concession, or that they will only bargain from a base point of no social interaction at all. And he argues that it is unclear even what Gauthier thinks is the relation between his discussion of ideal cases and actual cases in the world.

In "Rationality, Value, and Preference," Kurt Baier offers a critique of Gauthier's theory of practical rationality – that each person should maximize his expected utility in response to the choices he expects others to make – which he terms the "foundation" of "morals by agreement." Baier argues that the theory of practical rationality is flawed in at least two ways. First, Gauthier's account of preferences is inadequate to support the claim that rationality is the maximization of preference fulfillment. It is inadequate, according to Baier, because it does not correctly represent the connections between preferences and behavior. Second, the theory of practical rationality is flawed because Gauthier fails to give an adequate account of the process of reflection by which we arrive at settled preferences.

James S. Fishkin views Gauthier's *Morals by Agreement* as exemplary of the tendency of contemporary liberal theory to ground its claims in some thought experiment which either transports us to an imaginary choice situation or transforms our motivations. Most such theories, Fishkin argues, are vulnerable to at least one of two problems: they cannot plausibly show that one starting point for negotiations about principles is more appropriate than any other, or they cannot adequately exclude morally suspect preferences as the basis for choice. In "Bargaining, Justice, and Justification: Toward Reconstruction," Fishkin deploys the concept of a coercively structured situation to argue that Gauthier's theory is vulnerable to both objections. And he supplements his critique of Gauthier with an outline of an approach to liberal theory which, he argues, avoids both these problems.

In "Bargaining for Justice," Russell Hardin attacks the core of Gauthier's approach to the issue of distributive justice – the principle of minimax relative concession – on two fronts. First, Hardin argues that bargaining in accordance with this principle will either produce radically suboptimal results (i.e., a smaller social product than might be achieved under other circumstances), or will allocate the social product with little regard for the pattern of contributions that has produced it. In either case, rational agents are not likely to find the principle appealing. And second, the principle of minimax relative concession does not yield a unique outcome for bargaining situations involving more than two parties. Thus, we will find ourselves mired in a futile attempt to analyze the indeterminate number of outcomes that are possible in the real world.

James M. Buchanan, in "The Gauthier Enterprise," considers two different ways in which we might evaluate Gauthier's arguments. Buchanan identifies several problems in Gauthier's conceptualization of the bargaining situation – especially his account of who constitutes the community of bargainers and his view of the role that a theory of rights plays in defining the initial position from which bargaining proceeds. These problems lead Buchanan to conclude that Gauthier fails in his attempt to ground morality in the rational choice behavior of persons. However, he thinks that Gauthier is largely successful in delineating the moral stance that people must adopt if the liberal social order is to be preserved.

In "Constrained Maximization and Resolute Choice," Edward F. McClennen sets out to reconstruct Gauthier's argument in a way that meets what he takes to be a powerful objection. Part of Gauthier's task, as McClennen sees it, is to show that a rational agent will adopt a disposition to cooperate with others even in those cases in which defection is expected to yield him greater utility. McClennen argues that Gauthier fails to show that it is *possible* for an agent to do so: the same reasoning Gauthier uses to show that an agent will want to adopt such a disposition will also persuade the agent to act contrary to the disposition in cases to which it is supposed to apply. McClennen's solution to this problem is to develop the concept of context-dependent preferences and use it to provide parallel reasons for adopting such a disposition and for acting in the appropriate way in cases to which the disposition applies.

A crucial element in Gauthier's argument is the assumption that parties to the (hypothetical) bargaining process which grounds morals by agreement are plausibly construed as reasoning *self-interestedly*, i.e., that the preferences they seek to maximize are all self-regarding rather than other-regarding. In "The Relation between Self-Interest and Contractarian Ethics," Christopher W. Morris surveys a range of possible justifications for this assumption, and concludes that all of them are either inadequate or incompatible with other components of Gauthier's argument. And what is more, Morris argues, this assumption is likely to render morals by agreement unpersuasive (i.e., not likely to be agreed) to a great many people who do in fact have other-regarding preferences.

Laurence Thomas construes Gauthier's arguments as representative of a particular approach to moral philosophy. On this approach, it is first argued that some set of principles or constraints would be accepted by thoroughly nontuistic (i.e., selfish) people. Then it is argued that the affective capacities that people actually have make these constraints quite palatable. But Gauthier also holds that morality must bind regardless of the nature and content of our affections. In "Rationality and Affectivity: The

Metaphysics of the Moral Self," Thomas argues that Gauthier cannot have it both ways because to attempt to do so is to fail to take persons seriously. His argument is that tuistic and nontuistic persons are bound by moral constraints for different reasons and, thus, that it is inappropriate to ground constraints that are intended to bind tuistic persons in nontuistic considerations.

The final essay in this volume is an extended reply by Gauthier to his critics. Taken together, these essays represent a thorough treatment of what is undoubtedly an important contribution to the ongoing refinement of social contract theory.

CONTRIBUTORS

Gilbert Harman is Professor of Philosophy at Princeton University, where he is Chairman of the Committee for Cognitive Studies. With George Miller, he runs the Princeton Cognitive Science Laboratory. He is the author of *Change in View: Principles of Reasoning* (1986), *The Nature of Morality: An Introduction to Ethics* (1977), and *Thought* (1973). He is also the editor of *On Noam Chomsky* (1974), and, with Donald Davidson, of *Semantics of Natural Languages* (1972) and *The Logic of Grammar* (1975).

Kurt Baier is Distinguished Service Professor of Philosophy at the University of Pittsburgh. He received his D.Phil. from Oxford University in 1952, and has taught philosophy at the University of Melbourne and The Australian National University. He is a past President of the Eastern Division of the American Philosophical Association. Professor Baier is the author of *The Moral Point of View* (Cornell University Press, 1958) and coeditor, with Nicholas Rescher, of *Values and the Future* (The Free Press, 1969).

James S. Fishkin is Professor of Government and Philosophy at the University of Texas at Austin and a Fellow of the Center for Advanced Study in the Behavioral Sciences at Stanford. He holds a Ph.D. in philosophy from Cambridge University and a Ph.D. in political science from Yale University. Professor Fishkin is Associate Editor of *Ethics*, and the author of *Tyranny and Legitimacy* (Johns Hopkins University Press, 1979), *The Limits of Obligation* (Yale University Press, 1982), *Justice, Equal Opportunity and the Family* (Yale University Press, 1983), and *Beyond Subjective Morality* (Yale University Press, 1984).

Russell Hardin is Mellon Foundation Professor of Political Science, Philosophy, and Public Policy Studies at the University of Chicago. He is the author of *Morality within the Limits of Reason* (University of Chicago Press, forthcoming), and *Collective Action* (Johns Hopkins University Press for Resources for the Future, 1982), and the editor of *Ethics: An International Journal of Social, Political and Legal Philosophy*. His articles on rational choice, moral and political philosophy, and nuclear weapons policy have appeared in many journals and books.

CONTRIBUTORS

James Buchanan is Hobart L. Harris University Professor and General Director of the Center for Study of Public Choice at George Mason University, and the recipient of the 1986 Nobel Prize for Economics. Professor Buchanan received his Ph.D. from the University of Chicago in 1948 and has taught economics at Virginia Polytechnic Institute and State University, the University of California at Los Angeles, the University of Virginia, and Florida State University. He is the author of numerous books on economics and public policy, including *Fiscal Theory and Political Economy* (University of North Carolina Press, 1960), *Demand and Supply of Public Goods* (Rand-McNally, 1968), and *The Limits of Liberty: Between Anarchy and Leviathan* (University of Chicago Press, 1975).

Edward F. McClennen teaches at Washington University in St. Louis. He has published numerous articles on topics in decision and game theory, social choice theory, and social and political philosophy. In 1984, he served as Director of a Summer Institute on Public Choice Theory, sponsored by The Council for Philosophical Studies. His book, *Rationality and Dynamic Choice: Foundational Explorations*, is forthcoming from Cambridge University Press. He is currently working on a second book which deals historically and analytically with the concept of rational self-interest and its relevance for the justification of moral principles.

Christopher Morris is Professor of Philosophy at Bowling Green State University. Professor Morris received his Ph.D. in philosophy from the University of Toronto in 1977, and has taught philosophy at the University of California at Riverside, the University of California at Los Angeles, the University of Montreal, the University of Ottawa, and the University of Toronto. He has published numerous scholarly articles and reviews in such journals as *Ethics*, the *American Philosophical Quarterly*, the *Journal of Social Philosophy*, and the *American Political Science Review*.

Laurence Thomas is Professor of Philosophy at Oberlin College. He has taught philosophy at the University of North Carolina at Chapel Hill, the University of Maryland, Notre Dame University, and Harvard University. Professor Thomas has published numerous scholarly essays in such journals as the *Canadian Journal of Philosophy*, the *American Philosophical Quarterly*, the *Personalist*, and the *Journal of Value Inquiry*.

David Gauthier is Distinguished Service Professor of Philosophy at the University of Pittsburgh. The relationship of reason and morality has long been his primary intellectual concern, and provides the theme of *Morals by Agreement*. Having shown, as he continues to believe, that moral constraints have firm roots in rational agreement, he now hopes to explore the underlying account of reason, and the standard of rationality, that are presupposed by the theory of rational choice.

Social Philosophy & Policy 5:2 ISSN 0265–0525

RATIONALITY IN AGREEMENT
A Commentary on Gauthier's *Morals by Agreement*[1]

GILBERT HARMAN

Gauthier's title is potentially misleading. The phrase "morals by agreement" suggests a social contract theory of morality according to which basic moral principles arise out of an actual or hypothetical agreement. John Rawls defends a hypothetical agreement version, arguing that the basic principles of justice are those that would be agreed to in an initial position of fair equality.[2] I myself defend an actual agreement version, arguing that the moral principles that apply to a person derive from implicit conventions the person has accepted in dealing with other people.[3] Gauthier's view is different from either of these sorts of contract theory. Instead, he holds that certain basic principles of impartiality are prior to actual agreements. More precisely, he argues:

(a) rational people will agree to cooperate with each other whenever such cooperation yields a cooperative surplus;

(b) the terms of agreement will distribute the cooperative surplus in accordance with a principle of minimax relative concession (which normally requires an equal distribution of the surplus to all participants); and

(c) rational people will be disposed to cooperate with others who are similarly disposed to follow agreements that satisfy those terms.

1. SUMMARY OF THE ARGUMENT

I begin by summarizing Gauthier's main argument, as I see it. I omit an account of later chapters in the book in which Gauthier considers how the implications of his theory compare with ordinary moral opinions.

[1]David Gauthier, *Morals by Agreement* (Oxford: Oxford University Press, 1986). Subsequent references to this work will be indicated parenthetically in the text by *MA* followed by a page number.

[2]John Rawls, *A Theory of Justice* (Cambridge, MA: Harvard University Press, 1971).

[3]Gilbert Harman, "Moral Relativism Defended," *Philosophical Review*, vol.84 (1975), pp.3–22; reprinted in Jack W. Meiland and Michael Krausz, eds., *Relativism: Cognitive and Moral* (Notre Dame: University of Notre Dame Press, 1982).

Gauthier argues, first, that rational agents will acquire a disposition to cooperate with others who are similarly disposed, even in one time only Prisoner's Dilemmas, if they are able to acquire this disposition and if there is a good enough chance of distinguishing people who are thus disposed to be cooperators from others who are not so disposed.

Prisoner's Dilemmas occur when:

(1) participants can either cooperate or defect;
(2) it is better for all if all cooperate than if all defect; but
(3) any participant would do better to defect no matter what choice the others make.

One time only Prisoner's Dilemmas are to be distinguished from repeated Prisoner's Dilemmas either involving the same participants or occurring publicly enough so that participants know how each other have previously acted in similar Prisoner's dilemmas. In such repeated Prisoner's Dilemmas it may well be in a participant's long term interest to cooperate on a particular occasion, if that might encourage other participants to cooperate in the future. No such consideration of long term interest is relevant in a one time only Prisoner's Dilemma. Gauthier argues that it can nevertheless be rational to acquire a disposition to cooperate with others who are similarly disposed to cooperate in one time only Prisoner's Dilemmas. Whether or not this is rational depends, he argues, on the likelihood that one will be dealing with cooperators and the extent to which they can be recognized and distinguished from noncooperators.

Cooperation yields a cooperative surplus that can typically be divided among participants in various ways. Suppose equally rational participants try to reach an agreement as to how this surplus should be distributed. According to Gauther, they will agree to distribute the surplus in accordance with a principle that he calls minimax relative concession.

For each participant, we can compare the expected utility that person would receive from the base-point situation in which there is no cooperation[4] with the maximum expected utility the person could obtain from some possible way of distributing the cooperative surplus. The difference in these expected utilities is the participant's maximal claim on the cooperative surplus. The participant's expected utility from any other distribution of the surplus can be represented as a certain concession from that maximal claim. The participant's relative concession for that distribution is the fraction that concession would represent of a total concession down to the base point. Gauthier's principle of minimax relative concession says that a distribution is acceptable only if it minimizes the

---

[4] As we shall see in a moment, Gauthier later argues that the base point should be the expected utility of a situation of no interaction at all, cooperative or otherwise.

maximal relative concession made by some participant.

Suppose Gil and Lucy could cooperate with each other by playing one or another of various games. Suppose that each assigns a utility of 0 to noncooperation. Gil most prefers playing Twist and Lucy most prefers playing Twin. Gil's expected utility from their playing Twist is 10, Lucy's is 15. Lucy's expected utility from their playing Twin is 30, Gil's is 3. Gil's relative concession if they play Twist is 0; if they play Twin his relative concession is 70 percent. Lucy's relative concession if they play Twist is 50 percent; if they play Twin, her relative concession is 0. If these are the only options, then Gauthier's principle of minimax relative concession favors their playing Twist over their playing Twin, since the maximal relative concession if they play Twist is Lucy's 50 percent relative concession, as compared with Gil's 70 percent relative concession if they play Twin. Playing Twist rather than Twin minimizes the maximum relative concession.

If the cooperative surplus consists in a divisible good such as money or something that can be exchanged for money, and if the marginal utility curve of the divisible good (or equivalent in money) is flat for each person, then Gauthier's principle requires an equal division of the cooperative surplus among the participants.

Suppose Gil and Lucy find that people will pay to watch them play one game of Twist. Suppose that by now their enjoyment of playing for its own sake has declined to the point at which each is indifferent between playing or not playing, if no one is watching. Suppose also that neither Gil nor Lucy cares whether people watch, except for the money that people are willing to pay to watch. Suppose that Gil and Lucy will be paid a total of $50 to play Twist and suppose that, although Gil is much wealthier than Lucy, the marginal utility to either of an additional dollar now is the same as the marginal utility of an additional dollar after having first received some amount less than $50. Suppose that the utility of not playing is 0 for both. Gil's expected utility from playing and receiving $50 is 10, and Lucy's expected utility from playing and receiving $50 is 30. Then Gil's expected utility from their playing and each receiving $25 is 5, and Lucy's expected utility from that is 15. That is a 50 percent relative concession from both and represents the distribution which minimizes the maximum concession that must be made. So they should distribute the money equally.

Gauthier's argument for an equal division in this sort of case seems to be as follows. Under those conditions it cannot be rational to hold out for more than one's equal share, because that requires that it be rational for others to accept less than an equal share, which is incompatible with the assumption that participants are equally rational. Similarly, it cannot be rational to be willing to accept less than an equal share, because then it would be rational for others to hold out for more than an equal share, which again is incompatible with the assumption of equal rationality. So, rationality requires being willing to accept an equal share.

Recall that Gauthier has already argued that under certain conditions it is rational to acquire a disposition to cooperate with others who are similarly disposed. He now argues that the disposition it is rational to acquire is a disposition to narrow compliance, that is, a disposition to cooperate only on terms that are no worse than would be obtained from minimax relative concession. It is not rational to be more broadly compliant, so that one is disposed to cooperate on less than equal terms as long as one receives some benefit from cooperation. A disposition to be more broadly compliant would encourage others to cooperate on terms that were more favorable to them and less favorable to oneself. On the other hand, to be disposed only to cooperate on terms that are more favorable to oneself and less favorable to others than those determined by minimax relative concession would cut oneself off from other rational cooperators who, as has just been argued, will cooperate only on terms at least as good for them as those obtained from minimax relative concession.

Finally, Gauthier argues that the base point for calculating a particular person's relative concession for a particular distribution of the cooperative surplus should not be taken to be simply what that person would have in the absence of cooperation, but should rather be taken to be what that person would have in the context of no interaction at all with the other participants.

This can make a difference, because in the absence of cooperation among certain people some of these people might be benefiting themselves by worsening the situation of others. This worsening might involve taking things away from the others, doing things which pollute the resources of others, and so forth. So, it will often matter whether the base point for computing minimax relative concession is taken to be the position of no cooperation (allowing for whatever interaction would occur then) or the position of no interaction at all (as if the others were not to exist).

Gauthier argues that a rational agent will accept the proviso that minimax relative concession be determined from a base point of no interaction at all rather than just no cooperation in this case. His argument seems to be that if the agent were to be willing to cooperate on terms that permitted the base point to be other than the position of no interaction, that would only encourage others to benefit themselves at his or her expense in order to lower his or her base point in relation to theirs.

2. COMMENTARY

2.1 *The conditional disposition to cooperate in one time Prisoner's Dilemmas*

I accept Gauthier's argument that rational agents will acquire a disposition to cooperate with others who are similarly disposed, even in one time only Prisoner's Dilemma situations, if they are able to acquire this disposition and there is a good enough chance of distinguishing people who are thus disposed to be cooperators from others who are not so disposed. It is clear that there are conditions under which a rational agent would benefit from such a disposition, and I believe that the relevant disposition can sometimes be acquired simply by adopting a policy of such cooperation. A simple decision is then all that is needed.

How useful is this result? The disposition in question is a disposition to cooperate with others similarly disposed. It comes into play only if one has reason to believe that one is dealing with other cooperators and only if they have reason to believe that one is a cooperator. Normally, the only reliable way to tell whether someone else is a cooperator involves knowing to what extent the other person has cooperated on similar occasions in the past. But then the disposition is not normally going to come into play in one time only Prisoner's Dilemmas. It will normally come into play in situations involving repeated Prisoner's Dilemmas, which are situations in which cooperation can be defended by a straightforward appeal to long-term self-interest.

It is unusual to be in a one time only Prisoner's Dilemma situation with others that one has reason to believe are conditional cooperators, since the one time only aspect of the situation normally prevents one from having relevant evidence about the others. So, the concept of someone who is a conditional cooperator in such a situation will not normally be particularly salient to anyone. Since the concept of a conditional cooperator will not be a salient concept, people will not have formed policies involving the concept. So, few if any people will be conditional cooperators in the relevant sense. So, the conditions needed for conditional cooperators to cooperate in one time only Prisoner's Dilemmas will rarely if ever be met in real life.

Although I agree that under highly idealized conditions it could be rational to dispose oneself to be a conditional cooperator and then rational actually to act from that disposition, I do not agree with Gauthier's assumption (*MA*, pp. 170ff.) that, necessarily, if it is rational to acquire a disposition to do D in circumstances C, then it is rational actually to do D in circumstances C. This assumption is not universally true. Clearly, it is possible to imagine conditions under which it would be rational to take a pill that made one acquire a disposition to act irrationally in circumstances C.

Gauthier's defense of his assumption consists in dismissing a few proposed counterexamples. For example, he claims that it can be rational to carry out a threat of nuclear destruction if the threat has failed to deter the enemy (*MA*, pp.185–186)! I am willing to agree that it might be rational to do this if the rational agent has disposed him- or herself to carry out the threat by developing an intense desire to do so. But there are clearly other cases as well in which the disposition is a disposition to act irrationally.

In particular Gauthier says, "Imperfect actors find it rational to dispose themselves to make less than rational choices. No lesson can be drawn from this about the dispositions and choices of the perfect actor" (*MA*, pp.186). I agree. But then he continues, "If her [i.e. the perfect actor's] dispositions to choose are rational, then surely her choices are also rational." Here I disagree. There is no "surely" about it, as I have just observed. A perfect actor might have a good reason to take a pill that made her imperfect!

2.2 *Minimax relative concession*

The argument I have tentatively attributed to Gauthier for the principle of minimax relative concession is clearly unsound. I considered the (usual) case in which the principle requires an equal distribution of the cooperative surplus. The argument claimed that "it cannot be rational to hold out for more than one's equal share, because that requires that it be rational for others to be willing to accept less than an equal share, which is incompatible with the assumption that participants are equally rational. On the other hand, it cannot be rational to be willing to accept less than an equal share, because then it would be rational for others to hold out for more than an equal share, which again is incompatible with the assumption of equal rationality. So, rationality requires being willing to accept no more than an equal share." (This is my tentative interpretation, not a quotation of Gauthier's words.)

One thing is already wrong in the first step of this argument: "it cannot be rational to hold out for more than one's equal share, because that requires that it be rational for others to be willing to accept less than an equal share, which is incompatible with the assumption that participants are equally rational." It is not incompatible with the assumption of equal rationality to suppose that one party holds out for more than an equal share and that another party is then willing to accept less than an equal share in order to prevent a total loss. An assumption of equal rationality does not imply that participants have equal bargaining power in one or another sense of the phrase "equal bargaining power."

Gauthier later adds the specific assumption that "Our bargainers have no psychological strengths to exploit, or psychological weaknesses to be exploited" (*MA*, p.156). But that assumption is not specific enough to validate his argument for minimax relative concession, as we shall see in a moment.

Gauthier says, "Since each person, as a utility-maximizer, seeks to minimize his concession, then no one can expect any other rational person to be willing to make a concession if he would not be willing to make a similar concession" (*MA*, pp.143–144). The second part of this remark does not follow from the first, but we might simply add it as a further premise to Gauthier's argument. This extra premise says that the bargainers have equal bargaining power in the specific sense that each adopts the same attitude toward any given level of relative concession; all are willing to concede that much or none are. Then the argument seems to go through. But the added premise begs the question.

Consider the corresponding argument that results if appeal is made instead to a different premise, namely, the premise that the bargainers have equal bargaining power in the specific sense that each adopts the same attitude toward ending up with a given level of expected utility as the result of cooperation. The conclusion of this second argument is that the bargainers will agree to an arrangement leaving each of them equally well-off. This conclusion is different from that of the first argument if the bargainers do not start at the same level of well-being.

Consider also a third argument that appeals instead to a third premise: the bargainers have equal bargaining power in the specific sense that each adopts the same attitude toward conceding a given level of expected utility. The conclusion of the third argument is that bargainers will agree to an arrangement that divides up the cooperative surplus in a way that gives each participant an equal increase in expected utility. Assuming that the marginal utility of the distributed good diminishes as one's wealth increases, the conclusion of the third argument distributes more of the surplus to the participants who start out most wealthy, the conclusion of the second argument distributes more of the surplus to the participants who start out least wealthy, and the conclusion of the first argument distributes the surplus equally among participants.

The crucial premises in the second and third arguments require interpersonal comparisons of utility. Gauthier would reject such premises for that reason. In this context he says, "The absolute magnitude of a concession, in terms of utility . . . offers no basis for relating the concessions of different bargainers, since the measure of individual utility does not permit interpersonal comparisons. However, we may introduce a measure of *relative concession* which does enable us to compare the concessions of different bargainers, and which thus gives us a basis for

8 GILBERT HARMAN

determining what concession each must rationally make" (*MA*, pp.134–135). Of course, the controversy over interpersonal comparison of utilities has nothing to do with the purely logical point that I am making.

In any event, Gauthier does not seem to think his argument depends on the impossibility of such interpersonal comparisons. For he adds, "were we to assume a measure of utility permitting interpersonal comparisons, and were we then to be tempted by some principle of equal gain, we should remind ourselves that any such temptation could be countered by a principle of equal loss, in relation to one's claim. The unique acceptability of minimax relative concession is made evident when we balance gain in relation to non-co-operation with loss in relation to claim or potential gain" (*MA*, p.139).

Gauthier's suggestion that minimax relative concession has a "unique acceptability" suggests a different interpretation of his argument from the one with which I began. Perhaps he means to reason as follows: "The bargainers will settle on the most salient way of dividing the cooperative surplus. Minimax relative concession has a unique acceptability, i.e. salience. So they will settle on that."

But what is supposed to be "unique" about minimax relative concession? It is not the only possible principle, since Gauthier explicitly mentions two other possibilities. The other two possibilities are somehow not "acceptable"? Why not? Because they are equally acceptable. But all that follows is that neither of them can be *the* only acceptable principle. Gauthier's idea seems to be that there is a symmetry in these principles that makes it impossible that any one should be distinctively salient.

In any event, I do not agree that someone who finds equal gain a particularly salient principle will also find equal loss (in relation to claim) as salient. Indeed, I would think that most people would not find it so salient. On the other hand, in comparing equal gain with minimax relative concession, people may very well differ as to which is more salient.

Furthermore, to appeal to salience is to appeal to psychological factors that go beyond the rationality of the bargainers. It is true that salience plays an important role in bargaining.[5] But the salience of a given outcome is affected a great deal by past practice and various miscellaneous details of an actual bargaining situation. Salience is a psychological notion. What is salient to one person may not be salient to another. Inasmuch as the outcome of bargaining is determined by what is salient, it is not determined merely by the rationality of the participants, contrary to Gauthier's intentions in giving his argument.

[5]Thomas Schelling, *The Strategy of Conflict* (Cambridge, MA: Harvard University Press, 1960).

2.3   *The rationality of the disposition to narrow compliance*

A narrowly compliant person is disposed to cooperate only when the terms are (nearly) at least as good as could be expected from minimax relative concession. A broadly compliant person is disposed to cooperate whenever such cooperation yields some benefit in relation to universal noncooperation. Gauthier argues (*MA*, p.178ff.) that the narrowly compliant person is better off, because the broadly compliant person can be exploited by others who will insist on arrangements with the broadly compliant person that will give the broadly compliant person less than what is obtainable from minimax relative concession.

But it is far from obvious that a narrowly compliant person will do better than a broadly compliant person. Consider a broadly compliant person who insists on at least an equal share where that can be obtained but is willing to settle for what she can get from those who insist on more than an equal share even with narrowly compliant people. It would seem that this broadly compliant person gets all the benefits the narrowly compliant person gets as well as certain other benefits.

Gauthier says, "In refusing other terms [that provide less than what minimax relative concession would provide], she [the narrowly compliant person] does not diminish her prospects for co-operation with other rational persons, and she ensures that those not disposed to fair co-operation do not enjoy the benefits of any co-operation, thus making their unfairness costly to themselves, and so irrational" (*MA*, p.179). This is not obviously correct. She may very well diminish her prospects for cooperation when compared with the broadly compliant person, as I have just observed. Furthermore, although she deprives those who demand more than an equal share of cooperation with herself, which does deprive them of significant benefit, she does so at some cost to herself also, since she might have had some benefit from cooperation with these other people.

Later in the book, Gauthier gives an argument for the rationality of narrow compliance that parallels his earlier argument that bargainers will agree to minimax relative concession. He says:

> Since no one chooses to constrain his behaviour for its own sake, no person finds it rational to be more compliant than his fellows. Equal rationality demands equal compliance. Since broad compliance is not rational for everyone, it is not rational for anyone. . . . If some persons are less than narrowly compliant, then co-operation is possible only if others are more compliant. But this violates equal rationality. If some persons are more than narrowly compliant, then others would find it advantageous, and so rational, to be less compliant. But this again violates equal rationality. It is

rational for each person to be sufficiently compliant that society is possible if others are equally compliant; it is not rational for anyone to be so compliant that society is possible if others are less compliant; therefore it is rational for each person to be narrowly compliant (*MA*, pp.226–227).

In the previous section of this paper I have already discussed this sort of argument and noted its question begging character. I will come back to it again in the final section of the paper in considering the relation between ideal bargainers in idealized situations and real people in the real world.

2.4 *The proviso that the base point be one of no interaction*
Gauthier offers the following argument to show that the proviso must be accepted:

> The proviso, forbidding the taking of advantage, represents the weakest constraint rationally acceptable to persons who would avoid costly interaction with others, and the strongest constraint rationally acceptable to persons who would be free to benefit themselves. Thus the proviso reflects the equal rationality of persons who must constrain their natural interaction in order to enter into mutually beneficial social relationships (*MA*, p.227).

This argument is obscure and seems to assume that a person has a special desire "to avoid interaction with others that afford them benefits for which he pays the costs," special in that it is not just an instance of wanting to maximize utility.

Elsewhere (*MA*, p.194), Gauthier considers the proper initial condition for people who are at war. If the warring parties try to reach agreement taking as the initial bargaining position the actual position ahead of time, Gauthier says that such an agreement cannot be rationally acceptable to each party.

> [C]learly, an individual would be irrational if she were to dispose herself to comply, voluntarily, with an agreement reached in this way. Someone disposed to comply with agreements that left untouched the fruits of predation would simply invite others to engage in predatory and coercive activities as a prelude to bargaining. . . . We do not deny that, as long as her cost in resisting actual predation exceeds any benefit such resistance would bring her, the victim rationally must acquiesce. But if predatory activity is banned, then she no longer has reason to behave in a way that would maintain its effects (*MA*, p.195).

This is a difficult passage. First, we are told it would be irrational for her to be disposed to comply. Then we are told that she rationally must acquiesce. Finally, we are told that she no longer has any reason to acquiesce once predatory activity is banned. This final remark ignores the consideration that, if she stops adhering to the agreement, so will the others, and there will be a return to the status ex ante. So she does have a reason to continue to acquiesce.

I wonder if we are supposed to attach special weight to the word "voluntarily" in the remark, "But clearly an individual would be irrational if she were to dispose herself to comply, voluntarily, with an agreement reached in this way." Perhaps, "voluntarily" means "in the absence of coercion" or the threat of coercion.

Early in the book, Gauthier says, "If you seize the products of my labour and then say 'Let's make a deal', I may be compelled to accept, but I will not voluntarily comply" (*MA*, p.15). What is the force of "voluntarily" here? Surely, it can be rational to comply in some cases like this. The claim that such compliance is not "voluntary" sounds like a moral claim. But that is irrelevant to Gauthier's enterprise, as I understand it.

I agree that if a less well-off individual could be sure of the elimination even of the threat of coercion, that individual should reach that situation and then stop cooperating and bargain from the resulting position at that point. But it is hard to think of this as relevant if the point of the agreement is to end coercion, since as soon as the agreement is breached, coercion will be possible again.

To this, Gauthier says, "a return to the natural distribution benefits no one. The threat is unreal." I have two objections to this. First, if one party breaches the agreement, then the others lose any reason to keep the agreement with respect to that person. Second, the others may well have a good reason to dispose themselves to return to a state of nature with respect to anyone who violates the agreement, just as nations may have a good reason to threaten nuclear war under certain conditions. The threat can be just as real in both cases.

Suppose the only good is manna from heaven. Twice as much falls in A's territory as in B's. A and B are at war. As a result, they end up with the same benefits, worth about half the manna that falls on B. They make peace on the understanding that A will henceforth give a quarter of its manna to B, so that A and B now end up with the same amount, which leaves them three times as well off as during their war. Gauthier claims that it is irrational for A to adhere to this agreement, since it involves an "unproductive transfer" from A to B, a utility cost for which no service is provided (*MA*, p.197). But that is not so. The service is that B will refrain from attacking A. If B is disposed to attack unless this agreement is adhered to, it is rational for A to adhere to the agreement. And it is rational for B to be so disposed. Gauthier says, "The presence of unproductive transfers [of this sort] in otherwise co-operative arrangements is evidence of residual natural predation." But there need be no actual predation if the agreement is adhered to.

Gauthier also says, "The proviso [that "No person should be worse off in the initial bargaining position than she would be in a non-social context of no interaction"] ... must be accepted by each person for [rational] agreement to be possible." This is obviously false. It is not always irrational to agree to an arrangement that does not satisfy the proviso.

Gauthier argues that adherence to the proviso yields "fairer" agreements. But even this is not always so. Consider his own example (MA, pp. 211–213) of two people who discharge their wastes into the river. One lives upstream from the other. Gauthier's proviso says that bargaining between the two should not start from the status quo ante, but should include in the initial position full compensation to the downstream person from the upstream person for the upstream person's pollution of the stream. That brings the down stream person to the point he would have been at if the upstream person had not polluted at all. For example, the upstream person might pay to have the water purified. But this seems to put the down stream person at an advantage in further trading, since the upstream person has to pay a cost that the downstream person does not have to pay. A fairer principle would have them both pay half the costs.

2.5 How does the argument apply to the real world?

Early in the book, Gauthier says, "Our enquiry will lead us to the rational basis for a morality, not of absolute standards, but of agreed constraints" (MA, p.2). Is the envisioned morality supposed to be our (or someone's) actual morality, or is it supposed to be a hypothetical morality that would only exist under certain conditions? Is the argument that under certain conditions there could be such a morality? Or is it an argument purporting to justify certain actual constraints on us now, constraints which we have actually (?) agreed to?

For the record, my own view is that:

(1) all reasons have their source in desires, interests, intentions, and dispositions of the agent, where
(2) one accepts some of these desires, interests, intentions, and dispositions as a member of a group of people, and
(3) moral reasons always derive from the latter sort of desires, interests, intentions, and dispositions.

Sometimes Gauthier appears to accept a similar view. Sometimes he seems to advocate a different view that allows for other sorts of reasons, reasons which derive from the fact that one might have agreed to something under certain hypothetical conditions.

"The genuinely problematic element in a contractarian theory is not the introduction of morality, but the step from hypothetical agreement to actual moral constraint. . . . Why need [a person] accept, *ex post* in his actual situation, these principles [that would have been agreed to in a particular hypothetical situation] as constraining his choices?" (*MA*, p.9). I do not see that Gauthier ever answers this question. As we have seen, his specific detailed arguments concern highly idealized rational agents.

Yet there are many passages in which Gauthier seems to be advocating an account of actual morality for actual people in actual circumstances that is not a "mere fiction." For example, he says, "In order to take effective account of externalities, each person must choose her strategy to bring about a particular outcome determined by prior agreement among those interacting. This agreement, if rational, will ensure optimality. It may of course be implicit rather than explicit, an understanding or convention rather than a contract. But it is not a mere fiction, since it gives rise to a new mode of interaction, which we identify as co-operation" (*MA*, p.117). And he argues against an alternative view with the remark, "Although co-operators are concerned with the utility outputs rather than the strategic inputs of the outcomes among which they must choose, yet they are not passive in the process of agreement, and its strategic character may not be ignored in our analysis. . . . To suppose that the optimal outcomes are to be taken as indifferent, so that selection among them proceeds simply by lot, is to treat the process of agreement quite apart from its actual dynamic character" (*MA*, p.125).

But in fact Gauthier abstracts away from the actual dynamic character of human conventions. For example, he says that, "for co-operation to be rational, we must suppose that the joint strategy would have been chosen through [a bargaining] procedure, so that each person, recognizing this, may voluntarily accept the strategy" (*MA*, pp.128–9). Why must we suppose this? Is this supposed to be a moral "must"? If so, the theory presupposes something it is supposed to establish. If various different strategies might have resulted from antecedent bargaining, depending on accidents of the bargaining process, so that there is no joint strategy which definitely would have been chosen, that does not imply that each person cannot voluntarily accept the strategy agreed to.

He continues, "Co-operative interaction results from, and is determined by, the choice of a joint strategy. Each then chooses her own actions as required by that strategy; in so doing she is not bargaining with her fellows. Rather, choosing this joint strategy involves bargaining." But surely in real life it is not possible to separate cooperating from bargaining in this way. Cooperating and ceasing to cooperate and threatening to stop are part of the tacit bargaining that goes on all the time in daily life – and it is this sort of bargaining on which ethics is based, in my view.

He adds that, "In agreeing to a joint strategy the bargainers are concerned with the distribution of only the utility that each may receive over and above what she obtains in the initial bargaining position." This is supposed to hold "[i]n any bargain." But in an actual bargaining situation, some of the parties to the bargain may threaten (individually or collectively) to act so as to reduce the utility that someone has in the initial bargaining position. Indeed, this is characteristic of ongoing moral bargaining, in my opinion.

As I have already observed, Gauthier assumes that how compliant a person should be is determined entirely by how rational that person and the others are and is not affected by other differences in the psychology or situation of those involved. Of course, in an actual situation, the latter factors are important, so Gauthier's assumptions do not apply to actual situations. But then how is this supposed to be relevant to the real world?

Gauthier's assumptions about the relevant bargaining situation guarantee that it is a hypothetical bargain, not a real one, since each person is "fully informed. . . . Our bargainers have no psychological strengths to exploit, or psychological weaknesses to be exploited . . . bargaining is cost free . . . " (*MA*, pp.155–156).

Later he says, "We do not of course suppose that our actual moral principles derive historically from a bargain, but in so far as the constraints they impose are acceptable to a rational constrained maximizer, we may fit them into the framework of a morality rationalized by the idea of agreement" (*MA*, p.168). What is meant by "fit them into the framework"? What is the relevance of the hypothetical agreement? What sort of "rationalization" is involved? Is rationalization a good thing?

In my view, our actual moral principles derive from an actual bargain – a contemporary bargain, though, not a historical one. It is implicit but actual.

Chapter 7 begins with the story of a slave society that opts for cooperation instead, raising the question of what to take as the initial bargaining position. Once coercion of slaves is dropped, the agreement is repudiated by the slaves. Gauthier's moral is "that it is rational to comply with a bargain, and so rational to act co-operatively, only if its initial position is non-coercive" (*MA*, p.192). But that is so in this case only because coercion is abandoned as part of the bargain. If the coercion continued, it could still be rational for the slaves to act cooperatively within the framework of that coercion.

Against this sort of reply, Gauthier says:

> We should distinguish between compliance, as the disposition to accept fair and optimal co-operative arrangements, and *acquiescence*, the disposition to accept co-operative arrangements that are less than fair, in order to ensure mutual benefit. . . . Co-operation on terms less than fair is . . . less stable, in failing to gain the whole-hearted acceptance of all participants. Fair co-operation invites a full compliance which each does not stand ready to withdraw because of shifts in the natural distribution . . . (*MA*, p.230).

This assumes that it cannot be rational to acquire a stable disposition to acquiesce in less than fair arrangements. But Gauthier gives no argument for that assumption.

For a final example of the difficulty I have in understanding Gauthier's thoughts about the relation between the ideal and the actual, I note the following bizarre passage: "We may say that those possessing a superior technology are more rational than their fellows, in being better able to relate and devise means to their ends. . . . Our argument in support of the proviso, and in support of narrow compliance, rests on an assumption of equal rationality among persons which differences in technology deny" (*MA*, p.231). Inasmuch as the parties to bargaining are envisioned as having equal knowledge, and inasmuch as technology consists in knowledge, this is correct. But possession of technology can also mean possession of certain products of technology, e.g., bombs and guns. It is unclear how *that* is just a matter of rationality. The Spaniards who conquered the Indian civilizations of the Americas were not more rational simply because they had guns.

3. CONCLUSION

Gauthier's arguments concerning ideal cases are partially successful. Gauthier shows that it can be rational to dispose oneself to cooperate in one time only Prisoner's Dilemmas with others you identify as cooperators. However, he does not demonstrate that such ideally rational bargainers will agree to distribute their cooperative surpluses in accordance with his principle of minimax relative concession. Nor does he show that those who do thus agree should accept the proviso that takes the base point to be that of no interaction at all rather than just no cooperation in the present case. Furthermore, he does not show that rational agents will dispose themselves to adhere only to arrangements that offer them at least as much as would be provided by minimax relative concession plus the proviso. Indeed, it would often be irrational for an agent to restrict his dispositions in that way. Finally, it is unclear what relations Gauthier sees between his discussion of ideal cases and actual cases in the real world.[6]

Philosophy, Princeton University

[6]The research reported here was supported in part by research grants to Princeton University from the James S. McDonnell Foundation and the National Science Foundation under NSF grant number IST8503968. The views and conclusions contained in this paper are those of the author and should not be interpreted as necessarily representing the official policies, either expressed or implied, of the McDonnell Foundation or the U.S. Government.

Social Philosophy & Policy 5:2 ISSN 0265–0525

RATIONALITY, VALUE, AND PREFERENCE*

KURT BAIER

I. THE STRUCTURE OF MORALS BY AGREEMENT

Gauthier's magnificent book[1] erects a conception of morality, "morals by agreement," on the foundation of his own theory of practical rationality. This is as it should be if, as he claims, following Hobbes and others, there is an initial "presumption against morality" (*MA*, p.13) and no theory of morals "can ever serve any useful purpose, unless it can show that all the duties it recommends are also truly endorsed in each individual's reason" (*MA*, p.1), indeed, that it is a requirement of *rationality* that one always satisfy the requirements of *morality* (*MA*, p.5). This means, however, that the initial assumption against morality is inherited by his theory of practical rationality. His theory of morals therefore can serve a useful purpose only if his theory of rationality is sound. In this paper, I want to explore some of the more dubious aspects of that theory to see whether it can bear the heavy load of justification that "morals by agreement" places on it.

The foundation stone of Gauthier's theory of practical rationality is his conception of strategically rational choice in interaction. Individual actors are conceived of as mutually disinterested or, more exactly, "non-tuistic" (*MA*, p.87). Interaction is assumed to take place under three highly artificial conditions: (A) each person is strategically rational, i.e., maximizes her expected utility in response to the choices she expects the others to make; (B) all parties to the interaction know this of one another and know that they know; and (C) each chooses as if her knowledge of the grounds for choice were complete, shared by all, and known by all to be so shared (*MA*, p.61). Under these artificial conditions, natural interaction of such actors has nonoptimal outcomes, which "in 'Prisoner's-Dilemma-type'

* As always, I have benefitted greatly from discussion of some of these problems with Annette Baier, who also allowed me to read her review of Gauthier's book for the *Canadian Journal of Philosophy*. I have also benefited from reading and discussing with Paul Hurley his Ph.D. dissertation, in one of whose chapters he critically examines Gauthier's conception of preference.
  [1] David Gauthier, *Morals by Agreement* (Oxford: Oxford University Press, 1986). All subsequent references will be parenthetically indicated in the text by *MA*, followed by a page number.

situations may be little better than disastrous" (*MA*, p.82). Although no one is "able unilaterally to remove himself from the natural condition of mankind . . . everyone would benefit from ending a state of affairs in which it is rational to interact only on the basis of mutual utility-maximization" (*MA*, p.82).

Gauthier believes that if the world were or could be turned into a perfectly competitive market, then this problem would vanish. The invisible hand of the market would produce outcomes that are both utility maximizing and optimizing. The market thus would "constitute a morally free zone . . . within which the constraints of morality would have no place" (*MA*, pp.84, 261).[2]

However, the market "embodies a very special structure of interaction which cannot be all-embracing" (*MA*, p.84). Gauthier believes there are only two market failures, free-riding because of public goods, and parasitism because of externalities. It is because of these failures that we need, in addition to the structures that create a (nearly) perfectly free market, also a moral zone, a zone of justice in which the free-ridership and parasitism endemic to our natural condition are eliminated (*MA*, p.113). This is the zone of mutually beneficial cooperation. It is governed by the principle of justice, the principle of "not taking advantage of one's fellows, not to seek free goods or to impose uncompensated costs, provided that one supposes others similarly disposed" (*MA*, p.113). This applies both to interactions involving the infliction of harm and interactions for jointly producing an increased supply of goods and fairly distributing it. Gauthier derives two more specific moral principles, the *Lockean Proviso* which "prohibits bettering one's position through interaction worsening the position of another" (*MA*, p.16) and the *principle of fair bargaining*, namely, "*minimax relative concession*" (*MA*, p.137), or what comes to the same thing,

---

[2] It is not clear to me why the market is a morally free zone. One reason for this is that I am unclear about natural and market interactions. Natural interaction tends to degenerate into the use of force and fraud. Why is this? Is it because natural men are not rational, or is it because, though rational, they lack the social structures that make it irrational to engage in force and fraud? If the former, men must be trained to be rational, which assigns an important role to educators not sufficiently stressed in the book. For there one gets the impression that maximizing and only maximizing comes naturally. In any case, part of the education to be rational would include observing the prohibitions of force and fraud, which would normally be regarded as moral. If the market involves coercive social structures, such as the protection of property, then the market does not seem to be a morally free zone since, presumably, these coercive structures are approved by morality. Lastly, Gauthier does not say anything about those coercive social measures, such as antitrust legislation, which are widely regarded as necessary to counteract tendencies of market interactions to undermine the free market. The market thus seems to be a morally free zone in only a rather limited sense.

"maximin relative benefit" (*MA*, pp.155, 265)[3] which (he claims) fairly and impartially relates each person's concession made and each person's benefit received to his contribution to the surplus produced.

Gauthier then attempts to prove that those who adopt the principle of justice in such a way that they can be recognized as being disposed to cooperate, that is, being what he calls "constrained maximizers," are in a better position than straightforward maximizers to induce others to make mutually beneficial bargains with them. Hence, it would be rational for a straightforward maximizer to turn himself into a recognizable constrained maximizer. Thus, Gauthier modifies Adeimantus's claim that what is advantageous is *appearing* rather than *being* just, to read, roughly, that what is advantageous is *recognizably being just* because a person can appear to be just if and only if he is recognizably just. This is his account of why and when a rational person, i.e., a straightforward maximizer, would become a constrained maximizer, of what constraints he would impose on himself, of why these must be impartial and fair, and of why, being maximization-constraining, rational, fair, and impartial, they must also be moral.

His last point concerns the determination of what would be rational, fair, impartial maximization-constraining principles to govern the structure of any society. This determination involves choice from "the Archimedean point." That point is such that from it "one has the moral capacity to shape society" (*MA*, p.233). One is at that point if one is "a rational actor freed, not from individuality but from the content of any particular individuality,

---

[3] Gauthier uses these terms to refer to his solution to the bargaining problem. That problem arises in a situation in which two or more persons can, by cooperating with one another, achieve a joint product which is greater than what they can achieve if they do not cooperate. The problem is how to distribute the surplus. Every rational agent would most prefer to acquire the whole of the surplus and least prefer to acquire none of it. If a bargain is to be struck, one or all of the parties normally will have to make a "concession," that is, accept a share of the surplus less than the most preferred; no party normally can hope that the other(s) will make a "complete" concession. Gauthier develops a measure of the concession, which he thinks offers a basis for relating the concessions of different bargainers, which he calls "relative concession." It is the proportion that its "absolute magnitude" (the difference between the utility expected from the outcome originally claimed and the utility expected from the *proposed* concession) bears to the magnitude of a *complete* concession (*MA*, p.136). The problem then is to find a rational principle for determining "the concession" each person has to make. According to Gauthier, the principle is this: " . . . given a range of outcomes, each of which requires concessions by some or all persons if it is to be selected, then an outcome be selected only if the greatest or *maximum* relative concession it requires, is as small as possible, or a *minimum*, that is, is no greater than the maximum relative concession required by every other outcome." (*MA*, p.137).

In Ch. V. 4.3 (*MA*, pp.154–156), Gauthier attempts to show that the principle of Minimax Relative Concession "is equivalent to maximizing equal relative benefit [construed analogously to relative concession] when the latter uses up the co-operative surplus" (*MA*, p.155).

an actor aware that she is an individual with capacities and preferences both particular in themselves and distinctive in relation to those of her fellows, but unaware of which capacities, which preferences" (*MA*, p.233). Such a person must exhibit concern about her interaction with others, but her concern is necessarily impartial. Hence her choice of basic principles or social structures "must express the norms of justice" (*MA*, p.234). This approach starts from an impartial rather than a specifically individual standpoint. Hence, "If morality and rationality are in harmony, then ... Archimedean choice must select individual expected utility-maximization, constrained by the proviso and minimax relative concession. The impartial perspective of the ideal actor must cohere with the perspectives of rational individuals actually engaged in strategic choice" (*MA*, p.235).

II. "MORALS BY AGREEMENT" AND CONVENTIONAL MORALITY

Gauthier does not say much about the way these basic moral principles translate into middle-level precepts capable of guiding action. But he notes that "there will be differences, perhaps significant, between the impartial and rational constraints supported by our argument, and the morality learned from parents and peers, priests and teachers" (*MA*, p.6), and from "the 'plain duties' of conventional morality. Animals, the unborn, the congenitally handicapped and defective, fall beyond the pale of a morality tied to mutuality" (*MA*, p.268).

So far as I can see, there are other parts of our conventional morality he must reject, for instance, the principle telling us that we naturally *ought* to do certain things that are beyond the call of duty. For under which of Gauthier's moral principles could these be subsumed? Both the Proviso and Minimax Relative Concession tell us our rights and duties, not what goes beyond them. I shall not examine the question of whether moral desiderata, such as giving to charity or devoting part of our resources to helping people who have no rights against us, can be established from the Archimedean point. If they can, then there is an unjustifiable discrepancy between Gauthier's two ethical approaches, the approach via individual bargaining and the approach from the Archimedean point. If they cannot, both approaches diverge from our conventional morality.

I mention another part which I believe Gauthier cannot accommodate.[4] He distinguishes between the avoidance of mutually destructive conflicts and the cooperative creation of mutual benefits. By the latter he means "the production of an increased supply of goods" through cooperation

---

[4] In a review of Gauthier's book, which I received after I wrote this, Allan Gibbard makes what is essentially the same point (forthcoming in the *Times Literary Supplement*).

(*MA*, p.114). But what about Good Samaritan duties? Do "morals by agreement" allow bargains concerning not merely refraining from harmful intervention in other people's lives and cooperative production and distribution of the increased supply of goods, but also any duties of beneficial intervention? The Lockean Proviso specifically excludes this. Minimax relative concession would seem to be irrelevant, for there is no surplus product that needs to be fairly distributed on the basis of contribution. Again, I shall not investigate whether Good Samaritan duties can be supported from the Archimedean Point. At first sight, it certainly seems so. If it were possible, by taking out accident insurance, to secure an increased chance of being assisted when in danger, many would take out such a policy. If the recognition in a society of a Good Samaritan duty were to secure such an increased chance of the necessary assistance, would not the rational person at the Archimedean point be willing to pay her premium for receiving these benefits in the form of doing her share of helping others in danger, even though it may turn out in the end that she never needs such help herself? Does choice from the Archimedean point again diverge from choice from the rational individual's point of view, or do both diverge from conventional morality?

Of course, one can agree with Gauthier that moral philosophers need not and should not attempt to justify all of our conventional morality. For some of it, perhaps a large part, may be, and probably is, unsound. The history of our morality, including its views on slavery, status privileges, discrimination on the grounds of race and sex, poverty, violence, religious toleration, and many others, does not inspire unqualified confidence. It is implausible to treat the middle-level precepts of our public morality or of our personal moral convictions as the data of ethics, since these precepts surely rest on more general normative principles which, themselves, appear to stand in need of rational underpinning. Nevertheless, though not hard data, these precepts are normally backed by general principles that have carried conviction with many people over a long time. Their rejection would seem to need some explanation and justification, such as bringing to light errors or ignorance or blindness to fact, bias due to personal interest, emotional involvement, confusion, and the like. Or we might show that they are in conflict with general principles (or with their application to particular cases) that are derived from *unquestionably secure foundations*, such as the basic principles of practical reason. In that case, we must somehow weigh our belief in these supposedly secure foundations against our belief in those of our conventional or personal moral convictions that conflict with principles derivable from these foundations.

Gauthier presents his theory of practical rationality as the foundational rock on which "morals by agreement" rests. Let us, then, turn to the examination of that theory. Is it plausible enough to justify us in rejecting those principles of our conventional morality with which it conflicts? Is it at least superior to its main rivals?

III. PREFERENCE

Gauthier adopts the general framework of the theory of rational choice as developed in decision and game theory. "Practical rationality in the most general sense is identified with maximization. . . . The quantity to be maximized must be associated with preference . . . but the theory of rational choice defines a precise measure of preference, *utility*, and identifies rationality with the maximization of utility. . . . The rational actor maximizes her utility in choosing from a finite set of actions, which take as possible outcomes the members of a finite set of states of affairs" (*MA*, p.22).

However, Gauthier thinks that what is probably the most fully developed and widely accepted account of preference, namely, the economists', "does not suffice for moral theory" (*MA*, p.27). Why not? What flaws does Gauthier detect in the economists' account? On what grounds does he declare them flaws? How does he try to eliminate them? Does he succeed? Are there perhaps further flaws?

Neither the economists nor Gauthier make very clear what they mean by 'preference' and how their use is related to the everyday use. The reader, therefore, tends to fill in the gaps by relying on the everyday use, or even to be unaware of that use or to forget where they have told us explicitly to depart from it. It will therefore be helpful, before we look at the economists' account and Gauthier's modification of it, to remind ourselves briefly of some of the different things we often mean by 'preference' to see whether and when the economists and Gauthier have one or another of these in mind, and where they depart from these uses in some way or other, and if so, how this affects the plausibility of Gauthier's theory of rationality, since that plausibility may depend on what we mean by 'preference'.

For our purposes here, we should distinguish at least four different uses.[5] (These distinctions are mine, not Gauthier's.)

---

[5] I am not concerned to give an exhaustive account of the various everyday uses of 'preference' or a full account of the few I distinguish. My aim is only to distinguish the four uses which could plausibly be represented as both ordinary uses and uses Gauthier might have in mind. I believe, though I do not wish to argue this here, that the economists and Gauthier have broadened the use of 'preference' far beyond the ordinary, to include desires, motives, considerations, reasons, and perhaps more. I here completely ignore, because irrelevant, uses such as 'I would prefer tea' as a polite request, where it means, 'please give me tea', which is quite compatible with my hating tea and preferring other things offered to it, although such uses may make more plausible the economists' conception of "revealed preference."

(i) *Prima facie preferences*: 'I prefer the Bahamas over Italy, rock over Bach, the Republicans over the Democrats, the sea over the mountains, coffee over tea, Kant over Hegel, health over illness, pleasure over pain,' and so on. These are preferences for aspects of possible concrete situations. They are relatively stable and long-lived. Indeed, I would not be credited with having such a preference unless it were stable. It would be hard to establish that I have intransitive preferences, in this sense. I may, of course, say honestly at t_1, that I prefer apples to pears, and at t_2 that I prefer pears to oranges, and at t_3 that I prefer oranges to apples, but then either I am mistaken about at least one of these preferences, or one is not a settled preference, or one of them has changed between t_1 and t_3. Transitivity is a defining characteristic, not a merit of such preferences.

A particular prima facie preference can compete with others because a concrete situation may present alternatives each of which has aspects some of which are prima facie preferred and others not. My prima facie preference for a meat over a vegetarian diet may come into conflict with my preference for a diet that is healthy over one that is unhealthy, cheap over expensive, digestible over indigestible, and so on. Hence, every such prima facie preference may be in conflict with what I prefer on balance, all things considered.

(ii) *Given preferences*. An important subclass of prima facie preferences are those we find ourselves having, perhaps saddled with, even if we wish we did not have them, such as a preference for meat over vegetarian fare, or for smoking over not smoking. There are two different types of these: taste-based, such as my preference for veal over chicken, and inclination-based, such as my preference for eating over going hungry. They differ in that taste-based preferences are often relatively easy, inclination-based ones often relatively hard to ignore. I am not hooked on eating meat, let alone on eating veal rather than chicken. But I am hooked on eating rather than starving.

Given preferences are "brute,"[6] in the sense that they involve appropriate behavioral dispositions we do not adopt for reasons but find ourselves having on account of certain experiential aspects, namely, taste, or felt inclination.

(iii) *Enacted concrete preferences*, as in 'Jill preferred to sit out that dance rather than dance with Jack'. This implies that Jill acted from and in accordance with her concrete preference, which excludes two things: that she acted unintentionally or contrary to her preference, e.g., from weakness of will, as when, having decided she would not yield to his entreaties, she nevertheless does. It is not merely that Jill had a prima facie preference for

---

[6] To avoid confusion, I use the rather awkward term, 'given preferences', since Gauthier uses 'brute' to mean 'unconsidered'.

sitting out a dance rather than dancing with Jack, but also that that was her concrete, occasion-relative preference, taking everything into account that she actually considered. I assume that if she danced with Jack, we would have to infer either that Jill could not have preferred sitting out the dance, or that her preference had changed in the last minute, or that she had no settled preference at all.

Enacted concrete preference is close to the economists' use of 'revealed preference', for an enacted concrete preference infallibly reveals the person's concrete preference. If I am right, the only difference is that a person may choose or intentionally act in a certain way from weakness of will and so necessarily in accordance with her "revealed," but not necessarily her concrete preference. If I smoke yet another cigarette, that infallibly reveals my revealed preference, but does not necessarily enact and so reveal my concrete preference, since I may have smoked from weakness of will, succumbing to temptation, acting contrary to my concrete preference. If I succumb to temptation, I yield to the urge to smoke, even though in my judgment I had rejected the gains of yielding as sufficient grounds for doing so, hence as sufficient grounds for choosing to smoke, hence as sufficient ground for the disposition to smoke on this occasion, hence for the concrete preference to smoke then. My concrete preference was for adopting the dispositon I thought I had sufficient grounds to adopt, namely, not to smoke. From weakness of will I failed to enact it. (Of course, if I am wrong about the implication of 'Jill preferred to sit out the dance', then this remark does not exemplify what I call enacted concrete preferences.)

Concrete preferences should be distinguished from all-things-considered preferences. The former are dispositions based on grounds to behave in certain ways, but not necessarily on *all* grounds that are or that one thinks are relevant. We may know *that* we have not considered everything, and we may even know *what* we have not considered, e.g., the monetary cost.

That one *has* a concrete preference for a given alternative relative to a particular occasion does not entail that one *enacts* that preference on that occasion, since one may be physically forced not to or one may succumb to temptation. But doing something under duress (she handed over the money at gunpoint) or doing it from politeness (she decided to let it pass) are enactments of concrete preference. But such enactments of concrete preference must be reported in terms of *all* the matters taken into account. It might not be correct to say that she *preferred* to hand over the money to hanging on to it – indeed, it is very unlikely. What is more likely is that she preferred to hand over her money *and save* her life, over refusing to hand over her money *and risk* her life. Of course, concrete preferences are relatively short-lived, since they lapse when the occasion is past. Even so, they may not be firm or settled enough to be sure what they are, as when a person repeatedly resolves to give up smoking.

(iv) *First-order and second-order preferences.* First-order preferences are for states of affairs whose specification does not involve reference to anyone's preference, whereas second-order preferences are for states of affairs that do involve such reference. My preference for meat over vegetarian fare is first-order, my preference for my or your having a preference for vegetarian fare over meat is second-order. An important subclass of second-order preferences is what I call "distributive" preferences, that is, preferences concerning whose first-order preferences should be satisfied. The complete egoist has first-order preferences for the promotion of his own good over that of all other people's, and second-order preferences for the satisfaction of his own first-order preferences over that of all others, that is, entirely self-favoring distributive preferences. Altruists have other-favoring distributive preferences. Nontuists have rather peculiar distributive preferences: they have self-favoring distributive preferences when, though possibly only when, they exchange with others, whereas tuists presumably are those who have the same distributive preferences (some of them other-favoring) whether or not they are exchanging with others.

Typically, second-order preferences are not given (that is, taste-based or inclination-based), but are based on reasons or ideals. Take someone whose first-order preferences are those of a meatlover. Suppose that he would second-order prefer to have the sort of first-order preferences on account of which he would be called a vegetarian. Now there are two quite different kinds of basis for this second-order preference. One is that he thinks there is something wrong with his first-order preferences and that he finds it difficult to act in accordance with his second-order preferences as long as he has his old carnivorous first-order preferences. In such a case, he could conceivably (though perhaps with difficulty) achieve his ideal even without modifying his first-order preferences, as long as he acted contrary to them, because what his ideal requires is behavior – that he refrain from *eating* meat – not that he not like or want it more than meatless fare. His second-order "corrective" preference is based on the conviction that his first-order preferences for meat should not be acted on; the main or only reasons for changing his first-order preferences are that a change would increase the likelihood of his actually doing what he wants and thinks he ought, that it would lessen the cost to him of achieving this, and perhaps that it would raise the internal harmony and integration among his preferences.

The other case is one in which the person finds nothing wrong with his first-order preferences, except that they are the preferences of a *nonvegetarian*, and so contrary to his preferred self-conception. The difference is easier to see with a different ideal, say, that of macho. Suppose our man has nonmacho first-order preferences: he likes to have only one girl friend, treats her as an equal, helps in the house, likes looking after children but does not care whether they are his own, and so on. He realizes that he cannot become a macho man simply by acting *as if* he had the relevant first-order preferences. A real macho man is one who actually has them. So he must change them if he is to satisfy his second-order preference. One can be a merely "continent" rather than a fully "temperate"[7] vegetarian (in Aristotle's sense), but not a merely continent macho man. Justice is an ideal of the first kind, friendship and love are of the second kind. Plato, and probably Aristotle, thought that justice was of the second kind. Economic man is just only continently. In the last two chapters of his book, Gauthier can be taken to make a case for saying that the true liberal will often be temperately just.[8]

Note that if I *judge* that it is better for me, because it is better for my health, to have a vegetarian rather than a meat diet, then this is not tantamount to saying that I have a second-order preference for first-order (prima facie) vegetarian preferences. My judgment is primarily about *what I should choose and do, not about what first-order (prima facie) preferences I should have*. My judgment that I should live on a vegetarian diet does not require satisfying my second-order preference for having a first-order (prima facie) preference for a diet opposite to the one I now have. It would be irrational, because contrary to my judgment, if I acted on my (prima facie) first-order preferences, but it might also be irrational for me to try to satisfy my second-order corrective preferences, since working on my taste-based meat-preferences may be costlier than simply ignoring them in what I choose.

IV. REVEALED PREFERENCES

I return now to the economists' construal of preference and Gauthier's modifications of it. What normative role do economists assign to reason and value in human choice? Gauthier agrees with them that choice is rational if and only if it follows the maxim, 'maximize utility as a measure of

[7]According to Aristotle, a person is continent as long as she does what is morally required of her, even if it goes against the grain. She is temperate only if she has developed desires in harmony with what is morally required. On this view, only the temperate person is truly virtuous; the merely continent person is not.

[8] The distinction is deep-cutting. Ideals such as that of the macho, I call "aesthetic" (perhaps at the risk of being misunderstood) because their appeal does not depend on the way the preferences embodying it affect the well-being of the person who has the ideal and, above all, that of (all) other people. Nietzsche's forcefully expressed preference for the ideals that make up a master morality is aesthetic in this sense. The ideals of Christian morality are not.

preference', but argues that on their construal of preference as "revealed preference," this means no more than *act so that your action can be given a maximizing interpretation* (*MA*, p.27). It tells us to maximize but does not tell us *what* to maximize; if behavior can be given a maximizing interpretation, it maximizes something or other, but for the economist that is sufficient for rationality. Thus, the economists do not merely do what Gauthier approves of, namely, treat utility as a measure of preference rather than a standard for it, but also do what he rejects, namely, treat utility as a measure of choice rather than a standard for it. Economists thus manage to assign some role to reason and value in human choice – some choices can be irrational, for some revealed preferences may be incomplete or intransitive (*MA*, p.40) – but it is a rather limited one. This, apparently, is one reason why Gauthier rejects the economists' account of preference which determines this limited role.

His second reason for rejecting it is that on their account utility cannot plausibly be identified with value. Gauthier agrees with the view that what it is rational to maximize is *value*, not preference (*MA*, p.22), and identifies value with *coherent and considered* preference (*MA*, p.24). If preference satisfies these conditions, then "utility, as a measure of preference, is to be identified with value, and the maximization of utility with rationality" (*MA*, p.23). But economists do not require preferences to be considered but only coherent, and so their identification of utility, the measure of coherent preference, with value is untenable.

V. THE INADEQUACIES OF REVEALED PREFERENCE

What exactly is wrong with the economists' account? Gauthier gives several different explanations. One is that, on their account, the rationality of choices cannot be assessed by determining whether they maximize preference fulfillment (*MA*, p.26). But this is not quite fair to the economists. As they define 'preference', we *can* assess the rationality of choices by determining whether they maximize preference fulfillment: they do so if the choices allow of a maximizing interpretation. If they do, then they don't just maximize something or other, but they maximize preference, since preference is infallibly revealed in choice. So the real objection must be not that the economists cannot assess rationality on the basis of preference fulfillment, but that theirs is the wrong account of preference. And why is it the wrong account? Supposedly because it unduly restricts our evidence for what people's preferences are. "We accept the economist's assumption that rationality is to be ascribed to a person's behaviour in the absence of contrary evidence; we reject the extreme limitations on the evidence he allows" (*MA*, p.29). But by what standards is the evidence allowed by the economists *unduly* limited?

Gauthier, in a somewhat different context, makes a claim which could be treated as another explanation of what is wrong with the economists' account of preference and of why he thinks that the evidence they accept for what someone prefers is unduly limited: "We accept the general explanatory schema: choice maximizes preference fulfillment given belief. We reject the trivialization of this schema that results from denying independent evidential access to each of its terms – to choice, preference, and belief" (*MA*, p.30). However, in this explanation all the weight is carried by an explanatory theory that is by no means generally accepted.

A third explanation is explicitly normative: to identify maximization with revealed preference maximization is to *restrict unduly* the *normative roles* assigned to *reason* and *value* in the framework for understanding human action afforded by the theory of rational choice (*MA*, p.27). "If a person may behave in a maximizing way and *yet not fully rationally*, then maximization, although necessary, cannot be sufficient for rationality" (*MA*, p.27, emphasis added). Thus, the economists' standard of rationality is the wrong one because they wrongly allow all choices to be rational that maximize something or other which they call 'revealed preference'. Hence, on Gauthier's view, only the maximization of "genuine" or "real" preference fulfillment excludes the possibility that a person behaves in a way that maximizes preference fulfillment yet not fully rationally. In his view, a person might well act in a way that maximizes revealed preference, yet not rationally. But Gauthier does not defend this normative judgment. Unfortunately, his only claim that would make it plausible is false: "If reason and value are to play normative roles in the framework for understanding human action afforded by the theory of rational choice, then it must be possible to give the injunction to maximize *further content*" (*MA*, p.27, emphasis added). But as we have seen, this is not so. The economists' account provides enough content for the injunction 'Maximize' to afford a normative role to reason and value, for it means 'choose in such a way that your choice is capable of a maximizing interpretation'. But, clearly, this role is not one that Gauthier wants to accept: in his view, it allows *too many* choices to be rational. But Gauthier does not defend this normative judgment and I don't see how he could.

Of course, revealed preference is not what we ordinarily mean by 'preference', at least not in the context of rationality, and to the extent that the maximization of value as rational preference fulfillment is a plausible account of rationality, that plausibility is lost by so drastic a departure from usage. But I doubt whether Gauthier would want to argue that way and, as we shall see, his own account of preference also departs from what we commonly mean by it. It is therefore not clear, at least to me, why Gauthier thinks the economists' account of preference is inadequate for moral theory.

VI. GAUTHIER'S CONCEPTION OF PREFERENCE

Is Gauthier's conception superior to the economists'? Gauthier introduces both conceptual and operational distinctness of preference from choice by allowing that not only choice but also expression of preference provides evidential access to preference. However, on his view, these are two avenues of evidential access not to one and the same thing, preference, but to different dimensions (*MA*, p.27) or kinds (*MA*, pp.25, 30) of preference, each with its own independent measure. The preference that I (still infallibly) reveal to others (and myself?) by choosing an apple from a bowl of apples and pears is behavioral preference. The preference I express (and so reveal? to others? to myself? fallibly? infallibly?) when I say that I like apples better than pears is "attitudinal preference" (*MA*, p.27) or, simply, my "attitude" (*MA*, p.28). These two dimensions or kinds of preference may diverge: "Karen expresses a preference for reading philosophical works rather than watching situation comedies on television, but she spends her free time in front of her television set while her philosophical library gathers dust" (*MA*, p.28).

Now, as we saw, Gauthier believes that the rational person maximizes value, that is, his coherent and considered preferences. As we shall shortly see more clearly, having fully considered preferences involves having preferences which, among other things, are free of conflict between their behavioral and attitudinal dimensions (*MA*, p.23). "If a person's revealed and expressed preferences diverge, then her values are confused and she lacks an adequate basis for rational choice. . . . Lack of a measure common to behaviors and attitudes is a sign of irrationality. But we may not without further ado ascribe this irrationality to a person's choices because they fail to conform to her attitudes, or to her attitudes because they fail to express her choices. In specific circumstances one of these ascriptions may seem clearly justified. But in general we may conclude only that the divergence between choice and attitude indicates irrationality without locating it more precisely. For it would be overcome were either the person's choices to come to conform to what she expresses, or her attitudes to come to conform to what she chooses." (*MA*, p.28).[9]

[9] I assume that this means that it does not matter which of the two dimensions is made to conform with the other. For otherwise it is hard to understand why Gauthier thinks we can assume, with the economists, that a person's behavior is rational in the absence of contrary

Now, this account of preference is closer to common sense than the economists', for its introduction of expressed or attitudinal preferences accommodates uses of 'preference' other than the economists' revealed preference which, as we have seen, is close to, though not identical with, what I called enacted concrete preference. But the account of attitudinal and behavioral preference is still very far from our ordinary way of construing preference.

In the first place we normally distinguish sharply between the context of making a future choice and that of evaluating a past choice. In the first context, the chooser's task is to become aware of her relevant prima facie preferences – that is, those aspects of those states of affairs which alternative actions open to her will bring about and concerning which she has prima facie preferences. This will enable her to construct a concrete preference for an action as a means to a state of affairs which she prefers, given *all its aspects* concerning which she is not indifferent, e.g., (a) Jill's sitting out the dance as a way of avoiding dancing with Jack, or perhaps (b) as a way of avoiding disobedience to her mother, if the mother has strictly forbidden her to dance with Jack although she would have greatly preferred dancing with Jack to sitting out the dance.[10]

---

evidence which, on his view, would be absent if there were no divergence between the two dimensions of preference (*MA*, pp.28–29, 32–33). He thus seems to think that what matters for rationality is that there be no divergence between the two dimensions and that we can assume there is none unless there is contrary evidence, by way of such divergence. If it mattered which of the two dimensions had to be changed to harmonize with the other, rather than that there be harmony one way or the other, it would surely be hasty to assume rationality on the basis of outward harmony, since a person may have achieved harmony by modifying the wrong dimension. This is to say nothing about the implausibility of assuming that a person's expression of preference necessarily reveals his attitude, which Gauthier clearly identifies with attitudinal preference.

[10] Of course, as we saw, only the first case (a) could be correctly reported, by her or anyone else, with the words (a'): 'I (Jill) preferred to sit out the dance rather than dance with Jack'. The second case (b) would have to be reported as (b'): 'Jill preferred to sit out the dance and obey her mother rather than dance with Jack and disobey her mother', since the first report (a') would misrepresent her concrete preference in the second case (b). For in that case, (b) *she would have preferred dancing with Jack to sitting out the dance*, so *sitting out the dance* would be *counterpreferential* as far as that aspect of her choice is concerned, yet the first report, (a') 'Jill preferred to sit out the dance . . . etc.' implies that her choice was *according to preference* as far as that description of her choice is concerned.

It may perhaps be thought that Jill's behavior is not counterpreferential even in case (b). For though it is true that she *would have* preferred to dance with Jack, is it not also true that, *as things were*, she *did prefer not to dance with Jack*? Was her preference not for what she intentionally did, although *in other circumstances* she would have preferred to dance with him? Not so. To think so would be to confuse actual and hypothetical concrete preferences. Suppose I am offered a choice of a Golden Delicious apple or a pear and I choose the apple, but if the apple offered had been a Jonathan, I *would have preferred* the pear. Or suppose I am offered a choice of an apple and a pear, and I choose an apple, but *would have preferred* a pear, if I had just eaten an apple before that. Then 'I would have preferred a pear' means that *I would* have chosen *differently* either if the choice had been between *different alternatives* in the *same circumstances*, or between the *same alternatives* in *different circumstances*. However, in the

In the context of Jill's trying to make a preferential choice, she can normally ignore her actual behavior either in the past or in the future. Her task is, first, a "cognitive" one: to construct her settled concrete preference between the alternatives; and then a "practical" one: to choose and act accordingly. It would be a confusion to think that her preferences were confused if, having satisfactorily completed this cognitive task, she then failed in the practical. Of course if, from weakness of will, she finally does not act according to her concrete preference, then she acts irrationally, but not because she has confused preferences; she acts irrationally because she fails to act in accordance with (to enact) her concrete preferences.[11] Thus, in the context of making a preferential choice it surely would normally be irrational to try to bring one's "attitudinal," i.e., one's concrete, preferences into agreement with one's choices, rather than the other way around. For to what choices should she accommodate her attitudes? While she is trying to arrive at a preferential choice, she has not yet made the choice she is working on. If she is trying to predict what that choice will be, she is confusing her task as a chooser with that of an observer. And if she is trying to remember her past choices, surely those choices provide her with no adequate reason to modify her present preferences so as to conform with her past choices even if these choices correctly enacted her erstwhile concrete preferences. If her preferences have changed, she surely does not have to wait and see how she will act before she can tell what these preferences now are. Even in cases where she is deceiving herself about her preferences, she will think she knows what they are and act on them, though her pattern of choices may tell her that she has deceived herself. But that does not show that she has only a third-person access to her own preferences.

Let us now look at the situation from an observer's point of view. Once

case in hand, namely, (a) 'Jill would have preferred to dance with Jack' does not refer to different alternatives or circumstances. Her actual concrete preference, in this very case, between these very alternatives considered as such, and in these very circumstances, was for dancing with Jack. But since she intentionally sat out the dance, it would be misleading to report her behavior with the words 'Jill *preferred* – rather than *would have preferred* – to dance with Jack', for that implies two things: (i) her preference was for dancing with Jack and (ii) 'She chose and acted *from preference*', i.e., she did dance with Jack. But, of course, in the case in hand (ii) is false. So the conjunction is false, since the second conjunct is false. But, of course, this does not imply that the first conjunct is false. In fact, it is true. Her preference was for dancing with Jack, but she did not act *from* her concrete preference between *these alternatives*, but *for a reason* (her mother's prohibition), and this reason required counterpreferential action. Note, incidentally, that if the reason was adequate, her choice and the action based on it would not be judged irrational, even though they were counterpreferential.

[11] I here assume that at least one thing Gauthier has in mind when he speaks of attitudes, attitudinal preferences, or attitudinal dimensions of preference or expressions of preference, is (what I have called) concrete rather than prima facie preferences, and that by fully considered attitudinal preference, he means all things considered concrete preferences.

she has made her choice, we cannot infallibly infer her (behavioral) preference, since we cannot infer from observing her choice that it was a case of her preferring to do what she did. For one thing, she may have acted from weakness of will and so contrary to her concrete preference. For another, she may have acted in a way which was, *under some relevant description or other*, counterpreferential. Thus, even if somehow we know that she did not act as she did out of weakness of will but from and in accordance with her concrete preference, we do not know, simply by watching her act, under what description she preferred to do what she did. We observe Jill refusing to dance with Jack, but in turning him down, what she did may not have been a case of preferring to sit out the dance rather than dance with him, but a case of preferring to obey her mother rather than disobey her.

Thus, from the common-sense point of view, it is clear why we need something like Gauthier's attitudinal preferences. We need them in order to base (some of) our rational choices on them. Where it is rational to base our choices on our preferences, we need something other than behavioral preferences. Gauthier clearly thinks so, too, for as we have seen, in criticizing the economists' conception of preference he has in mind their failure to allow this role to our attitudes. But it is equally clear that in this context we need attitudes not in addition to, but instead of, behavioral preferences. "Behavioral preferences" or "revealed preferences" do not perform that sort of job at all. I believe Gauthier is mistaken when he says, "Yet we must not suppose that the economist's focus on revealed preference is simply mistaken. Certainly *choices reveal preferences*: a conception of preference that treated the linkage between preference and choice as merely accidental would be even more evidently inadequate than one that makes preference parasitic on choice" (*MA*, p.27). It is, of course, true that the linkage between preference and choice is not accidental, but that does not mean that choice always necessarily reveals preference, for the choice may be counterpreferential under all relevant descriptions – when it is from weakness of will – or we may not be able to guess under what description it is in accordance with preference. And in any case, this whole question of how an observer can, from Jill's choice, divine her preferences has nothing to do with Jill's own reliance, in making her choice, on her own preferences. She would be sadly misguided if she tried to infer her own preferences from her past or future choices or, for that matter, from her expression of preference. Jill is not related to *her* preferences in exactly the way the rest of us are related to them.

Thus, Gauthier seems to me wrong to assume, with the economists, that a person does not act irrationally if her choice is capable of a maximizing interpretation and if there is no diverging expression of (attitudinal) preference (*MA*, p.29). This assumption would be *tenable only if it did not matter in which way we reconcile choice and attitudinal preference*. But as we have seen, this matters very much. When we try to make a preferential choice we do not need to guess what we will choose or what we have chosen in the past, to gain behavioral evidential access to our preference, and when we assess the rationality of someone else's choice, we are not entitled to assume, from the absence of contrary expressed preferences, that the choice was rational, since the third-person assessment is an attempt to evaluate the performance of a rational chooser, that is, one who conforms his choices to his preferences, not the other way around.

Well, then, does Gauthier's distinction between behavioral and attitudinal preference remedy the major flaw in the economists' conception of revealed preference, namely, their failure to base the rationality of choice on whether choosers conform their choice to their attitudes concerning what their choices will bring about? It seems not, since the distinction he draws, with its suggestion of two kinds of preference having equal standing in a person's choice, obscures the logical priority of a person's attitudes both from a first-person and the essentially secondary third-person point of view. The suggestion that a person's choice infallibly reveals his behavioral preference, that a person can be assumed to be rational unless his expressed preferences diverge from his choices, and that he is rational if and only if he brings the two dimensions into conformity one way or the other, ignores the priority of attitudes, the dependence of the rationality of choices on their conformity with attitudes, and the essential secondariness of the third-person view.

Thus, it is not the case that a divergence between a person's expressed preferences and her choice is a sign of irrationality. Jill had a (prima facie) preference for dancing with Jack over sitting out the dance, yet her acting in this counterpreferential way was not irrational, if she accepted her mother's prohibition as an adequate reason not to satisfy her preference for dancing with Jack. Bringing her choice into agreement with that preference would not have made her choice more rational. The vegetarian's refusal to eat meat is not irrational even though he might have to say, in all honesty, that he much preferred a meat diet. It would not be rational to bring his choices into agreement with these prima facie preferences. Even if, as a result of these judgments about the preferability of a vegetarian diet, he comes to have a second-order preference for changing his first-order preferences, it may be irrational for him to bring these two types of preference (and expressions of them) into agreement with one another. Nor does it follow that there is no irrationality, if there is no divergence between the two dimensions, let alone between choice and expression of preference, since the person may have brought the wrong dimension into conformity with the other, as when the vegetarian, without finding any reason for changing his judgment, manages to reverse his second-order preference to conform to his first-order preference for and choice of a meat diet.

VII. COHERENT PREFERENCES

I turn now to Gauthier's second modification namely, the requirement that utility, to be identifiable with value, must be the measure of preferences that are both *coherent* and (fully) *considered*.

I shall not comment on coherence beyond noting, very tentatively, two things. The first is that the reason for imposing this constraint, namely, making it possible to define a precise measure of preference, seems, from the point of view of rationality, a rather dubious one. Have we found a measure of deterrence just because we can get statistics on recidivism and on nothing else that is relevant, or have we found a measure of intelligence because we have developed a manageable IQ test that gives numerical test results? It may, of course, be more useful for some purpose to redefine 'deterrence' or 'intelligence' so that we now have measures of these things instead of deterrence or intelligence in the ordinary sense. But it seems to me that it would be illegitimate in this context to make such a move. We want morality to be justified by reason, not by something else that happens to be measurable. It is not clear to me, therefore, that preferences that do not satisfy these formal conditions, whatever they may be, of coherence must be irrational and that their owner should modify them accordingly.

The second point to note is that some of these conditions, e.g., transitivity, are indeed independently plausible, at least at first sight, as conditions of rationality. They look like consistency conditions and these are readily accepted as tests of rationality. However, as I mentioned earlier, I have doubts about transitivity as a genuine normative constraint. As economists employ it, it is often used, in conjunction with a rationality assumption, to allow us to infer from a person's choices what her preferences as a rational chooser must be. But if we do not make that rationality assumption, and since transitivity can be tested only over time, it is hard to distinguish between someone's having a settled intransitive preference, or simply an unsettled (concrete) preference or a changed preference or no (settled) preference at all. But if that is so, intransitivity in this sense loses its intuitive connection with irrationality. For there is no reason to think that reason requires us to have settled rather than vacillating concrete preferences between, say, apples, pears, and oranges. It is only if we are committed to saying that choices reveal preferences that we must construe choices as preference-based and the intransitivity of choices – and their irrationality, as in the case of "the money pump" (MA, p.41)[12] – as due to the intransitivity of preferences. But if we drop the identification of choices with (revealed) preferences, we are not forced to this conclusion.

VIII. CONSIDERED PREFERENCES

Let me, then, turn to the second condition of the rationality of preferences. Gauthier says preferences "are considered if and only if there is no conflict between their behavioural and attitudinal dimensions and they are stable under experience and reflection" (MA, pp.32–33). We have already dealt with the question of the conflict between the two dimensions and have seen reason to doubt whether rationality requires us to bring the two dimensions into agreement one way or the other, or whether it is assured by our doing so.

What about stability under experience and reflection? In Gauthier's view, experience and reflection do two things. They ensure that the preference is a firm, clear, stable, or settled rather than a merely tentative one (MA, p.30). When a person has insufficient experience or has engaged in "incomplete" (the opposite of "full" [MA, p.31]) reflection, then although the preference thus based is his preference and the choice based on it "reveals his (behavioral) preference" (MA, p.30), what it reveals is *a preference of an inferior status*, one that may make one's choice "unsuccessful" (MA, p.31). Preferences revealed in such choices are to be regarded as tentative and as not a basis for determining the chooser's values. A person's failure to have sufficiently or fully experienced and considered preferences does not necessarily make her or the choices based on such preferences irrational. It all depends on whether the person's preferences and the beliefs underlying them are based on the greatest amount of experience and reflection possible for her in the circumstances (MA, pp.30f.).[13]

---

[12] If I have intransitive preferences, say, I prefer eating an apple to eating a pear, eating a pear to eating a peach, and eating a peach to eating an apple, then I shall presumably be willing to offer something, say, 1 cent, for trading my peach to a pear, my pear to an apple and my apple to a peach. By trading in this way, on the basis of my preferences, I arrive at my starting position at the cost of 3 cents. In this way, money can be pumped out of me, if I have intransitive preferences.

[13] It is not clear what we are to say about the rationality of these preferences themselves, as opposed to the choices based on them. On the one hand, "we may . . . speak of the conditions for coherent and considered preference as conditions of *rational* preference" (MA, pp.24–25, emphasis added), but on the other hand, choice based on insufficiently considered (experienced and reflected on) preference is not necessarily irrational (MA, p.31). This means either that being fully considered is not really a necessary condition of being a rational preference or that choices based on irrational preferences need not themselves be irrational.

I shall ignore the tricky condition of adequate experience and concentrate on Gauthier's requirement of adequate reflection. Unfortunately, Gauthier's remarks do not allow us to infer which of the various ordinary uses of 'preference' he has in mind, or whether, and if so how, his use departs from them. For instance, do we reflect in order to determine what our preferences in fact are or to determine what they ought to be? As far as given preferences are concerned, we obviously can distinguish these two questions. We may find that we have a preference for a meat diet over a vegetarian one but that, on reflection, we may conclude we ought not to have it. Are both preferences in Gauthier's sense? Are they confused?

And what about prima facie preferences which are not given, such as a vegetarian's preference for vegetarian restaurants which he necessarily has once he has convinced himself that he ought to be a vegetarian and has firmly adopted the vegetarian principle? And let us assume, to avoid problems about moral reasons, that he has become a vegetarian solely on grounds of personal health. Can we still distinguish between, on the one hand, the reflection which determines what preference we actually have and, on the other, the one we ought to have? Is Gauthier looking for what might be called a "propension," that is, a disposition which will be manifested in intentional action under a certain description on a certain occasion unless the person is prevented from acting in this way by physical force – something like revealed preference? Or is he looking for what I have called "concrete preferences," dispositions similar to propensions except that they are not manifested when the person acts from weakness of will? Or is he looking for what I have called "prima facie preferences"? Or is his reflection turned on the various relevant prima facie preferences so that he will come up with an all-things-considered concrete preference or propension?

We cannot here settle the difficult question of what exactly is the dimension (if there is one) on which practical reasons and preferences occupy different stretches, and where on that continuum the stretch of preferences ends and that of reasons begins, or whether and to what extent they overlap. But we should at least note that the two stretches *do not coincide*. If I prima facie prefer veal to chicken and therefore in a restaurant choose veal rather than chicken, I act both in accordance with preference and for a reason, the reason being that I prefer veal and that I see no reason not to act as I would if I acted from preference. If I had considered whether there were any reasons not to choose from preference in this matter and concluded that there were none, then I would have acted from preference and not for reasons. If I have no prima facie preference in this matter and choose chicken, let us say, because it is cheaper, then I choose chicken not from preference (that is, from preference for chicken over the other offerings) but for reasons.

Can we always transform any choice into a choice from (concrete) preference if we describe what we choose in such a way that *it includes all the facts awareness of which motivates us to choose as we do*? Is the preference the motivation to be reflected on, or is it that which results from the reflection, the propension to do whatever awareness of all the considered characteristics of the alternatives before us now inclines us to do? Or are there counterpreferential choices even if we are allowed to bring in all these aspects of the alternatives before us that incline us to choose one way rather than another?

Suppose the decisive aspect is that I believe that choosing A rather than B would be contrary to reason? Suppose I believe: (p) that it is *contrary to reason* to do anything that seriously harms my health; and (q) that smoking is a case of that. And suppose also that I have a strong inclination-based preference to have another cigarette right now. If I did not believe p and q, I would now have an inclination-based concrete preference for smoking over nonsmoking. But suppose that because I believe p and q, I do not now have that concrete preference. If I wanted to construe my behavior of smoking another cigarette as a preferential choice, I could not say I *preferred* not to smoke, for as far as the choice between smoking and nonsmoking was concerned, I preferred to smoke. I could construe what I chose as a preferential choice only by redescribing what I chose to do as, say, choosing the first alternative in a choice between the following two: (a) smoking and thereby acting contrary to what I took to be a compelling reason and (b) refraining from smoking and thereby acting in accordance with that reason.

But does Gauthier consider this a choice from and in accordance with preference? One reason for thinking that it must be is Gauthier's doctrine that "any choice reveals (behavioral) preference" (*MA*, p.30), but we have seen reason to reject behavioral preference as a dimension or type of preference. However, there is a better reason for rejecting it. For suppose I chose to smoke. Then, of course, my belief that I had a compelling reason not to smoke did not lead me to refrain. If my state of mind is to be described as having a (concrete) preference for not smoking, then I did not enact it, and so I acted irrationally because I acted contrary to my (concrete) preference. If it is one of not having this (concrete) preference, if on the contrary I had the opposite (concrete) preference which I did enact, then I also acted irrationally, not because I acted contrary to my (concrete) preference, but because, although I acted in accordance with it, my preference was contrary to what I believed to be a compelling reason. Thus, whichever way we construe concrete preference, it seems that our judgment of the rationality and irrationality of choice does not fit Gauthier's model of it: that a choice is rational if it endeavors to maximize value (*MA*, p.33), i.e., the measure of rational – considered and coherent – preference. For let us assume that my concrete preference is considered and is part of a set that is coherent. Then, surely, if that preference is contrary to what I regard as a compelling reason, I act irrationally even though I act in accordance with "rational," that is, considered and coherent, preference.

Does Gauthier perhaps want to say that my concrete preference *cannot be fully considered* if it is contrary to what I regard as a compelling reason? Suppose he does want to say that. Then he needs to make two significant modifications in his account of rational preference.

The first is to abandon the claim, taken over from the economists, that every "choice reveals (behavioral) preference" (*MA*, p.30). Instead, he would have to accept the common-sense view that there are not two dimensions or types of preference, behavioral and attitudinal, but only one type, attitudinal, and that choice and expression provide, mainly for others, highly fallible evidential access to that preference. In the case in hand, my choice to smoke does not reveal my fully considered concrete preference, but is contrary to it.

The second and more important modification is the introduction of practical reasoning into reflecting on preferences. But this upends Gauthier's theory. Instead of determining what is rational and what irrational choice on the basis of what we prefer, we have to say that rational choice is the maximization of the measure of rational preference, which involves reflecting on the preferences we have, which in turn involves asking ourselves what we have the best reason for doing, which requires us to operate with and according to what we regard as the best reasons, quite irrespective of what we *find* ourselves preferring after reflection, and it may require us to change or ignore these preferences.

But now let us reconsider the view we just supposed Gauthier to hold, namely, that one could not believe (i.e., correctly be said to believe) that one had a compelling reason not to smoke, yet smoke. This is a view of the type that has been called "Internalism," the thesis that there is some kind of necessary connection between someone's having a reason to do something and his doing it. However, on closer inspection, the type of Internalism we supposed Gauthier to hold does not seem plausible. Let us, for argument's sake, agree that a person does not really believe he has a compelling reason unless he somehow shows in his behavior that he believes he has such a reason. Even so, this does not entail that he always acts in accordance with that reason. Surely it is enough that he do something that shows that he believes it, e.g., he calls "Smokers Anonymous" or makes an appointment with his doctor about his smoking problem. Even that does not seem necessary. Surely, one can *believe* that one has a compelling reason to do something, e.g., not to smoke, yet do nothing about stopping one's smoking habit, provided only that one acknowledges that one is acting contrary to reason and that *there is an explanation* of why one is doing so, e.g., that one is too hooked on smoking, or is too lazy to do something about it.

A different objection may now be raised on Gauthier's behalf. It may be said that one's continuing to smoke cannot be irrational simply on the grounds that one believes one has a compelling reason not to smoke, but can be so only if that belief is true. But that belief could not be true unless one really had a propension to choose (A) rather than (B) of the following two alternatives: (A) to act in accordance with a compelling reason not to smoke and so not to smoke; (B) to act contrary to a compelling reason not to smoke and so to smoke. For having a propension to choose (B) rather than (A) shows that one does *not have* a compelling reason not to smoke, and so the belief that one does have such a reason must be false.

There are two replies to this. The first is that, on Gauthier's own showing, it may be rational for me to have a certain belief even if it is false, provided I have acquired it in a rational manner. It may, therefore, be rational for me to believe that, in the purported fact that smoking is seriously harmful to one's health and that it is contrary to reason to do what is seriously harmful to one's health, one has a compelling reason not to do it, even if this belief is false. After all, both beliefs are widely held, and so I may have arrived at these beliefs in a perfectly rational manner.

Secondly, the objection implies that the truth (or soundness) of this belief about reason and health depends on one's having the appropriate preference, that is, the concrete preference for doing what the supposed reason recommends, and on the preference being a considered one, i.e., one based on *sufficient* experience and reflection. But, as we have seen, this is operationally indeterminate. For how much is sufficient? Must one have had lung cancer or must one know many or some people who have died of it? Must one know about available treatments, analgesics, and so on? And what sort of reflection must one go in for? What question must one consider, or will any unstructured ruminations do? And for how long must one engage in it? There does not seem to be any genuine empirical way to determine when someone has sufficient experience or has reflected sufficiently to see whether or not he has a fully, or even sufficiently, considered concrete preference.

Even so, it may be objected, at any rate, a person cannot be said to believe that she *has* a compelling reason unless she believes that were she to have sufficient experience and to reflect sufficiently, she *would* have the relevant concrete preference. I very much doubt even this. For why should it not be enough that a person can *see* that health is an extremely important asset in her life – it need not be in everyone's life but simply in hers – and that she would be prevented from carrying out those important projects in her life on which she thinks its worthwhileness depends. Is not this enough to give one adequate reasons to think that one has compelling reason not to seriously harm one's health by smoking, quite independently of whether, on amassing sufficient experience and reflecting sufficiently, one were to *find* oneself *having* a corresponding concrete preference? Would one not, on the contrary, be inclined to say of a person who had come to think, by this sort of reasoning, that he had compelling reason not to smoke, yet failed to have the concrete preference which reason required him to have, that he would be choosing contrary to reason if he smoked: that it was simply irrelevant whether his choice was in accordance with or contrary to his concrete preferences? Would one not be inclined to say that what made his concrete preference rational was not that it was fully considered, but that it was a propension *in accordance with the outcome* of the reasoning, and not just *whatever* he came to be inclined to do *after reflection?* It is not sufficient for rationality that one should have reflected "sufficiently," that one's reflection has led one to *judge* that one *should* give up smoking, and that, after all this, one's strongest inclination is to smoke, and so one smokes. Rationality does not consist in those concrete preferences, whatever they may be, that one happens to end up with after sufficient reflection. Rather, it consists in having propensions *in accordance with the judgmental outcome of these reflections.*

IX. VALUE

The preceding ruminations bear on Gauthier's conception of value. It seems that by 'value' he means what we often mean by 'a person's values', which he identifies with a person's preferences provided they form a set that is both coherent and (adequately or fully?) considered.[14] He describes

[14] I believe there are important differences between a person's *values* and the *value* of persons or things, between these and the *excellence* of things and persons of a certain sort, e.g., knives and doctors, and all these and *the good* from a certain point of view, and that rationality relates in quite different ways to these things. But this is too big a topic to take up here, and so I am compelled to formulate my views in an oversimplified way. I have drawn some of the necessary distinctions in "What is Value," Kurt Baier and Nicholas Rescher, eds., *Values and the Future* (New York: Free Press, 1969), pp.33–67; "Value and Fact", *Ethical and Social Justice*, vol. IV, of *Contemporary Philosophic Thought*, Howard Kiefer and Milton K. Munitz, eds. (Albany, NY: State University of New York Press at Albany, 1968, 1970); and "Preference and the Good of Man," invited paper (submitted in 1974) for the von Wright volume of the *Library of Living Philosophers*, P.A. Schlipp, ed. (forthcoming). I have not found space in this paper to air my objections to tying rationality to maximization, but I have done so in "Maximization and the Good Life," *Ethics, Foundations, Problems, and Applications*, Proceedings of the 5th International Wittgenstein Symposium, 1980 (Wien: Holder-Pichler-Tempsky, 1981).

his own conception of value as "subjective" rather than "objective," and "relative" rather than "absolute."

(a) Subjectivism. That value is subjective means that values are considered preferences, and this means two things: that values are "registers of our fully considered attitudes to [certain] states of affairs given our beliefs about them" (*MA*, p.48), but that "the relation between belief and attitude is not itself open to rational assessment" (*MA*, p.48),[15] and that there is no "special realm of the valuable" accessible to a "unique 'value-oriented' cognition" (*MA*, p.49), as the objectivist maintains.

Clearly, Gauthier's subjectivism involves two criteria. One can accept the second without the first, though not the first without the second. One can agree – as I do – that there is "no special realm" of the valuable, yet believe that in some cases, though not all, the relation between belief and attitude is open to rational assessment. But if there were a special realm of the valuable accessible to unique value-oriented cognition, which presumably includes (as G.E. Moore thought) the cognition of the relation between having natural and value properties, then the relation between belief and attitude would be open to rational assessment. We would be given standards by which to judge whether the preferred accords with the preferable.

I believe that common sense allows the rational assessment of the relation between some beliefs and some attitudes, but not all. Thus, we do not allow any rational assessment of some of what I have called *given* prima facie preferences, e.g., those for the taste of apples over pears. Since most of the examples of preference offered in the literature are of this kind, the belief that all preferences are in this respect like given ones seems plausible at first sight. Even in this class, though, there are problematic cases, such as the masochist and the ascetic. These cases suggest that the preference "for pleasure over pain" is not wholly tautological – the preference for what is preferred – and also that, if someone had a genuine prima facie preference for (a certain) pain over absence of (that) pain, or for the absence of (a certain) pleasure over (that) pleasure he would have an irrational given prima facie preference, one such that if he based choices on it, they would be contrary to reason.

Furthermore, as I have already noted, when it comes to reflection, we do not allow any and every outcome of reflection to be rational. A person may

---

[15] This seems contrary to what we ordinarily do when we call certain emotions, such as fear or anger, irrational, or when we find paradoxical Hume's view, which Gauthier endorses (*MA*, p.48), that it is not "contrary to reason" – which Gauthier seems to identify with *irrational* – to prefer the destruction of the whole world to the scratching of one's finger. Gauthier attempts to explain this by distinguishing between irrationality and madness. I cannot discuss this here, but it is perhaps worth mentioning that in some of the best studies of the legal notion of insanity, which involves mental disorder, disease, or illness, it is construed as a form of irrationality. Cf., e.g., Herbert Fingarette's books on this topic.

indeed find that his life is not worth living, that preventing his death would not be doing him a service, would not benefit him, but we do not allow that such a conclusion is rational irrespective of what has gone into the reflection. If I want to commit suicide because I have a toothache, this would not be regarded as rational, even if I claimed I had carefully reflected on it (cf. *MA*, p.34). Would we not be entitled to say in such a case that I *could* not have reflected carefully *enough*? And does not this show that we know with greater certainty what the outcome of the reflection must be than when we have reflected sufficiently? Does not rationality mean more than that I have reflected even a long time? Am I rational in thinking that $5+7=13$, or $37698 \times 43621 = 12,375,855,018$, if I have reflected long enough? Surely, the first is irrational however long I have reflected on it, even though the second may not be.

This brings to light a distinction between accordance with reason and rationality, contrariety to reason and irrationality. The initial plausibility of Gauthier's claim, that it is not the content of particular preferences, but only 'the manner in which they are held, and their interrelation" that are the concern of reason (*MA*, p.75), rests at least in part on the failure to keep apart irrationality and contrariety to reason. For irrationality, but not contrariety to reason, may depend on the manner in which preferences are held. In our system of reasons, theoretical and practical, rationality and irrationality are only one type of assessment of a person's "performance" (what he believes, thinks, feels, prefers, intends, chooses, does, and so on) in the broad category of conformity with or contrariety to *reason*, that is, the balance of relevant pros and cons. Irrationality marks a particularly glaring or flagrant form, a flying in the face of reason, rationality a very broad range of performances from perfect rationality at the top down to the barest passing grade. There are quite a few other pairs of related evaluative epithets, such as prudent/imprudent, wise/unwise, sensible/foolish, consistent/inconsistent, and logical/illogical, that mark various other ways and degrees of accordance with and contrariety to reason. Our common-sense conception of rationality/irrationality does not define these terms directly by reference to interest, happiness, pleasure, desire, or preference, as Gauthier does, but defines it indirectly in terms of the balance of reasons, thus requiring a theory of what makes something a reason, whether theoretical (or 'cognitive', as I prefer to call it, to distinguish it from 'explanatory') – a reason *to* believe – or practical – a reason *to* act.

We are irrational, we fly in the face of reason, if our judgment runs counter to what we ourselves consider the overwhelming balance of reasons, as when we act perversely, cussedly, cutting our nose to spite our face, or when, from weakness of will, we continue to gamble, drink, smoke, to what we believe will be our certain ruin. By contrast, suppose that through inattention, carelessness, ignorance, or stupidity, we fail to perceive or work out the balance of reasons, and thus continue to gamble. Then, although our actions might not be irrational, they would still be contrary to reason. However, *pace* Gauthier, the concern of reason is not solely with rationality/irrationality, but with the whole range of ways in which one can perform in accordance with or contrary to reason.

Gauthier might argue that the person with masochistic or ascetic prima facie preferences is pathological, has a malfunction of the affections, or is insane (*MA*, p.25), but is not irrational, because his preferences are not held in an irrational, that is, ill-considered manner. But is not one of our reasons, perhaps the only one, for our wanting to call that person insane the fact that he has *these* prima facie preferences? Might he not be perfectly normal otherwise? And if he were, would we not have to abandon our claim that he was insane, but not the claim that his preference was contrary to reason, however long he had reflected on it?

It seems to me that common sense allows us to give rational assessments of the relation between some of a person's beliefs and attitudes, and so "to treat the content of preference as subject to rational assessment" but, *pace* Gauthier, this does not require "an objective conception of value" (*MA*, p.34), at least not in the sense of a special realm of the valuable. It requires only the belief that the community's beliefs of what are reasons for doing and preferring are more likely to be sound and so a better criterion of rationality than the individual's own reflection – unless, of course, that reflection is itself based on reasons which show the reason accepted by the community to be mistaken or subject to exceptions. Thus, I may have reason to think that it would be better for me not to cure my neurosis and stomach ulcers because this would dry up my philosophical inspiration. But then, this would itself be a rationally acceptable reflection. However, it would be thus acceptable not because I reflected sufficiently or for a long time, but because I surveyed and weighed relevant public reasons, and showed that a generally accepted prima facie reason – do what is necessary to promote your health – is overridden by another – preserve the conditions on which your special talent rests.

(b) Relativism. That value is relative means that value measures the place of some state of affairs in a person's preferences (*MA*, p.49). Different people's values may converge or diverge. "We have no good reason to suppose that the fully considered preferences of different persons over the same states of affairs would give rise to equivalent measures, even if we suppose the persons fully informed, fully reflective and experienced, and similarly placed to the states of affairs" (*MA*, pp.49–50).

Gauthier rejects Mill's "union of subjectivism and absolutism" (*MA*, p.52) because it passes from a seemingly relativist premise (that each person's happiness is a good to that person) to an absolutist conclusion (that the general happiness is a good to all persons), a transition which has generally been held to exemplify the fallacy of composition. This is not the place to investigate whether Mill could defend his subjectivist-absolutist conception by better reasons. Instead, I want to suggest that common sense embraces a conception of rational preferences which is neither exactly absolutist nor exactly relativist in Gauthier's sense. It operates on the principle that it is rational to act from preference except where there is sufficient reason to set preference aside, as when, let us say, a person has sufficient reason to set aside his preference for smoking, because he believes, on the basis of what he has read, that smoking will ruin his health, and that, going by what he has heard and thought, he believes that being ruinous to one's health is a very strong reason against doing something, stronger than the enjoyment derived from it and the unpleasantness that comes with giving it up. Common sense suggests two things: (a) that it is rational to follow what are generally regarded as reasons and how weighty they are, rather than ignore this and judge the matter on the basis of one's own independent reflections, because the public system of reasons has the backing of the experience and wisdom of many generations; and (b) that it is rational to depart from these public reasons only if one can show them to be mistaken, and not just because one does not like their outcome, e.g., that one has to give up smoking.

This is not absolutist, for there is no single state of affairs, comparable to Mill's general happiness that everyone has compelling reason to bring about. But nor is it relativist in the sense that the rational thing to do is whatever you prefer, that is, are most strongly inclined to do, after "sufficient" reflection. On the view I am suggesting, the rational thing to do is what you have *sufficient reason* to do, whether or not you prefer or are disposed to do it, after *sufficient reflection*. The conception is not exactly relativist, because rationality lies not in acting from and in accordance with the preference, i.e., propension, you have after reflection, but *in accordance with* the judgment you arrive at after *reasoned* reflection, that is, after determining which way the balance of reasons points.

X. CONCLUSION

There is much more to be said, of course, but perhaps I have said enough to cast sufficient doubt on the soundness of Gauthier's subjectivist-relativist theory of value and his theory that practical rationality is the maximization of value, that is, the measure of rational preference (rather than, as I think, action in accordance with the balance of reasons), and on his claim that these theories of rationality and value provide us with adequate reason to reject even plausible and uncontentious precepts of common-sense morality that are incompatible with "morals by agreement." I fear that, despite the rigor, precision, and cogency of this treatise, and despite the brilliant light it sheds on the logical connections between the central concepts he employs, some of them, including, I suspect, rationality, value, and preference as he construes them, will one day seem warped and off-beam to our descendants, if surely never "as strange . . . as The Form of the Good and The Unmoved Mover" seems to us (*MA*, p.20), as he himself fears.

Philosophy, University of Pittsburgh

Social Philosophy & Policy 5:2 ISSN 0265-0525

BARGAINING, JUSTICE, AND JUSTIFICATION: TOWARDS RECONSTRUCTION

James S. Fishkin

Part I of this essay will be devoted to Gauthier's principle of minimax relative concession. Part II will focus, more generally, on the variety of possible strategies available to liberal theory. In Part I, I will argue that the principle of minimax relative concession does not define "essential justice" as Gauthier claims. In Part II, I will argue that the difficulties facing Gauthier's strategy are common to other strategies of the same general kind. I will close by suggesting what I think may prove to be a more promising approach.

PART I: JUSTICE AND THE LOCKEAN PROVISO

Gauthier develops his account of the Lockean proviso[1] with the example of a person who has fallen into the water and is drowning.[2] Another person comes along and can either save him or continue walking. Following Nozick's earlier use of essentially the same example,[3] let us refer to the drowning person as Q and the person who could save him as P. A crucial question is whether Q got into the water on his own, or whether P had something to do with creating this baseline situation (e.g. whether P pushed Q in). Taking the perspective of P, Gauthier explains:

> The base point for determining how I affect you, in terms of bettering or worsening your situation, is determined by the outcome that you would expect in my absence. Worsening, and equally bettering, are judged by comparing what I actually do with

---

[1] All references to Gauthier are to his *Morals by Agreement* (Oxford: Oxford University Press, 1986); in subsequent notes and parenthetical references in the text, the title of this work will be abbreviated to *MA*. The term "Lockean proviso" refers to the morally appropriate baseline for bargaining. Central to Gauthier's position is that "the proviso prohibits bettering one's situation through interaction that worsens the situation of another. This, we claim, expresses the underlying idea of not taking advantage." [Gauthier, *MA*, p.205].

[2] Gauthier, *MA*, p.204.

[3] Robert Nozick "Coercion," Peter Laslett, W.G. Runciman, and Quentin Skinner, eds., *Philosophy, Politics and Society*, Fourth Series (Oxford: Basil Blackwell, 1972), pp.101–135, esp. p.115.

what would have occurred, *ceteris paribus*, in my absence (*MA*, p.204).

Gauthier does not actually apply the principle of minimax relative concession[4] to this example. He uses it solely to illuminate the Lockean proviso, the appropriate base line for bargaining. But those who had read Nozick's earlier treatment would be aware that P has, in similar cases, offered to save Q only if he is paid $10,000. Let us, however, imagine that our P has not only read Nozick on coercion, but also Gauthier on the case of Sam McGee, the prospector, and Grasp, the banker. Sam lacks the $100 to register his rich gold glaim and can only get it from Grasp the Banker. "[P]oor Sam", we are told, "will (rationally) have to offer Grasp a half-share in the claim" (*MA*, p.153). Minimax relative concession requires that the surplus (all the gold in Sam's rich claim) be divided equally by the new joint venture. In the two-person case, the maximum relative concession is minimized if they each give up half of their maximal claim. On this reasoning, it was enormously *generous* for Nozick's Q to settle for only $10,000! If Gauthier's P should be so kind as to pull Q out of the water (we might imagine P momentarily interupting his sunbathing on the shore by tossing Q a rope attached to the dock), he should, rationally, get *half of all* Q's *future earnings*. By the same reasoning as in the Sam McGee case, P should get half of the surplus produced by Q in his future life – a life which is about to become a joint venture with P. "Poor Q." This indentured servitude is merely the rational result of his poor bargaining position, defined by the unfortunate base line in which he finds himself (so long as it has come about through no fault of P).

Gauthier is correct to make the general point that "coercion" should not define the status quo in bargaining situations whose results we are to accept as morally relevant. However, I believe that Gauthier is incorrect to equate "coercion" in these bargaining situations with violations of his Lockean proviso. More specifically, Q is faced with a coercive structure of choice in which he is, literally, sinking without P's assistance. For P to demand $10,000, or worse, all that he could demand by Gauthier's bargaining principle, is not "essential justice." It is a form of extortion.

Figure 1 illustrates the analysis. The status quo is point 1. The Pareto-superior quadrant northeast of 1 is the surplus supplied entirely by Q's future earnings if his life is saved. (If P has other earnings, they are irrelevant to the argument; in any case, we might imagine that P has been

---

[4] Gauthier explains the principle of minimax relative concession as follows: "in any co-operative interaction, the rational joint strategy is determined by a bargain among the co-operators in which each advances his maximal claim and then offers a concession no greater in relative magnitude than the minimax concession" (the minimum maximum concession, *MA*, p.145).

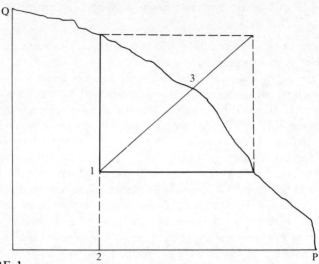

FIGURE 1

lolling around the beach, just waiting for such an opportunity). P's maximal claim is that he keep all of the surplus, without benefiting Q; Q's maximal claim is that he get all of it (perhaps in calculating the surplus, we have already subtracted a subsistence allowance for Q so that he can keep on working). By the principle of minimax relative concession, they settle on point 3 – splitting the difference so that Q and P will each be entitled to half of Q's future earnings. But they do this only because the status quo, point 1, is dynamic.[5] Q is sinking. He is threatened, if he does not come to an agreement with P, with ending up at point 2 (or whatever worse graphic representation for his fate you might like to pick). It is the threat of Q's move from 1 to 2 which forces him to agree, rationally, to 3. More generally, we might say that *when Q agrees to benefit* P *only to avoid what both know to be reasonably expectable disaster to* Q, *then* Q *has been subjected to a coercively structured bargaining situation.*

From this perspective, the difficulty with Gauthier's analysis is that some, *but not all*, coercively structured bargaining situations will be ruled out by his single-minded reliance on the Lockean proviso to identify coercion. Most obviously, if Q is in the water because P pushed him over the dock, then the disaster which is reasonably expectable for Q has been

---

[5] This kind of dynamic status quo also surfaced as a weakness in the theory of James Buchanan which Gauthier relies on at certain points. See Douglas W. Rae "The Limits of Consensual Decision" *The American Political Science Review*, Vol. LXIX, no. 4 (December 1975), pp.1270–94, esp. p.1289 for an incisive critique of the early version developed by Buchanan and Tullock.

caused by P and would not, according to Gauthier, define the morally relevant base line for bargaining. For such limited cases, Gauthier and I can agree that the Lockean proviso fulfills its task. However, the more general characterization of coercively structured bargaining situations would also accomplish the task, not only in the case where P has pushed Q in, but also in the case where he simply attempts to profit from Q's impending disaster by extorting an enormous concession. My position is that the situation is coercive in either case. A benefit to P is being extorted from Q by the threat of disaster. Whether or not P is the cause of the disaster, the dynamic character of the status quo for Q is the source of the threat from which P intends to profit.

A three person variation helps develop the point. A invites B and C to dinner. A decides to torture B until B agrees to a bargain whereby half of all B's future earnings will go to A. C is rather disgusted by this manner of entertaining dinner guests and points out that A cannot employ Gauthier's theory to legitimize this bargain because A is taking advantage of the situation in the sense ruled out by the Lockean proviso. A then replies that as a favor and gesture of friendship to C, he will refrain from torturing B if B makes the same bargain with C (donating half of B's future earnings to C). C is free to make such a bargain. A reasons, because C would not have violated the Lockean proviso – C would not be benefiting from a baseline in the bargaining where C has made B worse off (A has kindly done that for him). In my view, both A's proposed bargain with B and C's proposed bargain with B offer cases where someone is proposing to profit from a coercively structured situation. Both bargains are objectionable and neither could be represented as essential justice. But on Gauthier's view, if I understand him correctly, A's bargain is objectionable but C's would be perfectly legitimate.[6]

The contrast between violations of the Lockean Proviso and other coercively structured bargaining situations is clarified by variations on one of Gauthier's other key examples. Gauthier shows, amusingly and convincingly, the difficulty with a calculation of minimax relative concession from a base line defined by slavery. The calculation, one of the masters argues, is:

> What we need is a bargain with our slaves – we'll free them, dismantling all the coercive apparatus that slavery involves, and in return they will voluntarily be our servants. We'll benefit – better service, less expense, money saved for other uses, and they'll

---

[6] We might even imagine that once this hole in the Lockean proviso is discovered, A will regularly hold such dinner parties for C, and C will return the favor by holding them for A – permitting each of them to exchange chances to extort money from the unwitting third guest, all in full conformity with the theory and without violating the Lockean proviso.

benefit – no more beatings and chainings, and better living
conditions, since from the money we'll save in doing away with
coercion and the increased productivity we'll get from their willing
service, we can pay them wages better than the living allowance we
have to provide now, and still have the resources to put some *real*
pleasures into our lives (*MA*, p.190).

Gauthier denies the relevance of this application of minimax relative
concession to his theory because the slaves are worse off than they
otherwise would have been, were it not for the coercion of their masters.
Their masters violate the Lockean proviso. They profit from threat
advantage:

> We shall deny the relevance of threat behavior to rational
> interaction, and argue that, if the non-co-operative outcome
> involves coercion, then it must be constrained by removing the
> effects of that coercion if it is to serve as an initial position for
> bargaining to a joint strategy that rationally commands individual
> compliance (*MA*, p.192).

As he says at another point, "all effects of taking advantage must be
removed from the initial position" (*MA*, p.192). By contrast, my position
is that all coercively structured bargaining situations involve "taking
advantage"; they all involve "threat behavior" regardless of whether or not
they *also* involve violations of the Lockean proviso. However, Gauthier only
removes the "threat behavior" or the efforts to "take advantage" which
depend on violations of the Lockean provisio.

Returning to his example, suppose that there is a class of the very rich
coexisting with a ghetto underclass facing massive unemployment in a pure
market system (with no welfare-state apparatus). Just as in Gauthier's
example, let us assume that the rich want servants. The poor, who are
legally free to do as they please, may find themselves in a situation which is
coercively structured, just as surely as that of the slaves in the version
Gauthier finds objectionable. Like Q in our diagram, they may face a *status
quo* which is, itself, dynamic. If they don't find jobs, they can expect to
starve to death, just as Q, if he doesn't agree to P's conditions, can expect
to sink beneath the waves. So long as the rich have not, themselves, placed
the poor in this position, their prospective starvation is no more a violation
of the Lockean proviso than Q's drowning in the case where he found his
way into the water entirely on his own. Not offering Q a job is no more a
violation of the Lockean proviso than not offering to save him. But failure
for Q to obtain a job can be just as coercive and disastrous as failure to
throw him a lifeline out of the water.

The saga of the Joad family in Steinbeck's novel, *The Grapes of Wrath*, illustrates the point. No one violates the Lockean proviso. They are thrown off "their land" at the beginning of the story, but since they were sharecroppers, no property rights were violated. They journey to California to pick peaches, making a series of increasingly exploitative wage bargains. Each Pareto-superior move might well reflect the principle of minimax relative concession, but because their status quo is dynamic, their condition progressively deteriorates – taking them closer and closer to starvation (they are forced to accept less and less for more and more work, etc.). Because their bargains are coercively structured (in the sense defined earlier), those bargains are morally suspect. They are objectionable just as the bargain with the slaves was objectionable on Gauthier's own telling.

The point can be extended to our own time. Imagine that the U.S. had no welfare-state apparatus (none would be required by Gauthier's analysis). Black teen age unemployment has been running over 50 percent for years in most of America's major cities. What would minimax relative concession give to this urban underclass? What we do about this issue is, arguably, the crucial domestic problem of social justice facing the U.S. today. Provided that the advantaged have not violated the Lockean proviso in placing people into the ghetto underclass, the present desperate condition of the unemployed teenager defines the appropriate base line for bargaining in Gauthier's analysis. The results parallel with slavery into servant class example, with the one crucial difference that without violations of the Lockean proviso, the results would have to be endorsed by the theory.

However, one further contrast is worth pointing out. Members of the present ghetto underclass might well have no "rational" reason, in Gauthier's sense, to agree, even hypothetically, on a transition from a state of nature to civil society. The reason, quite simply, is that they have nothing to lose. Recently, Claude Brown produced a disturbing portrait of violent youths in Harlem. It included several accounts of how their violent behavior seemed rational. Brown challenged them with the following reasoning about how a life of crime was not in their interest:

> Every time he goes on the prowl, for a victim or an establishment, he runs the risk of one of three serious misfortunes: there is at least a 60% chance he will be killed, permanently maimed or end up doing a long bit in jail. And even if he succeeds in getting over nine or ten times for $1,000 or more, in a few days to a week at most he will be right back where he started – at the bottom of the hill. . . . Couldn't he see how futile it was?

Brown was startled by the response to this challenge by a youth whom he describes as not yet old enough to shave but who was doing a fifteen-year sentence for armed robbery:

> "I see where you comin' from, Mr. Brown" he replied, but you got things kind of turned around the wrong way. You see, all the things that you say could happen to me is dead on the money and that is why I can't lose. Look at it from my point of view for a minute. Let's say I go and get wiped (killed). Then I ain't got no more needs, right? All my problems are solved. I don't need no more money, no more nothing, right? OK, supposin' I get popped, shot in the spine and paralyzed for the rest of my life – that could happen playing football, you know. Then I won't need a whole lot of money because I won't be able to go no place and do nothing, right? . . . Now if I get busted and end up in the joint pulling a dime and nickle like I am (15 year sentence) then I don't have to worry about no bucks, no clothes. I get free rent and three square meals a day. So you see Mr. Brown, I don't really lose.[7]

This frightening example of philosophical reasoning from the more violent fringes of the ghetto underclass reveals a hole in Gauthier's basic inference: that minimax relative concession will provide a rational basis for social cooperation from a base line for bargaining defined by nonviolation of the Lockean proviso. This youth, let us call him X, can expect no surplus from social cooperation (as defined by the established institutions of civil society). X can rationally do better for himself by living in what amounts to a state of nature vis-a-vis the rest of us. First, his violence may be rewarded by robberies which go unpunished. Second, his status quo is so dreadful that the things we regard as punishments are regarded by him as rewards. In that sense, as he says, he can't lose. Complying with the law by joining civil society offers him only the prospect of unemployment or some job which he regards as far worse than what he can obtain by continuing in the state of nature. Because of his dreadful position, the social compact is not a rational bargain for him (in Gauthier's self-interested sense of rationality). Without the Lockean proviso having been violated, he finds himself in a position in which he has nothing to lose and everything to gain from *not* cooperating.

Once more, the difficulty is that Gauthier limits objectionable coercive situations to those which violate the Lockean proviso. When the proviso is violated, he is willing to grant that compliance is rendered irrational. However, what he says about that case might well be extended to this one:

> But compliance is rationally grounded only within the framework

[7] Claude Brown, "Manchild in Harlem," *New York Times Magazine*, Sept. 17, 1984, p.44.

of a fully co-operative venture, in which each participant willingly interacts with her fellows. . . . If persons are willingly to comply with the agreement that determines what each takes from the bargaining table, then they must find initially acceptable what each brings to the table. And if what some bring to the table includes the fruits of prior interaction forced on their fellows, then this initial acceptability will be lacking. If you seize the products of my labour and then say "Let's make a deal!" I may be compelled to accept, but I will not voluntarily comply (*MA*, p.15).

It is with this discussion that Gauthier introduces the Lockean proviso. But our ghetto teen-ager shows how an initially unacceptable bargaining situation may be created without any violations of the Lockean proviso. Compliance with the results may be no more "rational" in the purely self-interested sense than compliance in the case where poverty results from previous theft and in which Gauthier then says "Let's make a deal." Whether or not the extreme poverty results from previous theft, *X*'s situation is untenable and he need not rationally accept the bargain of minimax relative concession – as determined from *that* status quo – any more than Gauthier thought it reasonable for the slaves to accept a similar bargain from *their* debilitated status quo. In both cases, the benefits are so meager that civil society cannot plausibly be viewed as fruitful social cooperation. Judged from those baselines, the *non*compliance represented by the state of nature may well represent rational self-interested calculations.

Note that I am not claiming violence to be moral under these conditions; I am only denying that bargains inferred from such baselines represent either justice or rational self-interest. For Gauthier's argument to go through he must, of course, establish that they represent *both* justice and rational self-interest. For those who have nothing to lose, the no-agreement point is simply not to be feared as it is for the rest of us. For such persons, and under such terms, the social contract may not be viable.

Consider one further twist to the story. Suppose the members of our ghetto underclass all change their calculations because they have joined a religious sect whose leader commands them to accept civil society. They must all obey the law, find whatever employment they can, and donate the proceeds to the sect's coffers. If they fail to find employment, they are supposed to starve to death quietly, without complaint, and without any financial burden on the assets of the sect. They incorporate these new preferences as their own, delighted to be following the word of the Almighty.

Given their new preference structure, members of the sect come to view

civil society as a rational bargain. What does this prove? Only that with
sufficient indoctrination, it is possible for virtually any result to be upheld
by the preferences of some group. Gauthier has a modest defense against
this kind of argument, but it is only a modest one. It is that the preferences
must be "considered":

> Preferences are considered if and only if there is no conflict
> between their behavioural and attitudinal dimensions and they are
> stable under experience and reflection (MA, p.33).

There is no reason to assume that the members of our sect could not
plausibly claim their preferences to be "considered" in this sense. They
might, from that point on, be quite stable, consistent with their behavior,
and sustainable, on their view, in light of further reflection. The same
might be said about many other bizarre positions – moral, political, or
religious – which we, as outsiders, believe to be the result of indoctrination,
brainwashing, or sheer eccentricity. The criteria for considered preferences
specify nothing about the appropriate conditions for preference formation.
We are only given criteria for preference maintenance (stability) and
consistency with behavior – provided that those preferences survive
whatever questioning or scrutiny the person cares to engage in.

When our religious-sect story is added to the difficulties with the
Lockean proviso, two distinct issues emerge. First, there is the issue of
which hypothetical starting point is the morally relevant status quo from
which to evaluate rival principles. I will call this the *jurisdiction problem*.
Second, there is the issue that some preferences seem morally suspect as
the basis for choice. I will call this the *indoctrination problem*. Gauthier's
basic strategy is, I believe, vulnerable to both.

In Part II, I will try to place these difficulties in a more general
framework. I will end by suggesting a strategy which, I believe, is
vulnerable to neither the jurisdiction problem nor the indoctrination
problem.

PART II: LIBERAL STRATEGIES

I closed Part I with the argument that Gauthier's theory is vulnerable to
two fundamental difficulties – difficulties which I labelled the "jurisdiction"
and "indoctrination" problems. In this section, I would like to place this
claim within a broader framework. I will argue that Gauthier's vulnerability
is not surprising. In fact, any theory of his general kind must be vulnerable
to the same two difficulties. Furthermore, I will argue that the other
significant possibilities prominent in contemporary liberal theory are also

vulnerable to at least one, if not both, of these same basic problems. Finally, I will sketch the possibility of a quite different strategy which holds, I believe, the promise of avoiding both of these fundamental objections.[8]

Recent liberal theory has been distinctive for its thought experiments: transporting us to an imaginary situation or transforming our motivation so that we choose political principles under conditions in which only the morally relevant factors bear on the decision. Two kinds of imaginary devices have been employed to ensure impartiality – changes in the situation of choice and changes in the motivation (within which I include filtering requirements by which only certain motivations are selected, while the rest are prevented from bearing on the decision).[9] When the motivation for choosing principles has been altered or filtered in the interests of impartiality, I will classify it as "refined"; when people choose, or are imagined to choose, with unaltered motivation (as, realistically, we would expect to find them in actual life), I will classify those motivations as "brute." When the situation for choosing principles is the one in which those who must abide by the principles live together as an on-going enterprise, I will classify it as an "actual" choice situation. When the situation for choice is an imaginary one, held to be morally relevant, but not the situation in which those who must abide by the principles must live together as an on-going enterprise, I will term it "hypothetical."

These distinctions can be combined to produce the four-fold table pictured in Chart 1 below:

Motivations	Situation	
	Actual	Hypothetical
Brute	I	II
Refined	IV	III

Chart 1

An example of Category I is offered by actual consent theory. According to this approach, if people consent in real life, they are obligated to uphold

---

[8] This discussion is taken from a draft of my forthcoming book which is tentatively entitled *Reconstructing Liberal Theory*. In this section, I borrow substantially from my brief presentation in "Liberal Theories: Strategies of Reconstruction" A.D'Amico, ed, *Liberals on Liberalism* (Totowa, NJ: Rowman and Allanheld, forthcoming).

[9] Ackerman's theory employs neutrality as a "filter" on the motivations which can bear on the choice of principles. See the discussion below and Bruce A. Ackerman, *Social Justice in the Liberal State* (New Haven and London: Yale University Press, 1980).

the state; if enough (whatever that means) do actually consent, then the state is held to be legitimate and, somehow, everyone is obligated.[10] Motivation and situation are as we find them. Neither is subjected to some transformation in the name of impartiality or moral relevance.

Category II transforms the situation for choice, but not the motivation. Nozick's state of nature is a good example. We are to take the question of whether there should be a state at all to the "best anarchic situation one reasonably could hope for."[11] The motivations of people in this state of nature are not altered; they must be given a realistic construction. We are to assume that some would join protection associations voluntarily; others would choose to be independent. However, a major problem facing Nozick's argument is whether his scenario for the minimal state is compatible with a realistic construction of their preferences – whether, in particular, independents would be fully "compensated" in being forced to join the state.[12]

Category III transforms not only the situation, as in Category II, but also the motivations for choice in that situation. In Rawls's original position, agents are to choose principles of justice so as to maximize their shares of primary goods without knowing whom, in particular, they will turn out to be. They are endowed with an abstract preference for primary goods regardless of the details of their actual life plans; they will know the latter only after the veil of ignorance is lifted.[13] In Ackerman's space ship dialogues, entrants to a new world argue over the distribution of "manna" through a filtering device for relevant arguments (the "neutrality" assumption).[14] The perfectly sympathetic spectator of the classical utilitarians has both an imaginary vantage point (omniscience) and a postulated motivation (he reproduces in himself every pain and pleasure in the world and, hence, will prefer states of the world which maximize the net balance of pleasure over pain).

Of the possibilities in Chart 1, the basic difficulty with the *top row* categories (I and II) is that they are subject to *indoctrination problems* while

---

[10] A good account of these ambiguities, along with specimen illustrations, can be found in Pitkin, "Obligation and Consent" Peter Laslett and W.G. Runciman, eds., *Philosophy, Politics and Society*, Fourth Series (Oxford: Basil Blackwell, 1972).

[11] Robert Nozick, *Anarchy, State and Utopia* (New York: Basic Books, 1974) p.5.

[12] Can they be fully compensated by the protection services they have already refused (that is, after all, why they are independents)? But if they are not fully compensated, then have not rights been violated? Nozick might, of course, hypothesize that they *all* would simply love to join the state but this departs from the bounds of realism.

[13] John Rawls, *A Theory of Justice* (Cambridge, Mass. Harvard University Press, 1971).

[14] By "neutrality" Ackerman means "No reason is a good reason if it requires the powerholder to assert: (a) that his conception of the good is better than that asserted by any of his fellow citizens, or (b) that, regardless of his conception of the good, he is intrinsically superior to one or more of his fellow citizens." (p.11).

the basic difficulty with the *right column* categories (II and III) is that they are subject to *jurisdiction problems*. The only possibility offering the clear hope of avoiding both is Category IV (the left bottom quadrant). The proposal I will suggest here is an instance of that category.

The top row possibilities are subject to indoctrination problems because they take motivations as they are without any requirements specified for how they come to be that way. If people generally consent or accept an alternative because they have been brainwashed or manipulated, that result has the same standing as when they come to their conclusions after a fair and unbiased analysis. Preferences are "brute" in categories I and II. There is no mechanism built into these strategies for counteracting bias. In contemporary work this criticism applies, for example, to Tussman's use of actual consent theory[15] and to Walzer's *Spheres of Justice* (where the "shared understandings" current in the society determine the boundaries between "spheres" of life that ought not to be crossed).[16] It can also be applied to hypothetical choice scenarios involving brute motivations (Category II). If people accept a regime or a distribution because of indoctrination, then the legitimacy of brute motivations as a basis for choice has been undermined.

It is because of this inadequacy of brute motivations that the main thrust of thought experiments in liberal theory has been the *purging* of bias and indoctrination – the determination of what appears in the chart as "refined" motivation. Behind Rawls's "veil of ignorance," we cannot design principles so as to endow ourselves with any special advantage. We do not even know what our actual preferences are (nor do we know any other particular facts about ourselves). However distorted our actual preferences, they are not permitted to bear on the choice of principles in the "original position." Behind the "veil of ignorance," we must consider our own interests as if they were the interests of anyone, our class interests as if we were members of any class, our personal histories as if they were the product of any particular history of socialization. A similar purging of bias occurs in Ackerman's theory of neutral dialogue. Compatible with his notion of neutrality, we cannot even use our own theories of the good in giving reasons for one distribution rather than another. Various forms of utilitarianism address the same problem, although they are generally less successful. Because the perfectly sympathetic spectator of the classical utilitarians must reproduce in himself every pleasure and pain in the world, no one's pleasure or pain gets special consideration. But this is a less

---

[15] Joseph Tussman, *Obligation and the Body Politic* (New York: Oxford University Press, 1960).

[16] Michael Walzer, *Spheres of Justice: A Defense of Pluralism and Equality* (New York: Basic Books, 1983). For further criticisms along these lines, see my "Defending Equality: A View From the Cave" *Michigan Law Review*, Vol. 82, no. 4 (February 1984), pp.755–760.

adequate purging strategy. It escapes from some biases by counting all utility equally. But should the satisfaction of preferences induced by brainwashing and indoctrination count the same as those induced by autonomous reflection? Perhaps an "ideal" utilitarianism such as J.S. Mill's (which distinguishes higher and lower forms of utility) offers some response to this problem, but it does so only by positing a particular, controversial theory of the good.[17] In giving more than equal weight to some patterns of human development, Mill's strategy brings into question utilitarianism's claim to equal consideration – a claim which was, originally, at the core of its appeal.[18]

In any case, the general point is that a central motivation for the hypothetical choice strategies of Category III is that they provide a remedy (but sometimes only a partial one) for the indoctrination problems characteristic of Categories I and II. But when "refined" motivations are combined with "hypothetical" situations for choice, jurisdiction problems must be confronted.

The difficulty is that once we depart from actual life, we can appeal to any number of counterfactual situations. Even slightly different accounts of impartiality and slightly different notions of relevant claims or interests in these imaginary situations yield drastically different results.[19] *Which* imaginary court has jurisdiction when each can make precisely symmetrical claims?

Our critique of Gauthier in Part I shows how a theory at Category II can be vulnerable to both the jurisdiction and indoctrination problems. His requirement that preferences be "considered" is not an effective remedy for indoctrination, as we saw in the example of the religious sect. His account of bargaining from base lines established by nonviolation of the Lockean proviso faces the challenge of moral relevance: why should *this* base-line be accepted as the basis for choice, particularly when it includes some coercively structured situations which permit the extortion of some unacceptable results.

Category IV in Chart I offers the prospect of avoiding these difficulties, at least in their crucial aspects. The idea is to attempt to purge the actual

---

[17] For a critical discussion which argues that Mill stretches utility to the point of vacuity, see Isaiah Berlin, "John Stuart Mill and the Ends of Life," in *Four Essays* (New York: Oxford University Press, 1969). For a more sympathetic interpretation, see Richard Wollheim "John Stuart Mill and Isaiah Berlin: The Ends of Life and the Preliminaries of Morality" in Alan Ryan, ed. *The Idea of Freedom* (New York: Oxford University Press, 1979).

[18] For some useful observations on the intuitive appeal of the notion of equality at the core of utilitarianism, see Bernard Williams, *Ethics and the Limits of Philosophy* (Cambridge, MA: Harvard University Press, 1985), pp.105–6; Henry Widgwick *The Methods of Ethics*, Seventh Edition (London: MacMillan, 1963), pp.382, 420–42.

[19] For more on the jurisdiction problem see my *Beyond Subjective Morality: Ethical Reasoning and Political Philosophy* (New Haven and London: Yale University Press, 1984), Chapter Four.

ongoing society – rather than some imaginary counterpart – of bias and indoctrination bearing directly on fundamental questions of political authority. The notion of a *self-reflective political culture*, which I will suggest here, is intended to bring the self-purging dimension of liberal thought experiments home to the environment people actually live in, rather than merely to one they are asked to imagine.

This fact sharply differentiates my proposal from the purely hypothetical strategies (II and III). If the purging of indoctrination were limited to hypothetical scenarios, then the real people – namely, us – who are asked to embark on one imaginary journey or thought experiment rather than another – would need to question *our* capacity for evaluating the merits of the competing hypotheticals – each of which yields dramatically different prescriptions at the end of the journey.

Let us grant advocates of strategy III the benefit of the doubt. Strategy III (as opposed to II) clearly has the merit that it is explicitly designed to respond to bias and indoctrination. But the issue is how do we choose, in the first place, an *unbiased remedy* for bias and indoctrination? Unless a theory incorporates our requirement for a self-reflective political culture in the actual, ongoing society, its advocacy of any given hypothetical strategy is suspect. Suppose Rawls's (or Ackerman's or an enlightened utilitarian's) theory of justice were fully instituted. Part of what Rawls means by "a well-ordered society" is that people will come to believe in the merits of his theory of justice when they live with it in its fully realized form.[20] If that well-ordered society does not continually subject its governing theory to conscientious criticism and dissent, then its members must rationally question their capacity to evaluate the governing theory (compared to its serious rivals). In Rawls's state people would learn to take the question of the basis for justice to Rawls's original position; in Ackerman's state they would learn to take the question to the imaginary process of neutral dialogue (under the perfect technology of justice); in a fully utilitarian society they might learn to take such questions to the imaginary procedure of the perfectly sympathetic spectator. But to the extent that their *actual* society – however ideal according to the theory in question – fails to incorporate the self-reflective requirements we are proposing,[21] agents in that society face an unendingly controversial choice among competing hypotheticals intended to eliminate bias. It is not enough that the Rawlsian original position (or any of its rivals) is, itself, intended to eliminate bias. The problem is how to eliminate the bias in *our* choice of,

[20] See Rawls, "A Well-Ordered Society," Peter Laslett and James Fishkin, eds., *Philosophy, Politics and Society*, Fifth Series (Oxford: Basil Blackwell/New Haven: Yale University Press, 1979), pp.6–21.
[21] This notion of a self-reflective political culture is developed in greater detail below.

or susceptibility to, any particular thought experiment for eliminating bias rather than any other.

An agent in a self-reflective political culture is in a different situation. Unlike a person in Rawls's proposed just society (or that resulting from any of the other versions of strategy III), he has a compelling line of response to jurisdiction problems from hypothetical thought experiments – provided that they purport to bear on the question at issue (the question of whether there should be freedom of political culture in the demanding sense proposed here). First, he can respond that only *with* (or with at least) a self-reflective political culture are they (the advocates of any of the rival principles at issue) in a position to evaluate the claims of competing hypotheticals. Second, no argument from such a hypothetical can be conclusive to the point of obviating the need for continuing self-reflection on the part of the system. Advocates of rival theories who would presume to eliminate the conditions for actual evaluation within the system are foreclosing the dialogue even though they have no firm conclusions to put in its place. Hence, strategy IV offers a distinctive response to jurisdiction problems – but only on the narrow question at issue, whether the conditions of evaluation (for a self-reflective political culture) need to be continually maintained.

My position is that the particular version of strategy IV suggested here is necessary for solving what we will call the *legitimacy problem*. While proponents of more complete theories can reasonably disagree on a wide range of substantive conclusions, my proposed conclusion concerns only the distinctive conditions necessary for solving the legitimacy problem. The argument is on defensible ground if distinctive conditions can be linked to a general characterization of an unavoidable problem. The case is quite different with the hypothetical strategies of Category III. There, the general characterization of the problem (working through the political implications of impartiality or the moral point of view) leads to no definite results whatsoever. The problem in its general characterization is compatible with numerous, slightly different precise constructions which support incompatible resultant principles. The trick is to get distinctive conclusions from a general characterization of a problem which is unavoidable – so that the resulting conclusions have a firm basis.

Primary reliance on strategy IV does not, of course, rule out supplementary uses of any of the other strategies. In fact, as suggested here, only partial prescriptions follow from strategy IV – prescriptions for liberty of political culture in a demanding sense. While these prescriptions yield distinctive conclusions, they leave many controversial questions unsettled. My hope is to place the essential core of liberal theory on a firmer footing while leaving the rest untouched.

The key to the strategy is to situate the core propositions of liberal theory – certain requirements of liberty – at a different point in the argument. They are not offered as conclusions that follow directly from a postulated process of evaluation. Rather, they are necessary conditions for *conducting* the evaluation in the appropriate manner. In that sense, they follow indirectly, rather than directly, from the explicit process of evaluation. Once this distinctive location in the argument is revealed, the requirements of liberty take on a special status – one that insulates them from further criticisms that they may be unnecessary or should be abandoned.

They are protected from such attacks because the inevitably controversial and provisional character of moral argument within liberal theory prevents any particular prescription from being directly established by a moral evaluation with the kind of finality or conclusiveness that would obviate the need for continuing reexamination and reevaluation. Hence, the inconclusiveness and the indeterminacies familiar to critics of liberalism provide important support for the indirect strategy. They explicate the need to maintain the conditions for continuing, collective self-evaluation at the level of fundamental principles – regardless of the particular construction of those fundamental principles which we happen to accept at any given time.

The premise of my constructive argument is that justifications for state authority must be addressed to those who must live under that authority, those who must live with the claim, usually backed by overwhelming power, that the state's countless, pervasive effects on our daily lives are fully justified. The first question to raise about the state is not whether we have, in some sense, "consented" to it (tacitly, expressly, hypothetically, or whatever). Rather, it is whether the state has permitted us to be in a position where it is possible for *us*, in some reasonable fashion, to evaluate *it*. The state and its defenders are likely to limit what we can know about it, what we can know about the character of our relationship to it, and what we can know about the variety of possible alternatives to present policies and to the present system. All of these factors cloud our ability to evaluate the authority to which we have been subjected.

The first question of political philosophy is whether the *form of political culture* which is tolerated or supported in a given state is one that permits those subject to its authority to evaluate it – to determine from *inside* whether the authority to which they have been subjected is justifiable. If that authority is justifiable – according to arguments which it is rational for them to accept from within the political culture – then I will say that a solution to the *legitimacy problem* has been achieved. My basic claim will be that the legitimacy problem can only be solved in a *self-reflective political culture* – one that is significantly self-undermining as a result of unmanipulated dialogue. By "consistently self-undermining," I mean that the political culture subjects its supporting rationales to widespread, conscientious criticism. Such an airing of counterarguments directed at our institutions and policies is necessary if we are to be in a reasonable position to evaluate the case in favor. In that sense, only a system which is consistently self-undermining can rationally support itself.

I specify "unmanipulated" dialogue (in the definition of a self-reflective political culture), for when the state engages in (or permits) the manipulation of its own evaluation, it becomes reasonable for us, as members, to distrust the results. When voices have been silenced, or intentionally drowned out, our capacity to evaluate the case for the state and its policies has been severely impaired. Even if we are confident in whatever propositions are shielded from criticism, we are denied the opportunity to test those propositions against counterarguments; we are denied the kind of dialogue which would give us a reasonable basis for accepting those propositions in the first place. And if we were not already confident in those propositions, we must suspect them further when dissenting voices are persecuted or forcibly silenced. It is only reasonable to suspect the motives of those in power (or their allies) if they severely distort the public process of evaluating the power they exercise. The interests they have at stake are too great, the possibilities for self-serving rationalizations too apparent, for us to assume that we can blindly entrust our fate to them without the benefit of continuing debate and counterargument.

A self-reflective political culture continually purges itself of bias in its own favor. In doing so, it guards the intellectual freedom of its members to evaluate whatever positive case there might be for the state, its institutions, and its policies. The argument proceeds from (a) the general problem of political evaluation to (b) its characterization in terms of the legitimacy problem to (c) the requirements for freedom of political culture, for the intellectual liberties in the political sphere, which are necessary for solving the legitimacy problem. The basic idea is that justifications for political authority must be offered under conditions which permit those who live under that authority to arrive at some reasonable evaluation of it. Even if strong arguments were offered for the state but the conditions for evaluation were denied (for example, dissenters were persecuted, discussion was suppressed, newspapers were closed or bullied), no constructive solution to the legitimacy problem would be possible. Who could know what arguments had been silenced, what issues or protests might have arisen, were it not for the chilling effects of suppression? By denying its citizens the conditions necessary for a reasonable evaluation of its own authority, such a state, no matter what its other benefits, would also deny itself the possibility of solving the legitimacy problem.

The first step in the constructive argument is merely to grant that there are significant problems of political evaluation. This step amounts to little more than admitting that political philosophy exists as a subject matter. My strategy aspires to distinctive results by taking a second step, that of placing the locus of decision for those evaluations, not in the hands of some closely guarded elite, but rather in the public arena of the general political culture, available to all those who must live within the political system whose evaluation is in question. After all, they are the ones who must live with the countless everyday effects of the state upon their lives. For the state to subject them to this power, virtually inescapable within the confines of its territory, without permitting them the conditions necessary for any reasonable appraisal of it, would be to subject them to a kind of continuing, unreflective servitude. It would relegate them to a perpetual state of political childhood.

If the state could demonstrate conclusively and without room for reasonable disagreement that it knew best, that it had, in fact, justifiably settled all the important questions virtually for all time, then there might be a case for relegating its citizenry to this kind of continuing political childhood. But the requirements for justifying this kind of extreme mass paternalism are too great. Political theories which presume to make such claims inevitably overreach. There are inevitable limitations of normative evaluation which block this absolutist route to paternalistic suppression.[22]

My argument proceeds from the mere requirements for conducting a certain kind of evaluation. It does not rely on the conclusions of that evaluation but, rather, on the conditions necessary to conduct it. In that sense my strategy is *indirect*. The inconclusiveness in more straightforward, *direct* strategies – where a process of evaluation is conducted or posited and its explicit conclusions are prescribed – strengthens rather than weakens the argument. For the controversiality and incompleteness which inevitably apply to moral judgments provide part of the rationale for our having to continue the dialogue, for our having to view the direct results of political evaluation as provisional and open to reasonable disagreement. Hence, any tampering with the conditions for unmanipulated political evaluation would foreclose the dialogue prematurely – leaving us completely in the dark when we could barely see our way to our earlier, merely provisional conclusions.

As we saw from our discussion of Gauthier's jurisdiction and indoctrination problems, any thought experiment relying principally on

---

[22] For further arguments along these lines, see my *Beyond Subjective Morality* (New Haven, CT: Yale University Press, 1984).

purely imaginary scenarios is going to be open to continuing controversy. Slightly different interpretations of the conditions for choice or of the preferences bearing on that choice will yield radically different outcomes. By turning our attention to the possibility of a fully developed theory in quadrant IV, I mean to emphasize the possibility that refinement mechanisms can be incorporated into actual life so as to avoid both the jurisdiction and the indoctrination objections – objections which afflict proposals in the other three quadrants. To the extent that an adequate version of this kind of theory is developed, it will also yield "morals by agreement" – but in a sense quite different from the one proposed by Gauthier.

Government and Philosophy, University of Texas at Austin.

Social Philosophy & Policy 5:2 ISSN 0265–0525

BARGAINING FOR JUSTICE*

Russell Hardin

David Gauthier's *Morals by Agreement*[1] presents a partial theory of distributive justice. It is partial because it applies only to the distribution of gains from joint endeavors, or what we may call the 'social surplus' from cooperation. This surplus is the benefit we receive from cooperation insofar as this is greater than what we might have produced through individual efforts without interaction with others. The central core of Gauthier's theory of distributive justice is his bargaining theory of 'minimax relative concession' or MRC. Whether his theory is compelling turns essentially on whether MRC is workable and compelling. It is this issue that I wish to address.

Unfortunately, from what Gauthier has written about it, we cannot be fully confident that MRC is workable. The theory has in common with most formal bargaining theory that it is done entirely in utilities. In some contexts this can be risky because it masks too much of what is at issue. Formal bargaining theory is not about how to bargain but about what resolution of a bargaining problem rational bargainers should reach. It has been applied with compelling results to the problem of 'fair division', as for example, when you and I must decide how to divide the gift of cake that has been placed before us.

One of the great strengths of Gauthier's verbal discussion of the problem of distributive justice, however, is his recognition that the distribution of free gifts is not an analogue of our problem. When we investigate distributive justice, we are not concerned with how to allocate manna from heaven, but with how to allocate what we have first produced. The latter problem is more difficult because it inherently involves incentive effects: we are individually apt to produce more the more we individually get of what we produce. My contribution to the whole social product will be small, and my fraction of my contribution will be negligible. If what I get is a specific fraction of the whole social product and if my costs of

---

* This paper has benefited from discussions with many people, especially David Gauthier, James Buchanan, and others at the Bowling Green conference, and John Roemer.

[1] David Gauthier, *Morals by Agreement* (Oxford: Clarendon Press, 1986). (Henceforth, page number references to this book will be given parenthetically in the text.)

contribution are significant, then I would sooner not contribute and merely settle for my fraction of what everyone else contributes. Our problem, then, is to reward me directly for my contribution in order to secure it, and then to allocate to me my share of the remaining social product after each individual's contribution has been directly rewarded. This is the problem Gauthier sees as the central issue for a principle of distributive justice that is grounded in rational, self-interested calculation by all potential contributors and benefiters.

On this account the problem of distributive justice is the grandest of instances of the logic of collective action. It is not surprising, therefore, that Gauthier typically sees the issue as one of resolving Prisoner's Dilemma interactions, because the Prisoner's Dilemma is an analogue of collective action problems with perverse incentive effects that suggest that rational, self-interested individuals will fail to cooperate for mutual benefit.[2] The extraordinary value of Gauthier's theory, if it is compelling, is that it potentially resolves *all such problems*. Given that such problems seemingly abound, we must suppose that Gauthier's theory is wrong or that people have simply failed to understand their rational self-interest in cooperation. Perhaps even more impressively, we must suppose Gauthier has succeeded in cracking a problem that many of the best social theorists of the past two millennia have recognized as central but have failed to crack. It is an audacious supposition. If it is correct, Gauthier's result is, philosophically, world-historical. Although it would be pleasing to see and praise a world-historical move by a philosopher, I will argue that Gauthier's result is not compelling, that the theory he offers does not work for even the partial problem of distributive justice that he addresses.

MINIMAX RELATIVE CONCESSION

The most that anyone could claim from a joint effort would be the whole product minus the value of the contributions of other parties to it. The least one would accept would be the value of one's own contribution to it. What we have to divide, therefore, is the entire product of our joint effort over and above our contributions to it or, again, the social product. A bargaining theory or a theory of distribution could allocate this net product in any one of many ways. Gauthier supposes that rational bargainers would propose to allocate it by agreeing on how much each would concede to the others in order to get them to cooperate. Ideally, each would want the

[2] Mancur Olson, Jr., *The Logic of Collective Action* (Cambridge, MA: Harvard University Press, 1965); Russell Hardin, *Collective Action* (Baltimore, MD: Johns Hopkins University Press for Resources for the Future, 1982).

whole surplus but, practically, each would have to settle for less. The biggest concession one would make would be to settle for none of the gain; the smallest would be to insist on the whole gain. A reasonable compromise would be to have each bargainer settle for the same proportionate concession from full gain. Hence, *relative concessions* should be equal. When there are more than two parties involved, equality of relative concessions may not be possible or desirable, so that Gauthier stipulates that "an outcome be selected only if the greatest or *maximum* relative concession it requires is as small as possible, or a *minimum*, that is, is no greater than the maximum relative concession required by every other outcome" (*MA*, p.137). This is the principle of minimax relative concession, or MRC.

The core of Gauthier's theory is the claim that MRC provides the most compelling resolution of the problem of rationally, self-interestedly accepting a specific allocation of the social product. We need not here consider his arguments for why this particular bargaining theory – a variant of a particular one of the many extant bargaining theories – is the natural choice of a rational person. Rather, we need only consider whether MRC can do the job set for it. There are many reasons to question whether MRC is an adequate principle for allocating the social product (whenever this term is used without modifier, it is assumed to be net of all individuals' contributions to it). One of the most transparent is that it fails Gauthier's own demands in a problem that Gauthier himself analyzes for us. Another is to see what is masked behind the concern with pure utilities for gains. Consider each of these in the context of the cooperative effort of Adelaide and Ernest.

To explicate and justify his theory, Gauthier presents many examples to show how it works and to say why its results are compelling. One of these problems is a cooperative venture between Adelaide and Ernest. The venture is a variant of a mutual fund. Gauthier supposes that, for the range of their cooperation, "their utilities are linear with monetary values, so that we may give the payoffs in dollars" (*MA*, p.137). Each contributes something to the project, which returns gains above the contributions. If Adelaide were to receive all of the gains, she would get a value to her of $500. If Ernest were to receive all of the gains, he would get a value to him of $50. Under MRC Adelaide must concede $147 of her possible maximum gain and Ernest must concede $15, so that the net payoffs to them are $353 and $35, respectively, with rounding off to the nearest dollar. Adelaide's relative concession is 147 parts in 500 and Ernest's is 15 parts in 50, so that their relative concessions are equal.

Note how odd this result is. The total gain to Adelaide and Ernest, in dollars, is only $388. If Adelaide had received all of the gain, she could have paid Ernest considerably more than $35 while still having a net gain of more than $353 for herself. MRC seems to yield a perversely suboptimal result that genuinely rational bargainers should be able to avoid. In the actual world, bargaining without the possibility of side-payments in such contexts would be foolish. But Gauthier wants us to bargain cooperatively, which is to say, with the possibility of relevant binding agreements, such as that which Adelaide and Ernest would want to make in order to net more each from the possible total payoff of $500.[3] If Adelaide and Ernest bargain fully cooperatively, then the gain from their mutual effort should be $500, and each of them could claim to net this much at a maximum from the effort. In that case, they have identical MRC calculations, so that they get equal shares of $250.

If Gauthier permits the full range of side payments, MRC produces egalitarianism. As any reader must recognize, this does not seem to be Gauthier's sense of his own theory. If he does not permit side payments, he must severely restrict the market and permit radical suboptimality. If he permits full side payments, MRC loses its distinctive quality. The reason for this complication is that the mutual fund of Adelaide and Ernest involves money, which, to reverse a claim of Luce and Raiffa, behaves for all the world like the 'transferable utility' of Neumann-Morgenstern game theory.[4] When there is fully transferable utility over the space of possible outcomes, then the 'transferable utility value' of any coalition (e.g., of the whole set of players) is the maximum possible sum of payoffs in units of that transferable utility, and this whole sum is what the players should bargain over. For Adelaide and Ernest, this sum is $500; hence, the $50 payoff to Ernest that is joined with a zero payoff to Adelaide is of no interest and should play no role in their bargaining.

Transferable utility runs against the grain of the Raiffa-Kalai-Smorodinsky bargaining theory on which MRC is based. One might therefore suppose that the mutual fund of Adelaide and Ernest is a poor example for Gauthier to use. Against this supposition, however, note that transferable utility seems to fit many contexts to which any theory of distributive justice should apply. In particular, it is a central element of a money-based market. Hence, MRC may be ill-suited to general application to a real economy and arguably, therefore, also to the problem of distributive justice in a modern society. It makes best sense in relatively constrained two-person interactions in contexts outside the general market, such as contexts on which side payments are structurally or morally ruled out. In many such

[3] One might defend against this criticism by supposing that the payoff is actually some sharing of commodities, not of money. But Adelaide and Ernest may be presumed to have money with which to compensate each other for alternative allocations of the commodities in a way that would be far more optimal. This point will be considered below.
[4] R. Duncan Luce and Howard Raiffa, *Games and Decisions* (New York: Wiley, 1957), p.168.

contexts, of course, agreement of any kind is ruled out, so that MRC cannot be applied.

Now let us go behind the allocation of net gains to see how they might have been produced. Suppose the cost of their joint venture was $250 and that Adelaide paid $200 and Ernest $50. (Gauthier simplifies his discussion by assuming that their contributions are both $0 [*MA*, p.138].) Let us follow Gauthier to calculate their relative concessions. He says:

> The *relative magnitude* of any concession may be expressed as the proportion its absolute magnitude bears to the absolute magnitude of a complete concession. If the initial bargaining position affords some person a utility u^*, and he claims an outcome affording him a utility $u\#$, then if he concedes an outcome affording him a utility u, the absolute magnitude of his concession is $(u\#-u)$, of complete concession $(u\#-u^*)$, and so the relative magnitude of his concession is $[(u\#-u)/(u\#-u^*)]$ [*MA*, p.136].

Let us perform this calculation, as Gauthier does, without side payments. The value for u* for Adelaide is her contribution to, or opportunity cost of entering into, the joint effort, which is $200, as here stipulated. The value of u* for Ernest is $50. If Adelaide got all of the gains, she would receive a net of $500, hence a total of $700. If Ernest received all of the gains, he would receive a net of $50, hence a total of $100. The value of $(u\#-u^*)$ is $500 for Adelaide and $50 for Ernest. If MRC awards Adelaide a net of $353, she gets back a total of her costs plus this net, or a total $553; Ernest gets back his net of $35 plus his costs for a total of $85.

The interesting part of this derivation is that its bottom line of net benefits is in fact *wholly independent of the values of the costs to Adelaide and Ernest*. Suppose their costs are $10 for Adelaide and $240 for Ernest. Under MRC Ernest gets back his costs plus his net of $35 for a total of $275. Adelaide gets back her costs plus her net of $353 for a total of $363. Ernest's costs in dollars are twenty-four times Adelaide's, and yet her net benefit is ten times his. Indeed, if one of them had no costs, the allocation of net benefits would arithmetically be the same, although Gauthier seemingly rules this out (although in this example his own simplification, noted parenthetically above, assumes that both have no costs). He says, "Each person's claim is bounded by the extent of his participation in co-operative interaction. For if someone were to press a claim to what would be brought about by the co-operative interaction of others, then those others would prefer to exclude him from agreement" (*MA*, p.134).

Suppose we double the total contribution to get a proportionately larger net benefit, but suppose that the increased contribution comes from a *decrease* in Adelaide's contribution and *more than a doubling* of Ernest's contribution. The result is that both get net gains that are double their original net gains, even though Adelaide has contributed less than before. That makes her sound as though she were, in Gauthier's term, a parasite. We could as easily make Ernest seem to be a parasite. But Adelaide is a parasite only relative to the earlier cost-sharing scheme. What is the base from which we should draw comparisons to establish who is unfairly benefiting from a joint endeavor, to establish who is a parasite? What does it mean under the principle of MRC to say that "each person's claim is bounded by the extent of his participation"?

Would an allocation rule that allows such results as these be at all attractive to Gauthier's rational, self-interested bargainers? Knowing that these results are possible, a rational bargainer might wish first to bargain over the level of input each of us is to make. There is, in a typical case, no a priori unique level of total contribution and no unique rule for individual sharing of the total contribution.[5]

Of course, this is not the way an actual mutual fund works. Actual funds return gains (or, more commonly in the experience of many of us, losses) in direct proportion to contributions. Typically in such funds, no additional person's contribution at the margin makes any significant difference to the benefits received by other contributors. This is not unlike the way an actual society works in one important respect – a typical individual's contribution makes no significant difference to the rest of society, so that few if any of us could credibly threaten to reduce the welfare of others by withdrawing from the larger society. (Exceptions might be certain major political leaders, extraordinarily creative artists such as Mozart, or inventors such as Thomas Edison or Jonas Salk. Arguably, even the latter are often important to the rest of us only in speeding up advances that would come soon from someone else.) The real social product to be distributed may generally therefore be most of what there is. On Gauthier's MRC theory, the way this is distributed is virtually independent of the pattern of contributions that have produced it. If my contribution is enormous or piddling, I get repaid for that, and then I also get my MRC share of the net product, which, if generalization from two-person cases is apt, is likely to be equal to the MRC share of almost everyone else.

GOODS AND UTILITIES

At the outset, I noted that Gauthier's theory is a partial theory of distributive justice in that it covers only a part of what has traditionally

<hr />

[5] For further discussion of the range of such problems, see Hardin, *Collective Action*, Chap. 6, "Contractarian Provisions."

come under that rubric. It is also only a partial theory in another important sense: it is insufficiently specified to yield the results Gauthier wants from it. The omission from the theory may follow more or less naturally from the focus on utilities rather than on actual inputs and outputs, and perhaps from the simplification of thought involved in arguing from two-person cases. The real difficulties of the theory arise when we suppose that the inputs and outputs are not all instantly representable in monetary terms. Our inputs to the gross social product are generally in time, human capital, and various resources. Our outputs are various goods and services. MRC requires us to consider all possible allocations that can result from all possible patterns of contribution. One allocation might repay me in one bundle of goods for my contribution, and another might repay me in an altogether different but equally preferred bundle of goods for the same effort. The number of possibilities for a real society would be astronomically high even if we realistically restrict all inputs and repayments to lumpy, not infinitely divisible, quantities. A Hayekian would blanch at the very notion of the required data collection.

But note what could happen even in a small-number, simple society. My choice of what I get repaid for my contribution (to compensate me for my lost u*) will influence the value you put on the net remaining product. If there are only two of us, we could agree in principle to take in repayment – of all repayments to which we would be indifferent and which would be equivalent to our u*s – what would leave most value for distribution under MRC. If there are three of us, there may be no unique set of repayments that maximizes value for all of us. You may be indifferent between being repaid with, say, a car and an addition to your house. I will be better off in the end if you are repaid with a car; Jones will be better off if you are repaid with an addition to your house.

Note that Gauthier's condition on MRC for numbers larger than two does not meet this problem. This condition is that we take that allocation that involves the minimum-maximum, or minimax, relative concession to anyone. In the problem here, MRC might give each of us the same *relative* concession in each outcome. The relative concession will be calculated from the net product in that outcome. What is bothersome here, and unresolved, is that the absolute gain to me is greater in one outcome than in a completely different but possible outcome. Before we even get the use of MRC, we first have to decide which of these outcomes we are to enjoy. Perhaps we could apply MRC at this prior level, perhaps over and over until we get to that total allocation that yields minimax relative concessions as compared *not to what each could get in the status quo ante, but to what each could get in the best of all possible allocations*. These will not be trivial calculations. The Hayekian, having earlier blanched, may now turn purple.

Gauthier can credibly object that this surreal vision is not his program. But then he must put something else in its place in order to go on with that part of his program that he has given us.

CONCLUSION

What typically motivates our concern with distributive justice is how to redistribute the wealth that seems to get funneled through market or other processes to some persons far more than to others. Some of the difference seems to be a matter of harder work and might therefore be seen as deserved. Some of it seems to be a matter of talent and might therefore be seen, at least by some, as similarly deserved. But much of it seems to be the result of little more than luck, or what economists call "rent." One might wish to argue even then, as a libertarian or a conservative utilitarian might, that it would be destructive rather than beneficial in any sense to try to redistribute even that which accrues to luck, perhaps because it would be hard to trust the agency doing the redistributing to do it reasonably well. But this is not Gauthier's project, which is apparently to give an ideal prescription for just distribution of net joint product.

So what is net joint product in a large society? We cannot break it down into overlapping sets of dyadic net joint products. For example, even if we abstract away from genuinely public provisions of such goods as highways, we must grant, say, that factories have large numbers of inputs that go together to determine outputs and that we cannot disentangle the contributions of these inputs into dyadic or singular units. What is my status quo ante in the larger society? It must be either nothing or the leisure I forgo in helping to produce any joint social product. These questions conjure up some of the worst of dead debates. In particular, the question of the joint product suggests the labor theory of value and the question of my status quo ante suggests the state of nature. We may crudely address both questions at once by considering Richard Epstein's theory of just 'takings' by the government for public or other purposes. Epstein supposes that each of us would have a collection of goods if there were no effective government control, as represented in the first pie divided among us in Figure 1. The second pie has added to it the further goods we would have under a system of effective government control.[6] The additional goods would be vaguely analogous to Gauthier's cooperative surplus.

One must immediately sense from Epstein's "tale of two pies" that the second pie seems radically wrong if it is supposed to be drawn to the same

[6] Richard A. Epstein, *Takings: Private Property and the Power of Eminent Domain* (Cambridge, MA: Harvard University Press, 1985), p.4.

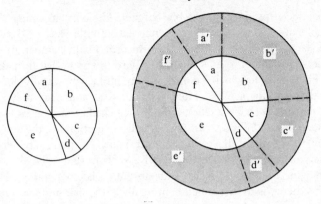

FIGURE 1   A Tale of Two Pies.*

Source: *From Richard A. Epstein, *Takings: Private Property and the Power of Eminent Domain* (Cambridge, Mass.: Harvard University Press, 1985), p.4, copyright 1985 by the President and Fellows of Harvard College.

scale as the first pie. It is only through the harmony of life under effective government control that we have achieved the extraordinary wealth of any modern society. The value of a square mile of Manhattan, Paris, London, or Tokyo today can have no analogue in any community in which there is no effective government control – compare it even to a square mile of Beirut, itself a product of a history of sometime government control. If the second pie is drawn to proper scale in its own right, then its inner circle would be indistinguishable from the point at the center of the present outer circle. What we have to distribute at all is virtually what we have at all. The status quo ante for every individual is essentially to have nothing but leisure. Hence, Gauthier's theory yields simple egalitarianism, and egalitarianism in utility at that. Gauthier supposes that his theory differs from John Rawls's Difference Principle in that it takes the status quo point into account, whereas Rawls wishes to distribute everything, including what was "mine" before the social cooperation.[7] It seems unlikely that this is a significant difference.

But perhaps this last move, reducing the status quo ante to virtually nothing, was too quick. It forces Gauthier's bargaining problem into a single-shot game in which we allocate everything. Perhaps what he wants to allocate are marginal gains more or less continually over time, rather than

[7] David Gauthier, "Bargaining and Justice," *Social Philosophy and Policy*, vol. 2 (Spring 1985), p.40.

the whole social product in one big bargain. Indeed, bargaining theory at the full-blown scale of the whole society makes little sense: "Bargainers," Gauthier says, "have no reason to be concerned with comparative overall preference-satisfaction."[8] Alas, then, it is hard to know what to make of his theory. The values to which I contribute are all heavily socially determined in several important senses. They are valued as much as they are only because there is such a society as ours in which they can be consumed or otherwise enjoyed. They are very much collective efforts in the sense that I build on what others have done. And many of them are essentially byproducts of activities that are otherwise socially supported. It would be idle to imagine what would be my state absent social cooperation. Hence, if Gauthier's theory is to be applied continually at the margin to various social cooperations as we go along, it wants some justification for the status quo from which we begin. Until we have that, we cannot get started with the application of MRC. As Gauthier notes of the publication of his book, he has come to an end, "aware that it is also a beginning" (*MA*, p.vi). The further trip may be a long one.

Political Science, Philosophy, and Public Policy Studies,
University of Chicago

---

[8] *ibid.*, p.39.

Social Philosophy & Policy 5:2 ISSN 0265–0525

THE GAUTHIER ENTERPRISE*

JAMES M. BUCHANAN

I. INTRODUCTION

I take it as my assignment to criticize the Gauthier enterprise. At the outset, however, I should express my general agreement with David Gauthier's normative vision of a liberal social order, including the place that individual principles of morality hold in such an order. Whether the enterprise is, ultimately, judged to have succeeded or to have failed depends on the standards applied. Considered as a coherent grounding of such a social order in the rational choice behavior of persons, the enterprise fails. Considered as an extended argument implying that persons should (and possibly must) adopt the moral stance embodied in the Gauthier structure, the enterprise is, I think, largely successful. Considered as a set of empirically falsifiable propositions suggesting that persons do, indeed, choose as the Gauthier precepts dictate, the enterprise offers Humean hope rather than Hobbesian despair.

Morals by Agreement[1] is developed in conceptually separate parts, which are made to seem more integrated than they need to be. The first, and most extensive, part of the book involves Gauthier's attempt to ground cooperative behavior in rational choice. In strategic interactions between persons *who possess defined and mutually respected initial rights*, the argument is that it becomes rational for each person to adopt a cooperative strategy. This part of the analysis falls within the theory of bargaining, and it is presented as such. The second part of the book, and much the more difficult part, attempts to extend aspects of the same argument to the *definition and assignment of initial rights* to persons.

I shall discuss the first of these two parts of Gauthier's argument in Sections II, III, and IV, with each section devoted to elaboration of a separate criticism. In Section V, I shall discuss the second part of the Gauthier enterprise involving the definition of rights. In Section VI, I shall

* I am indebted to my colleagues, David Levy, Hartmut Kliemt, Jennifer Roback, Viktor Vanberg, and Karen Vaughn for helpful comments.

[1] David Gauthier, *Morals by Agreement* (Oxford: Oxford University Press, 1985). Subsequent references will be by page numbers in the text.

present particularized criticism of the whole analysis that emerges from my disciplinary location as an economist. Finally, in Section VII, I shall discuss Gauthier's general perspective on social order.

II. COOPERATION AND THE DEFINITION OF COMMUNITY

As I noted, Gauthier presents his analysis of rational cooperation in the first part of his book as a contribution to the theory of bargaining. He seeks to demonstrate that the individual, who recognizes himself to be in a strategic interaction, will rationally choose that pattern of behavior that generates the cooperative outcome or solution. This demonstration is opposed to that which suggests that cooperative behavior in dilemma-like settings must exhibit a departure from individual rationality, defined as individualized utility maximization. Gauthier does not, of course, question the straightforward analytics of nonzero-sum games and the translation of objectified payoffs into their utility equivalents. His criticism is more general and, as carefully developed in his argumentation, it does carry considerable appeal. The individual, when placed in such an interaction setting, will exclude the off-diagonal or behaviorally asymmetric cells from his realm of feasible solutions. He will do so not out of any altruistic concern for his counterpart in the interaction, and not out of any expectation of repeated plays, but out of his rationally-grounded interest in his own payoff. The temptation to "take advantage" that emerges as the motivating force in orthodox treatments of dilemma-setting behavior is suppressed in an extended rational choice structure that embodies adherence to cooperative strategies as utility enhancing. Morals by agreement do not require other-regardingness or resort to supra-individualistic norms.

Descriptively, the Gauthier analysis applies to many areas of human interaction. I have often referred to the ordered anarchy that seems to define behavior in ordinary informal social relationships. We do not, as individuals, take advantage of each other each and every time that the occasion allows it. We do behave in accordance with precepts of mutual respect, and we brand as deviant the person who violates the mutuality norm.

There exist alternatives to the Gauthier enterprise that offer explanations for this behavior. Hayek suggests that we tend to behave in accord with certain codes of conduct, certain rules, that have emerged in a long process of cultural evolution, and that these codes or rules for behavior cannot be interpreted as products of any rational calculus.[2] These rules evolve

[2] Cf. F.A. Hayek, *Law, Legislation, and Liberty*, especially Vol. III, *The Political Order of a Free People* (Chicago: University of Chicago Press, 1979).

spontaneously, and direct our actions even though we cannot, consciously, understand them. I shall not discuss the Hayekian argument further here; I shall say only that in any relevant comparison my own sympathies lie with Gauthier. Generally, I applaud rational-choice reductionism, especially in its promise for ultimate institutional reform. Acquiescence before the inevitability of spontaneous evolution is a stance that holds, for me, little appeal.

My first, and most fundamental, criticism of the whole Gauthier enterprise lies, therefore, *within* the postulated structure of the argument.[3] I shall leave to the game theorists any dispute concerning the appropriate definition of technical rationality.[4] In the setting of *Morals by Agreement*, and for purposes of my argument here, I shall accept the essential elements in the Gauthier demonstration. My concern is nontechnically definitional. What does cooperative behavior mean in complex interaction settings that involve several possible interpretations of the set of players in the game, several, and competing, interpretations of the relevant community of persons within the strategic interaction, members of which might be "taken advantage of" by departures from cooperative strategies of behavior?

My point may be illustrated most directly with reference to the *Prisoner's Dilemma* in its classic, exemplary formulation where two prisoners are apprehended and suspected of a crime, but where there exists no hard evidence. The prisoners are led by the structure of the payoff matrix to confess to the crime. They do so, in the familiar argument, because they adopt individualized utility maximizing strategies. The Gauthier enterprise seeks to supplant the elementary logic here and to suggest that the prisoners will not confess, but that they will, instead, act on a rationally-generated disposition to cooperate.

Or so it would seem. But does the Gauthier enterprise really imply a nonconfession strategy on the part of the individual prisoner in a literally-interpreted version of the classic dilemma? The relevance of this question is immediately obvious when we observe that the "Confess-Confess" cell of the payoff matrix is presumed to be the *socially optimal* solution. The payoff structure with which the two prisoners are confronted is deliberately designed to offer incentives to the prisoners, who are presumed to have committed the crime for which they are charged, such that their predicted

---

[3] There are, of course, other approaches to explanation that do not rely on evolutionary processes and that do not involve incorporating behavior within the rational choice framework, as this is normally defined. These approaches usually involve redefinitions of the arguments in individual utility functions. For one such recent effort in this direction, see Dennis Mueller, "Rational Egoism versus Adaptive Egoism as a Fundamental Postulate for a Descriptive Theory of Human Behavior," Presidential Address, Public Choice Society, Baltimore, Maryland, March 1986 (Mimeographed, University of Maryland, 1986).

[4] See Russell Hardin's paper in this issue, which largely concentrates on such issues.

behavior becomes compatible with the socially desired outcome. The inclusive community, which includes those who are potential victims of crime as well as those who are potential criminals (partially intersecting sets) presumably selects an institutional–constitutional structure that imposes the dilemma on those apprehended upon the commission of crimes. If the Gauthier precepts for rationality are generalized over the whole community, should the individual prisoner confess?

The point can be clarified with a numerical illustration developed for instructional purposes by my colleague Charles Rowley, an illustration that will also prove useful in the analysis of Section III. In Figures 1 and 2, payoff matrices are presented for two identical firms that produce and sell a single product. The algebraically-defined cost and demand functions that generate these payoffs are specified in the footnote accompanying Figure 1.

In the two-by-two matrix of Figure 1, each firm has available two courses of action. A firm may behave cooperatively vis-a-vis the other firm, or it may act independently. If both firms adopt the cooperative strategy, the joint profit is maximized, as shown in Cell I of the matrix.

Is such cooperative strategy dictated by the Gauthier norm? If the firms cooperate one with another, joint profits are maximized, but consumers of the product suffer. Price is higher because output is restricted. Consumers are, in this setting, being "taken advantage of by the colluding duopolists. The Gauthier argument to the effect that cooperative behavior emerges

FIGURE 1

	Firm 2	
	Produce ½ profit maximizing output	Adjust output independently (Cournot)
Firm 1 Produce ½ profit maximizing output	$4050, $4050	$3375, $4500
Adjust output independently	$4500, $3375	$3600, $3600

* Profits in dollars.
** Industry demand function.

(1) $p = 200 - q_1 - q_2$

Firm cost function

(2) $c_i = 30 q_i$ $\quad i = 1,2$

from a rationally-generated disposition based on a recognition of the strategic setting seems highly plausible when the interaction between the two firms taken in isolation is examined. The same argument, however, becomes implausible in the extreme when the community of interaction is extended to include consumers as well as the two firms. The same behavior that is defined to be cooperative in the one community becomes noncooperative in the differently defined community.[5]

This is not a minor difficulty with the Gauthier construction. The problem of definition of the community of strategic interaction is a general one that cannot be readily avoided. There is no "natural community" for the application of the rationally-generated morality by agreement. Anthropologists and moral philosophers have long recognized the distinction between the norms for behavior of individuals toward members of the tribe and those for behavior toward strangers. The shift into what Hayek has called the "great society" and what I have called "moral order" require behavioral traits that are close cousins of those emerging from the Gauthier analysis.[6] My concern is with his attempted derivation of these norms from game theoretic or bargaining interactions in which the cooperative solutions are perhaps too readily identified. I have the same concern with the attempts to derive the evolution of cooperation from game-like settings.[7,8]

III. COOPERATION AND THE SIZE OF THE COMMUNITY

A closely related but conceptually distinct criticism involves the prospects for cooperative behavior on the part of an individual in a setting where the interaction clearly involves more than a critically small number of actors. Assume that there is no problem of subgroup versus inclusive-group cooperation, as discussed in Section II.

Here, the methodological constraints imposed by the analytical setting of

---

[5] Only after I completed a draft of this paper did my colleague, Viktor Vanberg, point out to me that an earlier criticism of a paper by Gauthier contains essentially the same argument that I have presented in this Section, even to the extent of utilizing the same examples. See, E. Ullman-Margalit, *The Emergence of Norms* (Oxford: Clarendon Press, 1977), pp.41–45.

[6] See my, "Moral Community, Moral Order, or Moral Anarchy," included in my book, *Liberty, Market and State* (Brighton, England: Wheatsheaf Books, 1985), pp.108–121.

[7] *Cf.* Robert Axelrod, The *Evolution of Cooperation* (New York: Basic Books, 1984).

[8] Critics have suggested that a disposition toward cooperative behavior, whether rationally or evolutionarily grounded, describes the behavior of persons generally, quite independently of the setting of interaction. The prisoners do not confess; the duopolists maximize joint profits. In this view, it becomes inappropriate to evaluate the results of such behavior against any notion of generalized "optimality" of "efficiency" for a more inclusive group. If this line of defense is taken, however, "cooperation," as such, may or may not be judged a character trait deserving of positive evaluation in all settings. Resolution of the dilemma present in subgames may create a dilemma in more inclusive games.

elementary game theory should be emphasized. Simple two-person games can, at best, offer insights into sources of behavior that may be generalized to large-number settings. The interaction of persons in two-person settings, taken literally, remains of relatively little interest. As the number of choosing–behaving units in an interaction increases, there is an exponential increase in the prospects for noncooperative behavior on the part of at least one of the parties. The relationship between the selection of cooperative strategies and the size of the group does not emerge from Gauthier's analysis.

Gauthier's prescriptive rule is that a player should adopt a cooperative strategy if his expected payoff from this pattern of behavior is higher than his expected payoff from the solution that embodies independent utility-maximizing behavior by all parties (MA, p.166). The rule does require that the probabilities of other players' choices of strategies be considered, but only for purposes of avoiding being "taken advantage of" rather than for those of "taking advantage." The prospects for attaining the off-diagonal cells in the simple two-person matrix are reckoned with, but only with reference to the lower of the paired payoffs in these cells.

The application of the Gauthier rule as well as the dependence of the strategy choice on numbers may be illustrated in the numerical example of Figure 1. (And, for present purposes, consider the firms in isolation from other possible players in the more inclusive economic game.) The Gauthier rule is that a firm should adopt the cooperative strategy if the expected value of the payoff is greater than that indicated in Cell IV, where all parties adjust behavior independently. Suppose that, in the two-firm model depicted, Firm 1 expects cooperative behavior on the part of Firm 2 with a probability coefficent of one-half. In this case, the Gauthier rule would dictate cooperation because ($4050 plus $3375)/2 exceeds $3600. The expected value from cooperation is $3718; that from independent adjustment is $3600.

Suppose, however, that there are three identical firms rather than two, with product demand and firm cost functions unchanged. In this setting, even if the expectation remains that each firm will behave cooperatively with the *same* probability coefficient of one-half, the Gauthier rule will dictate adoption of a noncooperative strategy. The computations yield an expected value of *$1950* from cooperation against an expected value of *$2025* from independent adjustment of behavior. (Details of the computations are provided in the Appendix.) In order for the Gauthier rule to dictate continued adherence to a cooperative strategy as numbers in the interaction increase, the probability of any one player adopting the cooperative strategy must *increase*, which seems to counter common-sense notions about the way persons behave.

The numerical example extends the numbers only from a two-party to a three-party interaction. As numbers increase beyond small-number limits, the prospects for cooperative behavior, even on the part of those persons who try to behave in accordance with Gauthier's rational morality, will disappear in many situations. This apparent flaw is critical to the Gauthier enterprise, because it is the potential breakdown of the ordinary two-person relationships of the competitive market that gives rise to the necessity of some morality that exhibits comparable properties of reciprocation without concern. Coase-like bargaining can be depended on in small-number spillover relationships; it is precisely the difficulties of market-like bargaining that create the problem in large-number settings.

IV. THE RATIONALITY OF RETRIBUTION

A third criticism is closely related to those discussed in Sections II and III above. In the Gauthier idealization of society, individuals rationally take on a disposition that prompts them to refrain from taking strategic advantage of others when such advantage seems profitable in the orthodox utility-maximization sense. The functioning of this social order requires general adherence to such rational morality by a sufficiently large number of the community's members to make both free riding and parasitic behavior the exception rather than the norm.

In this construction there is no room for whom we may call the moral entrepreneur; there is no means through which the individual, acting singly, can enforce the precepts of rational morality on others. The whole enterprise would seem to be more promising if it incorporated some role for individual entrepreneurship.

If we are willing, with Gauthier, to jettison orthodox utility maximization as a necessary and central feature of the very definition of rational behavior, we may ask why the extension of rationality need stop at the point where the individual takes on the disposition not to take advantage of others in strategic interactions. Could not arguments be advanced on Gauthier-like bases for the possible development of a rationally-generated disposition to behave *retributively* toward those persons who violate the contractarian precepts? Why not punish those who depart from the cooperative norms?

The virtue of this extension of something akin to the Gauthier enterprise lies in its ability to incorporate a role for the individual as moral entrepreneur, as enforcer of cooperative norms for behavior on the part of others. The attainment and maintenance of the cooperative solutions to strategic interactions can be guaranteed by adherence to rationality by a

FIGURE 2

Firm 2

		Produce 1/2 profit maximizing output	Adjust output independently (Cournot)	Produce 1/2 competitive output
	Produce 1/2 profit-max output	I $4050, $4050	II $3375, $4500	III $2025, $4050
Firm 1	Adjust output independently	IV $4500, $3375	V $3600, $3600	VI $1800, $2700
	Produce 1/2 competitive output	VII $4050, $2025	VIII $2700, $1800	IX $ 0, $ 0

much smaller set of the community's overall membership than that required under Gauthier's more limited model.

The point may be illustrated in the matrix of Figure 2, which adds a row and column to the matrix employed in Figure 1. The example is identical with that of Figure 1; there are two identical firms producing a homogeneous good. For present purposes, I shall ignore any concern about consumers, as expressed in Section II. The row and column additions indicate the payoffs to the two firms when one or the other firm, or both, adopt what we may call a retributive strategy. In this case, we define such a strategy to be production of one-half of the industry output that will satisfy the requirement that marginal cost equal price. When both firms adopt this strategy, profits fall to zero, which is the competitive solution where the benefits to consumers are maximal.

Is it not as plausible to impute, as rational, a strategy that dictates such retributive behavior to the firm upon observance of noncooperative behavior on the part of the other party as it is to impute comparison with the independent adjustment position as the benchmark or fallback option? Look carefully at the numbers in the matrix cells of Figure 2. Suppose that the two firms are initially in the cooperative solution of Cell I, but that Firm 2 tries to take advantage and shifts the outcome to Cell II. If Firm 1 recognizes this potential for deviance on the part of Firm 2, it may have built into its response pattern a disposition to impose punishment; it shifts the solution to Cell VIII, where the payoff to Firm 2 is reduced considerably below that attainable in independent adjustment (Cell V).

By comparison with the simple tit-for-tat sequence confined to the four upper left cells of the matrix, the potentially deviant party, in this case Firm 2, is guaranteed a net loss in the sequence of plays. By contrast, and ignoring discounting, Firm 2 breaks even in the tit-for-tat sequence, as does Firm 1, the enforcer. By communicating that it has rationally disposed itself to behave retributively, and making this strategy credible to Firm 2, the enforcing firm has established an incentive structure such that the cooperative solution will tend to be maintained without explicit adherence to any cooperative strategy on the part of Firm 2. The latter knows that it must lose in the sequence to be followed out if it departs from cooperation; it also knows that it loses relatively to Firm 1 in the process, although Firm 1 will also suffer losses.

I shall not extend the argument further since I have discussed this sort of strategic behavior elsewhere under the labels "samaritan's dilemma" and "punishment dilemma."[9] My reason for bringing this discussion to bear on the Gauthier enterprise is to suggest that, once the model extends rationality beyond the limits of orthodox utility maximization, there seems no reason why rationality may not be attributed to a retributive strategy as well as to the more restricted reciprocal strategy advanced by Gauthier.

I am not clear concerning Gauthier's possible response to this third criticism of his argument. He may well accept, in certain cases, the extension of the rationality norm to retribution. He does suggest that deterrence is rational, and that it remains rational to carry out even a failed threat. I agree. But he does not sufficiently emphasize that a retributive strategy is not an initiating threat strategy. The enforcer does not threaten others so long as they behave cooperatively. To communicate a strategy that will punish those who might take advantage is quite different from a strategy that employs threats as a means of taking advantage. Nor does Gauthier recognize that the retributive strategy, by comparison with his strategy of reciprocation, can produce social stability without the necessity of general adherence on the part of most parties to interaction.[10]

V.   THE DEFINITION OF A PERSON

The criticism advanced in Sections II, III, and IV are independent of any derivation of a theory of rights. So long as there exists some mutually

---

[9] See, "The Samaritan's Dilemma," *Freedom in Constitutional Contract* (College Station: Texas A & M University Press, 1977), pp.169–180; "The Punishment Dilemma," Ch. 8 in *The Limits of Liberty* (Chicago: University of Chicago Press, 1975), pp.130–146.

[10] I have limited the discussion to behavior that involves the threat of punishment for individual departure from a pattern of cooperative behavior. A more inclusive treatment would, of course, include moral indoctrination of the ordinary sort, designed to instill feelings of guilt and shame in those persons who might be otherwise inclined to defect.

acknowledged set of initial positions from which social interaction commences, precepts for individual behavior within this interaction may be analyzed. The Gauthier enterprise would, indeed, have been ambitious even if it had been limited to this extent. The enterprise goes much further, however, and includes the effort to outline a normative theory of rights, a theory that derives the definition of the initial positions from which rational bargainers start.

I find this part of Gauthier's work to be basically incoherent. My criticism can best be discussed with reference to Gauthier's treatment of my own argument as developed in my book, *The Limits of Liberty*. I employed the concept of the "natural equilibrium" distribution in Hobbesian anarchy. This distribution is that which tends to emerge in the total absence of agreed-upon or accepted rules defining individuals' rights, endowments, or boundaries. I argued that this distributional equilibrium offered the only base point from which conceptual agreement among persons on some delineation of rights, some assignment of things and acts to "mine and thine" categories, could be grounded. Such agreement emerges because parties recognize that there are gains to be secured from a cessation of investment of resources in predation and defense. A set of rights comes to be established prior to the emergence of exchanges of these rights among holders, a second stage of contract that will further increase expected utilities.

David Gauthier fully understands and appreciates my analysis, including its purpose in my enterprise. For his own enterprise, however, he is critical of my construction because of its alleged failure to incorporate some recognition of the illegitimacy of coercion in the preagreement or Hobbesian setting. Gauthier's criticism is superficially appealing, and I should acknowledge here that it is probably shared by most of the philosophers who examined my argument. Why should the slave, who is coerced by the master in the preagreement equilibrium, agree on terms of a contract that will permanently preserve the preagreement advantage of the master? Despite the fact that both master and slave improve their positions by a removal of restrictions in exchange for continued work for the master on the part of the slave, Gauthier argues that no such agreement could be justified from a rationally-based morality.

The Gauthier criticism fails because, in my view, it does not account for the basis of the alleged coercion in the anarchistic setting. Why should the slave be in the master's chains? Clearly, he is enslaved only because of some inability to enforce more favorable terms of existence. The slave does not, presumably, possess a viable exit option, one that would allow him to carry on with an independent and isolated existence. There is no benchmark of independent existence that will define the presence or absence of coercion. If the slave cannot survive independently, can he be said to be coerced? Suppose, however, that the slave could have lived independently, but that he has been captured against his will. Despite our civilized sense that the master's act of enslavement is unjust, hardheaded analysis here must conclude that independent existence for the slave was not feasible, and that any such existence was fantasy, given the presence of the potential master.

Gauthier's reluctance to accept the preagreement base for the measure of cooperative surplus stems, in part, from his desire to make his precept of rational morality extend to include compliance with agreements or contracts once they are made. The slave who had been captured against his will in the preagreement setting would never, rationally, comply with the terms of an agreement that would preserve the advantages of the master. Note, however, that the extension of rationality discussed above in Section IV can extend to compliance. Recognizing the prospect that the slave might not rationally comply with an agreement, the master, before agreeing to terms, can communicate to the slave that any departure from the terms will bring punishment. And, indeed, the agreement itself may include the establishment of an effective enforcement agency.

I acknowledge that my own construction is conceptually *explanatory* in a sense that Gauthier may not intend for his justificatory alternative. For his purposes, the independent existence of the individual provides the normative benchmark from which cooperative gains are counted. In my enterprise, by contrast, parties to potential contract commence from some status quo definition of initial positions because, quite simply, there is no other place from which to start. This existential acceptance of the status quo, of that which is, has no explicit normative content and implies neither approbation nor condemnation by any criteria of distributive justice. My contractarian explanation allows me to justify the emergence of institutions of cooperation, and with respect to the constraints on individual behavior within these institutions, I should find some Gauthier-like rule to be necessary, whether this rule be adhered to voluntarily or enforced by the sovereign. My analysis embodies the justice of natural liberty, to employ Adam Smith's fine terminology, and at some levels there are parallels with the apparently more inclusive and more ambitious Gauthier enterprise. I commence from the status quo distribution of rights and I do not apply criteria of justice to this distribution. My emphasis is almost exclusively placed on the *process* through which potential changes may be made, rather than on either the starting point or the end point of change. Gauthier extends his justificatory analysis to the initial distribution from which cooperation commences, and he seeks to establish that the distribution qualifying as "just" is only indirectly related to that which may exist.

Although his enterprise here does not require rectification as extensive as that of Robert Nozick (see below), the definitional problems raised by the Lockean proviso in Gauthier's usage are more serious than those required by Nozick. Past injustice must remain potentially relevant in both enterprises.

How is past injustice defined? For present purposes, let me address this question within Gauthier's justificatory framework. A person has been unjustly treated if he has been taken advantage of, if his well-being has been reduced below that level which he might have attained in an independent and isolated existence totally apart from those persons with whom he has been forced to interact. Some version of a secession criterion for exploitation is useful, and, indeed, it is one that I have also invoked in recent papers.[11] But it is surely heroic to imply that the individually attainable level of well-being in isolation from social interaction is more than a tiny fraction of that which is secured by almost anyone in complex modern society. The secession criterion, even if it extended to apply to groups rather than to individuals singly, may offer little or no support to those critics of the existing distribution of rights among persons, and hence little or no warrant for differential bias in the sharing of cooperative gains to rectify past injustice.

In concrete application, the Gauthier version of the Lockean proviso may be empty in the sense that it generates results equivalent to those that emerge, much more simply, from my own existential usage of the status quo. Consider an example. *Neither* the relatively rich man *nor* the relatively poor man could earn more than a pittance in isolation from the social exchange nexus. Any person's "natural talents" are specific to the social exchange nexus in which he finds himself. Almost all of the income enjoyed by any person stems from the cooperative surplus produced by social interaction. Despite observed wide disparity in levels of well-being in the status quo, the observed distribution falls well within the inclusive bargaining set outlined from the initial positions defined by Gauthier's proviso.

If we seek to go behind "the justice of natural liberty," it is necessary squarely to face up to the distribution of rights and endowments, as such. It is, of course, legitimate to inquire into the separate stages in the historical process through which the status quo distribution has been generated. And contractarian criteria of fairness may be applied to any or all of such stages. To label a single stage of development in the historical process as "unfair" (*e.g.*, the capture and bondage of slaves) may imply some noncontractarian

¹¹ "The Ethical Limits of Taxation," *Scandinavian Journal of Economics*, vol. 86 (1984), pp.102–114; "Secession and the Sharing of Surplus," with Roger Faith (mimeographed 1985).

attribution of "unfairness" to the end state defined by *that which exists*. But such an attribution does not, in any way, remove the normative legitimacy of evaluating potential changes from *that which exists* in terms of procedural criteria for fairness (actual or hypothetical agreements) that are equivalent to those procedures that may have applied historically to earlier stages in the process. Rectificatory redistribution, if effectuated, must as a process, involve violation of the contractarian or agreement criteria for fairness, and it is on this process that my own emphasis lies.

As observed, the status quo distribution has been generated through a complex process of political–legal evolution, deliberative political action, preference shifts, economic development, and social change. It is appropriate to ask to what extent does the observed pattern embody precepts of fairness? And if fairness criteria have been violated at earlier stages of the process that generated that which exists, do these historical violations in themselves offer justification for violations in some process of rectification? Or is it best to concentrate on the process as it operates from the here and now?

I submit that the contractarian exercise does not require rectification of prior injustices before application to relevant forward-looking questions. The relevant questions must, ultimately, be answered empirically, with reference to the general attitudes expressed by the community's members. "Equal chances," "fair shakes," "equal treatment for equals," "play by the same rules," "equality before the law," "careers open to talents" – these seem to me to be principles of procedural fairness that find widespread acceptance. They are fully consistent with, and indeed are required by, the Gauthier enterprise, including the appended Lockean proviso.

As I noted earlier, rectificatory redistribution may be nonexistent even on full acceptance of the Gauthier argument. By contrast, Gauthier's characterization of the market as a morally free zone may be misinterpreted as an indirect defense of the distributive patterns emergent from market interactions. Close examination of his argument reveals that persons are to be justified (by the proviso) in receiving only the values of their external marginal product, values that exclude rents.[12] As his discussion (*MA*, p.276) makes clear, the baseball free agent who may earn $500,000 from each of several major league clubs is not "entitled" to this total. If his nonbaseball alternative is the $20,000 salary of a truck driver, the $480,000 is rent that emerges only from the exchange nexus and is, therefore, subject to sharing in accordance with the Gauthier bargaining norm,

---

[12] For related discussion, see James M. Buchanan and Robert Tollison, "The Homogenization of Heterogeneous Inputs," *American Economic Review*, vol. 71 (March 1981), pp.23–30; also, my paper, "Coercive Taxation in Constitutional Contract" (mimeographed, Center for Study of Public Choice, George Mason University, September 1985).

minimax relative concession. If, in turn, the genuinely isolated prospect for the person is not $20,000 but $5,000, the inclusive measure of rent increases to $495,000. As this numerical example suggests, application of the Gauthier norm may require very substantial distributive departures from those patterns that are emergent from the market process as it operates.

If rents assume major quantitative significance in the reward structure of the market, the Gauthier precept for the sharing of the overall cooperative surplus may seem to be both equally arbitrary with and not too different from the familiar difference principle advanced by Rawls. Implicitly, Rawls assumes that the isolated individual can produce no value and that all observed income is "social rent." In the absence of incentive-induced feedbacks on the production of value, the Rawlsian principle generates equality. The Gauthier principle generates inequality only as related to differentials in the capacities of persons to produce values in isolation one from another. In practical application, the two positions seem much closer than Gauthier's discussion might suggest.

Although they disagree on the specific sharing principle, both David Gauthier and John Rawls seek to go beyond the criterial usage of con- tractual agreement as the test for distributive fairness. Both philosophers seek to define "that principle upon which contractors will agree," a step that I have tried consistently to avoid. My own contractarianism is, therefore, more limited, and it enables me to acknowledge that any one of several sharing principles may emerge from an ideally conceptualized agreement, including those of Rawls, Gauthier, and others that embody much less redistributive thrust.

VI. THE MARKET AS A MORAL FREE ZONE

The idealized relationship between the individual buyer and the individual seller in competitive market exchange is a cornerstone of the Gauthier enterprise. In this relationship, mutual gains from trade (cooperation) are realized, and these gains are shared between the parties in a determinate manner, without other-regardingness on the part of either party, without resort to transcendental moral norms, and without costly investment in bargaining. As so idealized, it is not surprising that this basic market relationship appeals to David Gauthier, the modern moral philosopher, in much the same way that it appealed to Adam Smith, the moral philosopher of the eighteenth century. (A damning indictment of twentieth century moral philosophy emerges when we recognize that David Gauthier's appreciation of the moral content of the exchange relationship is the exception rather than rule within the set of his disciplinary peers.)

The crowning discovery of the eighteenth century lay in the recognition that the spontaneous coordination properties of the market remove dilemma-like opposition of interests among persons from wide areas of social interaction, thereby eliminating the necessity of pervasive and overriding political direction of individual activity. Adam Smith stressed, however, that these properties of the market, properties that allow for the self-interested behavior of persons yet generate socially beneficial results, require an environmental setting of the appropriate "laws and institutions." Individual rights must be guaranteed; contracts must be enforced; fraud in exchange must be prevented. There need be no inconsistency between the enterprise of Adam Smith and that of David Gauthier. Smith might well agree with Gauthier's implied inference that the formal structure of the law must be complemented by a rational morality that incorporates reciprocal respect among persons in the relevant nexus. Adam Smith, along with most of the economists who have followed him, might be more skeptical than Gauthier concerning the relative importance of the two influences. We recall Smith's differentiation between the behavior of the Dutch merchant constrained by the discipline of continuous dealing and that of the once-encountered rude Scots highlander.[13]

Although he does not make the point directly, Gauthier's analysis implies that the set of social relationships classified as "the market" will more or less emerge naturally from the self-interested behavior of participants and, further, that within this set of relationships there arises no possible conflict between the precepts for rational morality and straight-forward utility maximization. A participant in exchange will refrain from taking advantage, from cheating on the agreed terms of trade. If, however, we should remove the protective legal umbrella, Adam Smith's "laws and institutions," the basic elements of the Prisoner's Dilemma appear in even the simplest of exchange relationships. The whole of the Gauthier enterprise would have been strengthened by an explicit recognition that the market relationship offers the exemplar of rational morality, rather than a "morally free zone." As Adam Smith emphasized, men *trade*; animals do not, despite recent empirical evidence demonstrating that animals have well-ordered utility functions and that they exhibit some sense of property rights. Is not the very existence of exchange the best proof that something like Gauthier's rational morality applies to normal behavior within market relationships?[14]

There is, of course, a major difference between the idealized market relationship in which each participant is a price taker and those

<hr />

[13] See, Adam Smith, *Lectures on Jurisprudence* (Oxford: Clarendon Press, 1978), p.538.

[14] I am indebted to my colleague, David Levy, for discussion on these points.

relationships characterized by the absence of exogeneously-determined terms of trade. In the competitive setting, the dilemma-like elements of potential conflict arise only with respect to the prospects for gains from cheating in carrying out the terms of contract, the type of cheating that cannot be wholly prevented except in the imagined abstractions of the general equilibrium economists, abstractions that Gauthier seems to have imbibed somewhat too uncritically. In general equilibrium, producers' rents are absent and all owners of inputs secure returns equal to opportunity costs. But, as the discussion of rents indicated in Section V above, opportunity cost *within* the market nexus is far removed from opportunity cost outside the nexus. As presented, Gauthier's argument suggests that distributional conflicts arise only in noncompetitive settings where prices are indeterminate. In any less abstracted conceptualization of market process, both producers' and consumers' rents are ubiquitous, and the apparent distributive neutrality of markets emergent from Gauthier's sharing norm disappears.

For basically the same reasons, Gauthier is too enthusiastic about the properties of the market in its institutional role as the eliminator of externalities *in the sense required by his enterprise*. So long as the inclusive economic nexus can be factored down into simple two-person or two-unit buyer–seller deals, there is no requirement that the rational morality of the two parties do more than secure some sharing of the cooperative surplus. The morality must extend to take on a heavier burden only in those settings where "markets fail" in the sense that such a factoring down cannot take place, or where there are external effects on persons who are not primary participants in the simple exchange processes.

The examples are familiar. The discharge of toxic waste into the stream kills the fish. The person who takes such action is "taking advantage" of others with whom he is not primarily dealing, and he must refrain from taking such action by some explicit resort to the rational morality of Gauthier. To the extent that rights are exhaustively assigned, however, the need to call on such an explicit sharing norm is not required. The implication is clear that such externalities are relatively rare.

The market does allow persons to act without direct regard for the interests of others, and, over very extensive areas of interaction, this process does generate results that are welfare-maximizing for the whole community of persons. The market process fails in this respect only in the presence of relevant externalities. But these are only a small subset of the set of all externalities, if this term is defined simply as the imposition of noncompensated harm or benefits on parties who are not primary participants in exchanges. The conventional distinction in theoretical welfare economics is that between *technological* and *pecuniary* externalities, that is, between those actions that directly affect the utility or production functions of parties outside the exchange, and those actions that affect such parties only through changes in terms of trade, or prices. This distinction is broadly recognized also in the traditions of the common law. The market fails in the standard sense when the first sort of externalities are present; the market works only because the second sort of externalities can be disregarded.

The question for moral theory is whether or not there exists a means of making this distinction. The point is closely related to that which has already been discussed in Section II above. How can a person know the difference between the two sorts of noncompensated harms or benefits that his behavior imposes on third parties? An example may be helpful here. Suppose that I enter into simple exchange dealings with construction firms, wholesale grocers, employees, and others and open up a hamburger stand on the corner of Main and Broad streets. In so doing, I impose noncompensated capital losses on the existing owner–operator of the Burger King franchise on the opposite corner. This person is a third party to my transactions, and this third party is harmed by my behavior. This is clearly a *pecuniary* externality. But am I taking advantage of the Burger King franchise in any sense that would require me either to refrain from acting, or to share the cooperative surplus in accordance with some norm? Economic theory tells us that I need not do so, and that any attempt to force me to do so, either in formal law or in a derived morality, would be harmful to the welfare of the community as a whole. To be able to make the required distinction between noncompensated harms and benefits that would and those that would not invoke the application of some rational morality seems beyond the limits of the plausible, even within the acknowledged confines of the Gauthier enterprise.

VII. THE ENTERPRISE ASSESSED

I have advanced several fundamental criticisms of the Gauthier enterprise, based on my understanding of it. These criticisms are intended to be relevant primarily, if not exclusively, to the interpretation of the enterprise as an effort to ground the morality necessary for orderly social interaction in precepts of rational choice behavior. Recall, however, that this was only one among three sets of standards for evaluating the Gauthier effort that I enunciated in the first paragraph of this paper. By the second set of standards, my judgment of the inclusive enterprise is favorable. I shall defend this judgment in this section, and I shall make a few comments on the third set of standards suggested.

Broadly construed, the Gauthier enterprise represents an attempt to fill a major gap in our understanding and explanation of how we act and how we should act in social relationships one with another. I am convinced that social order, as we know it, would collapse overnight if all persons, or even a large share of persons, should suddenly commence to behave strictly in accordance with the utility-maximizing models of orthodox choice theory, and within the constraints only of formal legal enforcement structures. We need only refer to the statistics of crime and punishment. It is much easier for our formal models to explain why persons commit crimes than it is to explain why persons do not do so.

By comparison with David Gauthier, I am much less concerned with whether or not the behavioral norms required for what I have called the "moral order" can or cannot be grounded in some extension of rational choice. As I have indicated, I am skeptical of his success in this respect. I am concerned, however, with the presence of such norms in the behavior of persons with whom I must interact in the complex socio–political– economic nexus of modern life. Gauthier shares my conviction that the norms emergent from his enterprise, or some that are roughly similar, are necessary for the liberal social order. If his effort is reinterpreted as offering an argument, even if oblique, in support of this proposition it should carry much more weight even to those who remain highly skeptical of his more ambitious enterprise. Clearly, we must understand (to the extent that it is possible) the sources of the moral norms that provide the cement of liberal society if we are to think about constructive improvement or even constructive prevention of further erosion.

So interpreted, Gauthier is a *moral* constructivist, whose enterprise is distinguishable from many other moral philosophers by its individualist– contractarian foundations. By way of comparison, my own position is that of a *constitutional* constructivist, whose enterprise builds on the same individualist–contractarian foundations. But my emphasis is placed on the rules that constrain behavior, rather than on the norms for behavior itself. In this rough classificatory schemata, Rawls combines elements of both moral and constitutional constructivism, still within the contractarian framework. The three of us, Rawls, Gauthier, Buchanan, seem clearly to be closer to each other than either of us is to the nonconstructivism of Nozick or Hayek.

By my third set of standards, I suggest that the Gauthier enterprise offers Humean hope rather than Hobbesian despair. Recall that Hobbes wrote amid the turbulence of revolutionary mid-seventeenth century England; Hume worked out his ideas in the relatively well-ordered Scotland of the eighteenth century. It is far easier to imagine the empirical reality of a rational morality in the Scotland of David Hume and Adam

Smith than it is to model Puritans and Cavaliers as agreeing on precepts for sharing the cooperative surplus. Both Hobbes and Hume were individualist in their rejection of supraindividualist sources of value; one offers reasons for constraints, the other offers reasons for abiding with those that exist.

The enterprise of David Gauthier has both Hobbesian and Humean elements. Does the enterprise presuppose that we live in a social environment nearer to the Scotland of Hume than to the England of Hobbes? Is the community of social interactors sufficiently well defined to make any system of morals by agreement viable? Is a rational morality independent of history, of culture, of institutional–constitutional structure? Perhaps we do have a *moral* obligation to answer these three questions affirmatively.

ARITHMETICAL APPENDIX

In a shift from the two-firm to the three-firm interaction with product demand and firm cost functions unchanged from the example in Figure 1, joint profit maximizing industry output will, of course, remain unchanged at 90 units. In the three-firm setting, this output will be shared equally among the three identical firms, with each firm producing 30 units. The price remains at $110 per unit, and each firm's profit becomes *$2700* [(30 × $110) − (30 × $20)]. This is compared with the *$4050* profit in the two-firm setting. In considering whether to adopt the cooperative strategy by the Gauthier rule, the firm must compare the expected payoff under this strategy with that which is predicted under fully independent adjustment by each of the three firms.

Payoff for Firm 1
if it adopts cooperative
strategy

Behavior of Firm 2	Behavior of Firm 3	Prob.	Profit to Firm 1
C	C	1/4	$2700
C	N	1/4	$1800
N	C	1/4	$1800
N	N	1/4	$1500

Expected value of payoff *$1950*

Consider, first, the prospects if Firm 1 cooperates, which, in this case, means setting output rate at 30, which is one-third of the joint profit maximizing output. The firm expects that each one of the other two firms will behave cooperatively with a probability of one-half. There are four possibilities, with probabilities indicated below, with C and N referring to cooperative and noncooperative strategy choices.

Values for the profit for Firm 1 are computed by postulating that all firms with N strategies maximize profits subject to the C firm's retention of joint profit maximizing output.

Payoff to Firm 1 if it adopts
independent adjustment strategy,
and same strategy is adopted by
other two firms

$2025

Value computed by postulating that each of three firms adjusts output independently to outputs of other firms.

Center for Study of Public Choice, George Mason University

Social Philosophy & Policy 5:2 ISSN 0265–0525

CONSTRAINED MAXIMIZATION AND RESOLUTE CHOICE*

Edward F. McClennen

1. INTRODUCTION

In *Morals By Agreement*, David Gauthier concludes that under certain conditions it is rational for an agent to be disposed to choose in accordance with a fair cooperative scheme rather than to choose the course of action that maximizes his utility.[1] This is only one of a number of important claims advanced in that book. In particular, he also propounds a distinctive view concerning what counts as a fair cooperative arrangement. The thesis concerning the rationality of adopting a cooperative disposition is, however, logically independent of his substantive view of a fair cooperative scheme and is itself central to the project as a whole. Gauthier's concern is to establish that certain moral principles are those that fully rational, self-interested persons would agree to take as regulative of their dealings with one another – that a contractarian approach, in this sense, can provide an adequate basis for a theory of morality. As he remarks at the very outset:

> ... [the] genuinely problematic element in a contractarian theory is not the introduction of the idea of morality, but the step from hypothetical agreement to actual moral constraint. Suppose that each person recognizes himself as one of the parties to agreement. The principles forming the object of agreement are those that he would have accepted *ex ante* in bargaining with his fellows, had he found himself among them in a context initially devoid of moral constraint. Why need he accept, *ex post* in his actual situation, these principles as constraining his choices?[2]

The defense of the claim that it is rational to be disposed to cooperate and,

---

* An earlier version of this paper was presented at a symposium in honor of the publication of David Gauthier's book, *Morals By Agreement*, at the 1986 Meeting of the Central Division of the American Philosophical Association. I am indebted to Gauthier himself, Geoffrey Sayre McCord, David Falk and other members of the Triangle Workshop on Ethics (Chapel Hill, NC), and an anonymous referee, for very helpful comments.

[1] David Gauthier, *Morals By Agreement* (Oxford University Press, 1986). Hereinafter referred to as *MA*.

[2] *MA*, p.9.

hence, to constrain one's disposition to choose so as to maximize utility, is thus crucial to the whole project:

> Indeed, if our defense [of this proposition] fails, then we must conclude that a rational morality is a chimera, so that there is no rational and impartial constraint on the pursuit of individual utility.[3]

I share Gauthier's commitment to a contractarian approach to morality, and I think it is possible to interpret moral principles as principles upon which rational, self-interested persons can agree. I also share his view that it is crucial to such a project to show that rational persons will dispose themselves to choose in a cooperative manner. My concern, as it turns out, is not with conclusions but, rather, with arguments. Specifically, I think that the case for the rationality of cooperative dispositions has not been made as effectively as it might have been. While Gauthier has clearly shown that rational, self-interested persons will *want* to develop the capacity to interact cooperatively with one another, it is less clear that he has shown, at least as effectively as he might, that they *can* cooperate. This is the problem that I shall address in this paper. I want, however, to approach this matter in a cooperative spirit by exploring a way in which the argument Gauthier offers might be reformulated so as to make the thesis of the rationality of cooperative dispositions even more secure.

2. GAUTHIER'S CONCEPT OF CONSTRAINED MAXIMIZATION

On the account that Gauthier offers, to be disposed to cooperate is to be disposed to choose, in certain cases, other than the course of action that would maximize one's own (expected) utility. Gauthier is prepared to acknowledge, of course, that the maximizer of utility will find it rational to enter into agreements with others and, under a wide range of circumstances, will also find it rational to comply with these agreements. The standard argument, however, which Gauthier rejects, is that it will be rational to cooperate in any such situation *only if* the utility one expects from acting cooperatively is at least equal to the utility one would expect, were one to act instead on one's best individual strategy. Gauthier argues that if this argument goes through, it defeats cooperation in a significant class of cases and, thus, precludes agents from securing benefits that such cooperation would make possible.[4]

---

[3] *MA*, p.158.
[4] *MA*, pp.166–167.

Gauthier characterizes the standard argument as recommending that one always pursue a policy of *straightforward* maximization, that one always choose an action that maximizes utility given the strategies of those with whom one interacts. Against this, he argues that a rational agent should adopt, in certain situations, a policy of *constrained* maximization, which involves choosing in accordance with a fair cooperative scheme.[5] A constrained maximizer does not unconditionally choose in accordance with such a cooperative scheme. In a specific situation in which the cooperative scheme calls upon him to do some action, his expected utility from doing that action must be judged by him to be greater than the expected utility of his and everyone else playing their best individual strategies. Suppose now that he anticipates that others will definitely not cooperate; then, typically, his expected utility from cooperating himself (when others do not) will be less than his expected utility from no one cooperating. Under such circumstances, he will not cooperate. Thus, whether he cooperates or not will depend (in part) upon his expectations concerning what others will do.

Gauthier argues that what a constrained maximizer (CM) will do does not always coincide with what a straightforward maximizer (SM) would do in the same situation. The example he offers is one in which both parties know that how each chooses in a particular situation has no bearing on how well each can expect to do in other interactions and which has the structure of a Prisoners' Dilemma (PD) game.[6] In this kind of situation, an SM will choose not to cooperate, while a CM will choose to cooperate, if he believes that the other agent will also cooperate. Indeed, he will cooperate so long as he thinks that there is sufficient probability that the other will cooperate.[7]

The issue, then, is not whether a CM policy is distinct from an SM Policy. Rather, the issue is whether it is rational for a person to become a CM, i.e., to adopt the disposition in question, or to remain an SM. This is to be settled, according to Gauthier, by determining which choice of a disposition has the higher expected utility, taking the choice of a disposition by others as a fixed parameter:

> In parametric contexts, the disposition to make straightforwardly maximizing choices is uncontroversially utility-maximizing. We may therefore employ the device of a parametric choice among dispositions to choose to show that in strategic contexts, the

---

[5] What counts as a fair cooperative scheme is the subject of Chapter V of *MA*.

[6] See *MA*, p.170.

[7] Thus, for example, while both an SM and a CM can be expected to employ tit-for-tat in iterated PD games, a CM will, while an SM will not, cooperate on the last round of a finite interaction, if he expects that the other player is a CM.

disposition to make constrained choices, rather than straightforwardly maximizing choices, is utility-maximizing.[8]

The problem of choice in Prisoners' Dilemma situations is thus to be
"resolved" by showing that when the decision problem is recast as one in
which an agent must choose a disposition (to choose), taking the choice of
a disposition by others as fixed, then straightforward maximization calls
upon one to adopt the disposition of a constrained maximizer.

Now, in choosing between dispositions, Gauthier argues, one need
consider only situations in which the dispositions would yield different
behavior: more specifically, where there are (fairly distributable) gains to be
had from cooperation and where there are additional gains for the player
who defects while the other does not. Gauthier invites us to consider, then,
an individual who is faced with the problem of deciding which disposition
to adopt in a situation having the following features: the greatest utility for
the agent will be realized if others adhere to the cooperative scheme while
he defects unilaterally, but the outcome of everyone cooperating yields him
greater utility than does the outcome of everyone defecting from the
cooperative scheme. Stated somewhat more formally, let u be his expected
utility, if he and the other players act on individual strategies; let u' be his
expected utility, if he and the other players act in accordance with the
cooperate scheme; and let u'' be his expected utility, if he acts on an
individual strategy and the other players act in accordance with the
cooperative scheme; then the defining characteristic is: $u'' > u' > u$.[9]

Gauthier suggests that, for cases in which the relevant utility values
satisfy this constraint, there are two conflicting lines of argument that can
be brought to bear on the question of which dispositon to adopt:

> *Argument (1)*: Suppose I adopt straightforward maximization.
> Then if I expect the other to base his action on a joint strategy, I

---

[8] See *MA*, p.183. Such a conclusion, it should be noted, is consistent with his remark that
the "constrained maximizer does not reason more effectively about how to maximize her
utility" (*MA*, p.170). A CM is not simply an SM in his most effective guise. Nonetheless, the
disposition expressed by a CM is to be defended on the grounds that, within the class of cases
to which it is to apply, it is a more effective way to maximize expected utility. That is, from the
ex ante vantage point, where the agent deliberates whether to be a CM or an SM, the option of
becoming a CM has associated with it a greater expected utility. The essential point is
presumably that one's disposition to choose affects the likelihood of being in situations in
which mutual advantages can be secured. A straightforward maximizer must expect to be
excluded from cooperative arrangements which he would find advantageous. A constrained
maximizer may expect to be included in such arrangements. He benefits from his disposition,
not in the choices he makes but in his oppportunities to choose.

[9] Notice here that no mention is made of the outcome that would result were the individual
in question to act on the cooperative strategy while the other player acts on an individual
strategy. That is, the analysis abstracts from the possibility that the deliberating agent
mistakenly thinks the other player will be cooperative. I shall return to this point shortly.

defect to my best individual strategy, and expect a utility, u''. If I expect the other to act on an individual strategy, then so do I, and expect a utility, u. If the probability that the other will base his action on a joint strategy is p, then my overall expected utility is $[pu'' + (1-p)u]$.

Suppose I adopt constrained maximization. Then if I expect the other to base his action on a joint strategy, so do I, and expect a utility u'. If I expect the other to act on an individual strategy, then so do I, and expect a utility, u. Thus, my overall expected utility is $[pu' + (1-p)u]$.

Since u'' is greater than u', $[pu'' + (1-p)u]$ is greater than $[pu' + (1-p)u]$, for any value of p other than 0. . . . Therefore, to maximize my overall expectation of utility, I should adopt straightforward maximization.[10]

To interpret this argument for a relatively simple setting, suppose that I have chosen to be an SM and that I expect to encounter a number of distinct two-person PD situations, in some of which the other participant is a CM, and in some of which he is an SM. For those cases in which I encounter a CM, I can expect that he will act on the joint strategy; and on the hypothesis that I am an SM, I will choose my best individual strategy and expect a return of u''. For those cases in which I encounter an SM, since I am an SM myself, I will defect, i.e., choose my best individual strategy, and expect a return of u. If, then, I only know that there are CM and SM persons out there in proportion p to $1-p$, my expected return, from the decision to be an SM, is: $pu'' + (1-p)u$. Notice that in this case, it is of no consequence whether in any particular situation I can identify my counterpart player to be a CM or an SM: regardless of his disposition, as an SM myself, I always choose my best individual strategy.

Suppose, on the other hand, I choose to be a CM. For any case in which I encounter another whom I can identify as a CM, I will expect that he will base his action on the joint strategy, and as a CM myself, I will do so also, expecting a return of u'. For any case in which I can identify the other is an SM, I will expect him to play his best individual strategy, will respond by playing my own best individual strategy, and will expect a return of u. Finally, if the population is mixed, so that I expect to encounter CMs in proportion p to $1-p$ of SMs, then my expected return per encounter is $pu' + (1 - p)u$. Since u'' is greater than u', regardless of the proportion of CMs to SMs (so long as there are some CMs out there), my expected return from being an SM is always higher than my expected return from being a CM. Notice here, by way of contrast with the case of being an SM, that the

[10] MA, pp.171–172.

argument presupposes that I am able to correctly identify whether the person with whom I am interacting is an SM or a CM.

Gauthier suggests that this line of reasoning does not go through smoothly.[11] The agent who tries to anticipate the behavior of others must recognize that those others will be disposed to cooperate only with those whom they suppose to be similarly disposed. This means that the probability p of the others basing their action on a joint strategy will itself be in part a function of their expectation concerning what disposition the agent has chosen, and this expectation, in turn, will be in part a function of how the agent does choose. Thus, the probability of others acting cooperatively is not independent of the agent's own choice of a dispositon. But, Gauthier argues, the validity of the argument rehearsed above presupposes probabilistic independence in this respect. To put the point another way, Gauthier's agent assumes that he will correctly diagnose the dispositions of each person with whom he interacts and adjust his strategy accordingly. As I already noted, for the case of the agent choosing to be a CM, the calculations presuppose that the agent in this instance never makes a mistake himself, i.e., never treats one who is an SM as if he were a CM. The calculation abstracts from the possibility of the agent himself, as a CM, being exploited by the other – thereby getting presumably less than even u. But if the agent assumes himself to be infallible, then he should attribute similar powers to other fully rational agents, in which case he must reexpress the formulas above as $pu'' + (1-p)u$ and $p^*u' + (1-p^*)u$, and acknowledge that in the former, regardless of the proportion of those with whom he interacts and who are CMs, p will be very small, while in the second, p^* will simply be equivalent to the proportion of CMs to total population.

Gauthier now takes up a second argument, which incorporates these considerations:

> *Argument (2)*: Suppose I adopt straightforward maximization. Then I must expect others to employ maximizing individual strategies in interacting with me; so do I, and expect a utility, u.
>
> Suppose I adopt constrained maximization. Then if others are conditionally disposed to constrained maximization, I may expect them to base their actions on a co-operative joint strategy in interacting with me; so do I, and expect a utility, u'. If they are not so disposed, I employ a maximizing strategy and expect u as before. If the probability that others are disposed to constrained maximization is p, then my overall expected utility is $[pu' + (1-p)u]$.
>
> Since u' is greater than u, $[pu' + (1-p)u]$ is greater than u for

[11] *MA*, p.172.

any value of p other than 0. . . . Therefore, to maximize my overall expectation of utility, I should adopt constrained maximization.[12]

It is clear that Gauthier does *not* have in mind the following interpretation of the last step in the argument: in each particular case I might not know for certain whether I was encountering a CM or an SM person – but could only assign a probability to his being such a person. In the face of uncertainty about whether the person with whom I am interacting is a CM or an SM, I must reckon with other possible cases, specifically the case in which I (as a CM) believe I am interacting with a CM, when in fact the other is an SM. In that case, I will end up with presumably even less than u, say u^*, and this will have to enter into my calculations. Gauthier does turn to consider this case, but his remarks suggest that the original version of the argument is to be read as involving no uncertainty on the agent's part as to the disposition of the person with whom he is interacting, a point already implicit in the analysis, since the possibility of the agent being mistaken, and thus ending up with less than even u, is not raised in the passage quoted above.

3. CONSTRAINED MAXIMIZATION UNDER CONDITIONS OF TRANSPARENCY

Under conditions of perfect information concerning the dispositions of the person with whom I interact, Argument (2) is very powerful. It says, in effect, that a CM will be able to realize gains from situations involving another CM which an SM will not be able to realize and that a CM will do just as well against an SM as would another SM.[13] Argument (2) also takes into account what Argument (1) ignores – the difference between the way in which another player who is a CM can be expected to interact with an agent, depending on whether he judges the agent to be an SM or a CM.

But, Gauthier notes, Argument (2) also involves an important presupposition. The argument turns on the consideration that how others will interact with the agent depends on the agent's own choice of disposition. But this presupposes that his choice of disposition is known by others, and nothing has been said that precludes a person from deceiving others in this regard (or others simply making a mistake). Gauthier suggests that this objection can be defeated by a particular maneuver. Suppose we

. . . take our persons to be *transparent*. Each is directly aware of the dispositions of his fellows, and so aware whether he is interacting

---

[12] *MA*, p.172.
[13] Implicitly, then, this is also a dominance argument.

with straightforward or constrained maximizers. Deception [on this hypothesis] is impossible.[14]

In this instance the case for constrained maximization allegedly goes through. Under conditions of transparency, an agent who anticipates interactions with others will have a utility maximizing reason for choosing to become a CM. Suppose that he projects that a number of persons will not adopt the cooperative disposition, but that he knows he will be in a position to identify them subsequently, if and when he interacts with them. If, in addition, he supposes that whatever choice of disposition he himself makes, this will be something that others will be able to ascertain then it will pay him to become a CM, so long as he expects that there are others among those with whom he will have to interact who are CMs. That is, under conditions of perfect information, adopting the cooperative disposition is a dominant strategy – one can never do worse, and if one encounters any other CM, one will do better. To see this, recall that the disposition in question is simply a commitment to cooperate only in so far as one has reason to believe that others will do so as well. One who is disposed to cooperate with others insofar, but only insofar, as he believes that others will also cooperate – but who is in a position to know when the other is, or is not, a cooperator – will behave towards noncooperators just like one who has decided to be an SM. Thus, having chosen to be a CM costs him nothing in these situations. He does just as well as an SM would do. But, of course, he does better in encounters with others who are CMs.

It still remains the case, of course, that in specific situations that arise and to which this disposition is applicable, what each then does has no implications for other choice situations. Thus, presumably, long-run considerations do not apply. It is not that I must cooperate in such a case so as to ensure that others will be willing to trust me in other similar situations. But still, here and now, before I face these situations, that I will then (*ex post*) in each such situation be transparent means that I now (*ex ante*) have a compelling reason for becoming a CM.

4. CONSTRAINED MAXIMIZATION UNDER CONDITIONS OF TRANSLUCENCY

Gauthier goes on to point out that to assume transparency is to rob the argument of much of its interest: transparency does not characterize the real world. He is thus led to explore a weaker assumption, which he characterizes as "translucency" – the assumption that agents can in a reasonably large proportion of cases correctly identify the dispositions of

[14] *MA*, pp.173–174.

others.[15] When agents are translucent to each other, so that each has at least probabilistic knowledge of who among those with whom he interacts are CMs and who are SMs, it may still be rational to choose to be a CM.

Here matters are, however, considerably more complicated. Those who have chosen to develop the disposition to cooperate will face the real prospect of being taken advantage of by SMs who pass themselves off as CMs. Of course, it is still the case that those who develop the disposition and who can find others in the environment who are also so disposed will benefit thereby. Thus, the person who contemplates adopting the disposition to cooperate faces a trade-off between expected gains (from being able to cooperate with others who are also disposed to cooperate) and expected losses (from noncooperators who will take advantage of him).[16] In this case, then, whether one does better, in terms of expected return, to become a CM will depend very much on one's estimate of the proportion of deceptive SMs to CMs in society, the relative frequency of one's encounters with members of each group, the probability of being mistaken about whether a given person is a deceptive SM or a CM, the magnitude of the gains and losses in each case, *and* one's estimate of one's ability to effectively play the role of a deceptive SM.

There is something worrisome about this part of Gauthier's argument. The conditions under which the most rational policy is to be a CM may be more constrained than Gauthier himself indicates in his book. This is the thrust of an interesting article by Geoffrey Sayre McCord. He suggests that while a CM policy may win out over an SM policy in pair-wise comparison, under conditions in which persons are relatively translucent to one another, it is still the case that other policies may do even better from a utility-maximizing point of view. In particular, there is what Sayre McCord describes as the "trans-opaque" policy, which involves deliberately sending up all sorts of misleading signals to the effect that one is a CM, while continuing to be an SM.[17]

It would seem, in fact, that under a wide range of circumstances, those who contemplate whether to develop the disposition or not will face a familiar coordination problem. Clearly it will be in a given agent's interest – regardless of what disposition he decides to cultivate in himself – to encourage others to develop a truly cooperative disposition. But it is less obvious that it would be rational to cultivate this disposition within himself. From a parametric point of view, if others develop the disposition and he adopts the strategy of only appearing to develop it, while

[15] *MA*, pp.174–177.
[16] Gauthier explores this problem at great length in the book. See in particular, *MA*, pp.174–187.
[17] See his "Deception and Reasons To Be Moral," *American Philosophical Quarterly* (forthcoming).

actually remaining disposed to always choose in a strategic manner, he will benefit. On the other hand, if others adopt the same strategy, it is also clearly in his interest to only appear to be cooperative. Thus semblance, rather than the real thing, may well be the best strategy, regardless of what others do. Of course, if all reason in this manner, then the real disposition to cooperate will never take root, and instead of a successful transformation of the way in which persons deal with one another, there will be extensive free-riding coupled with highly sophisticated forms of hypocrisy. Still, even if this is understood as the natural outcome of rational calculations on the part of each, it simply poses for the members of the group the same dilemma all over again. All will do worse in this case than they would have done if each had simply decided to become a CM.

5. A PROBLEM: CAN DISPOSITIONS BE CHOSEN?

Sayre McCord has correctly diagnosed, I believe, a weakness in the version of Gauthier's argument that presupposes translucency. My concern, however, is that there is another weakness, one that applies even under a presupposition of transparency. Whatever the problem with choices made under conditions of translucency, it might seem that Gauthier has at least shown that under conditions of transparency the best approach from an expected utility-maximizing point of view will be to adopt a CM disposition. Now, I think it is true that even those who hold the more traditional view of rationality can accept the claim that those who are able to become CMs will secure benefits not available to those who are SMs. Where the problem emerges is over the inference that Gauthier now proceeds to make, namely, that having established the benefits of being a CM, one can conclude that a rational agent will adopt and act on such a disposition. The defender of the more traditional view can be expected to insist that he has established something less than this.

Consider once again a situation in which a CM really is distinct from an SM. More specifically, consider a classic Prisoners' Dilemma game in which some sort of precommitment or enforcement mechanism is not available and choices are to be made simultaneously. The critic can argue that while the agent may judge *ex ante* that under conditions of transparency a CM's expected return would be higher than that of an SM (in environments in which he interacts with other CMs), the agent cannot expect to effectively implement such a policy. On the usual account, the would-be CM must anticipate that when the *ex post* occasion for choice finally arrives, his rational choice of action (not disposition) will be to behave just as the SM would. But since he can anticipate this, he must anticipate that the choice of a disposition lies beyond his reach. He can say the words, "I shall be so disposed to choose," but he cannot effectively choose to be so disposed.

One can thus argue that Gauthier has correctly diagnosed *ex ante* expectations but that he has not offered any analysis of how, *ex post*, when the time comes for execution of the policy chosen, the agent can follow through. If it is expected utility – calculated from the *ex ante* point of deliberation over policies – that judges a CM policy to be superior to the SM Policy, it is also expected utility – calculated from the *ex post* point of choice of a course of action – that will judge implementation of SM superior to implementation of CM. It would seem, then, that the agent must realize that, notwithstanding the best of intentions, when push comes to shove he will continue to be an SM. Granted this, of course, he must also expect that under conditions of transparency his counterpart player will realize that he is not capable of following through on such a policy and, hence, that he is not to be trusted. The cooperative solution, then, absent the usual sort of enforcement mechanism, is simply not feasible.[18]

The problem, I want to suggest, is that expected utility calculations at the *ex ante* point (point of choosing dispositions) do not appear to suffice to determine how a rational agent will actually dispose himself with respect to future choice. Preference (or utility) as judged from a particular point in time may well govern choice at that point; but it is unclear how this can serve to regulate choice at other, subsequent points. The difficulty here, I think, can be traced back to the nature of parametric reasoning. The essence of such parametric reasoning is this: (1) the agent is presumed to have an antecedently specifiable preference ordering over the set of all possible outcomes of action, (2) rational choice consists in selecting a feasible course of action whose associated outcome is maximially preferred, and (3) the set of background considerations that condition any moment of choice function essentially only to restrict the set of feasible actions – they do not shape in any way the agent's preference ordering over actions. Within that sort of model, antecedently specifiable preferences for outcomes that are realizable at the time of choice determine the preference

---

[18] To be sure, there will clearly be situations in which it will pay to be disposed to be cooperative. If being cooperative towards others engenders a cooperative response from others, it may well be that, in straightforward utility-maximizing terms, the agent's best strategy is to be cooperative. Imagine, for example, a version of the standard PD game in which each agent is permitted to revise his strategy choice in the light of information about how the other player has chosen – with reconsideration terminating only when each player has "stood pat" with his last announced choice, and where these announced choices are then executed by a referee. Under those conditions, the rational solution will be for each to cooperate – since the rules in question preclude unilateral defection. But in such cases, it can be argued, a CM is simply an SM in a more effective guise. That is, what a CM policy calls upon the agent to choose is exactly what an SM policy calls upon him to choose.

ordering of actions available at that point in time. It is possible, of course, to reason parametrically at time t to the conclusion that one should take steps to preclude choosing in a certain way at some future point in time. Consider, for example, Ulysses, who has himself tied to the mast, and instructs the crew to ignore any pleas on his part to be untied. Thus, present choices can shape a future feasible set, but they cannot, it would seem, shape future preferences for actions.

The logic of parametric reasoning, then, makes it difficult to render coherent the idea that conclusions reached thereby have in and of themselves any force that extends over time. Within a parametric framework, it would seem that a decision at some *past* time t to adopt a disposition can have no carrying power – that it can have no direct bearing on the question of what the agent should do here and now at time $t + 1$: that decision is determined by consulting what outcomes still remain feasible at time $t + 1$. Thus, one who reasons parametrically at one point in time to the conclusion that he should adopt a certain disposition, will be disposed, it would seem, to reason parametrically also at some subsequent point of choice (in a situation to which the disposition chosen is to apply), and this will lead to choice inconsistent with the disposition that the agent putatively adopted at the *ex ante* choice point. In this way, it would seem that parametric reasoning about dispositions will be undercut by parametric reasoning about situations to which the disposition (putatively taken to be in place) applies. That is, *ex ante*, reasoning about dispositions will be undercut by *ex post* reasoning about cases.

To clarify what is at issue here, consider the following modified version of the sort of PD situation that Gauthier fixes upon (as discussed above in Section 2). The specific modifications I have in mind involve interpreting the problem as explicitly sequential in nature, and specifying payoffs such that the problem of dispositions confronts only the agent under consideration and not his counterpart player. Employing the usual conventions for representing a sequential choice problem, consider the decision tree given in Diagram 1, with monetary payoffs to each player.

On the assumption that, at least *prima facie*, each player prefers more to less money, the other player's most preferred outcome is reached by both cooperating. *His* problem, however, is simply that if he initiates such a cooperative venture by playing C at n_2, he has to worry that the agent will respond with D rather than C at n_3, which would result in his receiving the outcome that he least prefers, $10. If, on the other hand, he plays D at n_2, then he can expect the agent to respond with D, and his payoff will be $20, which is preferred to $10.

Now, it would seem that the agent at n_1 would prefer to be disposed to cooperate (at least if his disposition would be known to the other

DIAGRAM 1

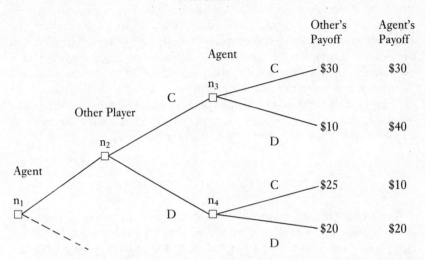

player – which it would be under conditions of transparency), for then he could expect a cooperative response from the other player, and a return to himself of $30 instead of $20.[19] Suppose, however, the agent were to find himself at n_3, facing (*ex post*) a choice between C and D. By reference to antecedently determinable preferences for monetary amounts, he prefers the outcome of D to the outcome of C (i.e., prefers getting $40 rather than $30). But, then, by appeal to the principle of parametric reasoning he can be expected to choose D rather than C. Under conditions of transparency, of course, the other player will expect the agent to choose in this fashion, and this anticipation will condition what is, from the standpoint of n_2, a feasible outcome. The other player would prefer, of course, getting $30 to getting $20, but given his anticipation of how the agent would choose, were he at n_3, $30 is simply not a feasible outcome (nor is the outcome that yields him $25). Among outcomes that are feasible, $20 and $10, the former is preferred, and hence the other player can be expected, again by appeal to the principles of parametric reasoning, to choose D at n_2.

Gauthier's agent, then, can say to himself and to the other player that he would like to be disposed to cooperate, if and when n_3 is reached, but there is no reason for either to believe that he can be so disposed. By hypothesis, the CM policy differs from the SM policy precisely in that the former calls

[19] To be sure, it is also true that *ex ante* he would most prefer that the other player trust him while he defects from the cooperative arrangement. But the assumption here is that this possibility is not open to him: under conditions of transparency, he cannot hope that the other player will act cooperatively when he himself is known to be an SM.

for the agent to abstain from taking the action that maximizes his preferences for outcomes in this type of situation. The utility values given above in Section 2 express this: the utility of the outcome of the intersection of SM and a cooperative commitment by other players (u'') is greater than the utility of the outcome of the intersection of CM and a cooperative commitment on the part of others (u'). On the standard account of utility, which Gauthier accepts, to say that u'' is greater than u' is to say that from the *ex post* vantage point at which he must actually make a choice, the agent prefers the outcome of defecting to the outcome of cooperating.[20] Thus, Gauthier's agent faces a dilemma.

6. CONTEXT SENSITIVE PREFERENCES

The argument just rehearsed threatens Gauthier's whole project. He needs to show that a rational agent will become a CM. It appears, however, that he has only shown that a rational agent would want to be a CM, not that he can be so disposed. Despite this, I remain convinced that the type of contractarian theory of morality to which Gauthier is committed can be defended. What I propose to do is develop an alternative approach (or reinterpretation of his argument), one which still yields his conclusions regarding the rationality of acting on cooperative schemes.[21]

One can begin by recalling that Gauthier is content to make an appeal – at the level of the choice of dispositions – to parametric reasoning. The discussion of the last section suggests that such an approach cannot be confined to that level, that it will also apply at the level of choice of action as well, thereby undercutting the conclusions established at the level of dispositions. I suggest, then, that if one is to avoid the problem posed in Section 5, one must restructure the argument so as to avoid the appeal to parametric reasoning. More specifically, since what is central to parametric reasoning is that antecedently definable preferences for outcomes feasible at time t are controlling for rational choice at time t, it is precisely this assumption that must be challenged.

To return to the example presented in Section 5, one can acknowledge

[20] What supports the assumption that u'' is greater than u', that the agent prefers the outcome of unilateral defection over the outcome of mutual cooperation? On the traditional way of thinking about this sort of problem, the notion is that it is just such an order of preferences, and hence utility values, that generates the problem to be analyzed. The most familiar version of this type of problem is, of course, the standard PD game. The agent is presumed to prefer fewer years in jail to more. Those who prefer more years to fewer, or who prefer that both get only a few years to one getting many years in jail while the other goes free, do not face a standard Prisoners' Dilemma.

[21] The approach developed here is treated in much greater detail in my book, *Rationality and Dynamic Choice: Foundational Explorations* (Cambridge University Press, forthcoming).

that typically an agent will, of course, prefer the outcome of unilateral defection to that of cooperation, namely, \$40 to \$30. But it does not follow that one must take those preferences for outcomes as completely determinative of the preferences that the agent has for the actions open to him within the context of this kind of interactive situation. That is, granted that the agent prefers getting \$40 to getting \$30, when amounts of this sort are abstractly considered, it does not follow that these preferences determine his preference for D over C at n_3 and, hence, his choice of an action at that point in the decision tree.

Notice, first of all, that there is no logical contradiction in supposing that all of the following is true of the agent: (1) when he considers the possibility of receiving this or that amount of money, his preference, *ceteris paribus*, is for more rather than less money; (2) at time t, under conditions of transparency, he prefers to be disposed to cooperate rather than to defect at time $t + 1$; and (3) at time $t + 1$ he is disposed to cooperate. If it is pointed out to him that there is a certain tension between (1) and (3), one could imagine him to respond that while he would be disposed to choose the course of action that would realize for him the larger amount of money, if he were to confront such a choice outright, he is not disposed to choose in such a manner within the context of a decision problem of the sort under consideration. That is, he could argue that his preferences over options available to him within a decision tree are sensitive to context: how he would choose, were he to face a situation just like that at n_3, except *de novo*, i.e., not against the background of the interactive situation defined by the full tree, is different from how he would choose at n_3, i.e., within the context of that decision tree.

This is a possible story. Of course, matters cannot be left there. The crucial question concerns what might motivate an agent to have such a preference, i.e., to prefer not to defect, even though, abstractly considered, he prefers the outcome of defection to the outcome of cooperation. Clearly, some account must be given since, otherwise, the appeal to a preference for cooperating rather than defecting would be purely *ad hoc*. Moreover, since I share with Gauthier a commitment to the project of showing morality to have a rational basis, not just any account will do. That is, some stories that could be told here would not help to advance that project. Of course, if the story to be told really does advance that project, it can be asked whether I have really offered a new argument or merely offered a way to rephrase his. Finally, if what I have proposed is a genuine alternative, then it must be shown still that it is not open to an objection parallel to the one raised against Gauthier, namely, that while the agent might prefer at time t that he choose the cooperative alternative at time $t + 1$, at time $t + 1$ itself, he will find himself preferring to defect rather than cooperate.

7. CONTEXT SENSITIVE PREFERENCES AND RATIONALITY

I want to suggest that there is an account that satisfies these various concerns. As Gauthier himself makes clear, the problem in a typical PD situation is that an agent who is unable to cooperate is thereby precluded from gains that would be available to him were he able to cooperate and others were assured of this. Now, under conditions of transparency, he can be assured that others will be aware of his dispositions. Under such conditions, then, the agent has an interest in developing an effective disposition to cooperate and, hence, an operative capability of preferring, and choosing, the cooperative course of action. He has that interest precisely as a result of coming to realize that, under conditions of transparency, it is a preference on his part for defecting that precludes his realizing certain benefits that it otherwise would be open to him to secure.

Recognition of something like this point is, oddly enough, implicit in the way in which the standard theory of rationality deals with such situations. On the standard account, it is acknowledged that rational agents who know each other to be such will have to forgo benefits that would otherwise be available to them and, hence, that such agents will be motivated to make arrangements that will permit them to coordinate on mutually advantageous outcomes. Thus, for example, it is predicted that rational agents will adopt surveillance and enforcement devices. It is rational to do this, so the standard argument goes, because they can secure additional benefits thereby. Now, if the prospect of additional benefits can motivate persons to adopt various surveillance and enforcement devices, then it must also be capable of motivating them to secure those additional benefits at the least cost possible – since achieving the same benefits at lower cost amounts to securing even greater benefits. Surveillance and enforcement mechanisms, however, typically involve expenditures of scarce resources, while an arrangement under which each constrains his *ex post* choice, that is, takes his *ex post* preferences for actions as contextually shaped in the manner discussed above, will achieve the same outcome without the expenditure of those scarce resources. In this respect, the standard approach sets out but then short-circuits a plausible line of argument: it appeals to the notion that rational agents will always move to secure desired outcomes at the greatest savings possible, but then fails to carry that argument to its logical conclusion.

Here, it seems to me, is a plausible account of why rational agents will, at least under conditions of transparency, come to treat their preferences among feasible sets of actions as sensitive to more than just their preferences for the corresponding outcomes of those actions. Contextual dependency is here to be understood as a "strategy" to be employed in interaction situations for securing greater benefits. Since the ultimate criterion to which appeal is made is increased benefits, this account treats the emergence of such an attitude as due to *endogenous*, not exogenous, factors: that is, such context dependent preferences for actions can be understood as rooted in the disposition to maximize, to seek additional benefits wherever possible. Alternatively put, the agent who develops such context dependent preferences for feasible actions is no less a maximizer of his preferences over outcomes than is the agent who proceeds always to reason parametrically, since it is with a view to improving his prospects that he comes to adopt such an approach to interactive choice situations. It is simply that he views such consequences from a different perspective than does the agent who reasons parametrically. The latter maximizes with respect to his preferences for outcomes in an incremental fashion, while the former maximizes his preferences for outcomes in a more holistic fashion.

8.   THE STABILITY OF SUCH DISPOSITIONS

Gauthier's agent reasons parametrically from his *ex ante* position about the adoption of a disposition. But what he judges from that *ex ante* position is that adoption of the disposition in question would maximize his preference for what is then the set of feasible outcomes. Subsequently, when called upon to act on that disposition, the feasible set is different, and it would seem that a new judgment is called for, one that may prescribe choices in conflict with what the disposition requires. Thus, it would appear that the decision made earlier with respect to a disposition is unstable.

The analysis I have offered would be subject to a similar objection if I had to make appeal in connection with *ex ante* deliberation to the principle of maximizing with respect to preferences for given, i.e., feasible outcomes, that is, if I had to assume that the agent reasoned parametrically at the *ex ante* point of deliberation. No such appeal needs to be made. On the account I have offered, there is no presumption as such that evaluation at any point in time must be based on parametric reasoning – hence, there is no particular reason to suppose that the agent must parametrically reevaluate at the *ex post* choice point.

The case for preferring at the *ex post* stage to cooperate rather than defect can be made in a different way altogether. In place of Gauthier's model of an agent who, it seems, must reason parametrically at each point in time, one can consider a different model altogether, predicated on the notion that the agent is a being who continues over time, with concerns that have some continuity to them. Such an agent can be understood to view himself as deliberating over alternative *plans*, i.e., sequences of choices to be made over time and subject to various contingencies, as choosing some particular plan, and then proceeding, at least in the normal course of events, to make specific choices (at different points in time) that serve to execute or implement the plan chosen. What is characteristic of such an agent is that his *ex post* preferences among available actions are disciplined or shaped by what he judges, from the perspective of plans taken as wholes, to be the best plan to pursue. If such an agent is successful in this regard, then it can be said that what he chooses *ex post* to do is consistent with what he resolved (or planned) to do. Such an agent can be described as a *resolute* chooser.[22]

Contrast this with the agent who reasons in the more traditional manner. If he supposes that he will, at each choice point, reason parametrically with respect to preferences for outcomes, then he must project that he will choose *ex post* to defect rather than act in accord with the cooperative plan. Thus, for such an agent the cooperative plan is not feasible: it calls upon him to make a choice subsequently that he now expects that he will not make. If the *ex post* choice is one that he *now* judges it would be advantageous to make, he may investigate ways in which to precommit – to change the future choice situation in some manner or other so that the choice in question can be made – say, by introducing special incentives in favor of the choice in question, or constraints on other options (as when Ulysses has himself tied to the mast to ensure that he "chooses" not to follow the Sirens). However, whether he simply regards certain plans as not feasible, or takes steps to precommit himself, his behavior is in marked contrast to that of the resolute chooser, for instead of disciplining *ex post* choice to chosen plan, he disciplines his adoption of a plan to what he projects will be his *ex post* preference.

The problem is simply that such an agent, unlike the resolute agent, must either forgo certain opportunities or expend valuable resources. That is, parametric reasoning works against the continuing interests of the agent. Agents who are capable of adopting and carrying through on plans will do better, over time, than do those who always reason parametrically. Alternatively put, if one thinks of the self as separable into discrete time-slices, then a resolute approach – a commitment to chosen plans – recommends itself on the grounds that each of the relevant time-slices can judge himself to be better off if the plan is adopted and followed than if no

---

[22] For an earlier statement of the implications of resolute choosing for such situations, see my paper, "Prisoner's Dilemma and Resolute Choice," F. Campbell and L. Sowden, eds., *Paradoxes of Rationality and Cooperation: Prisoner's Dilemma and Newcomb's Problem* (Vancouver: University of British Columbia Press, 1985).

such plan is put into effect, i.e., if choice is always based on parametric reasoning of the moment. The case for the disposition to act on plans is thus to be made by reference to the interest that each and every time-defined self has in such an approach, and not simply by reference to what the *ex ante* self judges parametrically to be the superior plan.

9. WEAKNESS OF WILL AND RESOLUTE CHOICE

The argument I have just rehearsed presupposes that the individual can act on a plan, and this presupposes, in turn, that he recognizes himself as a continuing entity, as possessing some sort of identity over time. Notice, however, that the argument does not presuppose that successful interaction involves a parallel recognition of distinct selves as somehow part of some greater unity, some social whole. If the argument I have constructed is successful, a capacity on the part of each individual to discipline sequences of choices to adopted plans will suffice to make cooperation possible, at least in a certain range of cases.[23]

Talk of being resolute, of course, suggests a connection to a very old problem: the problem of weakness of will. One way to pose the objection to the model that Gauthier has adopted is to note that it implies that the agent must, by hypothesis, exhibit weakness of will. Gauthier's model has this implication, since he supposes that it is parametric reasoning from preferences for outcomes that motivates the agent to adopt the new disposition. Thus, the very principle of choice which is introduced to recommend adoption of a new disposition recommends its abandonment in the very contexts in which it is to be operative.

This is not to say, of course, that on the alternative proposed here the agent faces no problem of weakness of will. What I have done is simply to offer a model in which the burden of presumption has been shifted. On the more standard view, weakness of will with respect to dispositions turns out to be the result of the operation of rational motivation (in the form of the principle of parametrically maximizing with respect to preferences for outcomes). On the view proposed here, weakness of will, while still possible, will have to be understood in terms of a *failure* of rational motivation.

---

[23] Notice also that the criterion of rationality to which appeal is made is a criterion of individual rationality, not group rationality. The argument is that rational persons who know those with whom they interact to be rational owe it to themselves to choose cooperatively, for by so doing they advance their own interests.

10. PSEUDO-SOLUTIONS AND AD HOC EXPLANATIONS

Gauthier supposes that rational agents will adopt and act on a disposition to constrain their choices in certain circumstances; thus, his agents choose within the context of certain decision problems by reference to more than simply their preference ordering over the outcomes to be associated with those actions. What is central to the notion of contextually sensitive preferences, as characterized in the previous section, is that the agent's choice of an action is responsive to more than just his preference for outcomes. Moreover, there is a natural bridge from his argument to mine. Gauthier's intention is to convince us that the agent can come to choose to be a CM rather than an SM, where this is understood to mean not simply that he agrees *ex ante* to coordinate with others, but actually follows through and does *ex post* what the cooperative scheme calls upon him to do. Suppose that Gauthier is right and the agent now acts as a CM. If the agent is a CM and chooses accordingly, from the perspective of preference revealed by behavior (choice), he is appropriately interpreted as maximizing utility (preference) in that situation in a straightforward manner. If choices reveal preferences, Gauthier's claim that an agent can behave as a CM can be reinterpreted plausibly, then, as a claim that such an agent is capable of basing his choice on preferences that are context sensitive.[24]

The economist Amartya Sen has recently cautioned against employing a revealed preference concept in this manner to provide a solution to PD situations.[25] Sen is prepared to acknowledge that those who cooperate may indeed be revealing a preference for cooperation – if it turns out that they are, say, sufficiently concerned for the welfare of the other participants. He insists, however, that a PD problem arises precisely because it is presumed that the agent is *not* concerned with the welfare of the others – but only with his own welfare or interests.

One can mark here what appear to be two distinct, although closely connected issues. One concerns whether certain ways of arguing that rational agents should cooperate in a PD situation might be dismissed on the grounds that the reasons cited imply that those who are so disposed do not face a genuine Prisoner's Dilemma. The second is whether some particular account of how persons might come to cooperate in such a situation could be faulted on the grounds that it "resolves" the problem in

---

[24] Since on the account offered here a rational agent does not ever act contrary to the preferences he has for actions at the time of choice, and, correspondingly, does not choose other than a utility-maximizing action, it is perhaps misleading to describe him as a constrained maximizer. He maximizes in an unconstrained sense his preferences for available actions, although not his preferences over (separately considered) outcomes.

[25] Amartya K. Sen, "Behavior and the Concept of Preference," *Economica*, vol. 40 (1973), pp.241–259.

a purely *ad hoc* manner. It would seem, for example, that those who are concerned about the welfare of others and who are led thereby to act in a cooperative manner can be said, in so behaving, to reveal their concern for others. However, if one supposes them to cooperate for that reason, then they do not really face a PD situation. Moreover, such a "resolution" of the problem has the air of being *ad hoc*.

The model I have proposed is subject to neither of these objections. Following Sen, I start with the assumption that the agents' preferences for *outcomes* conform to the pattern of a classic Prisoners' Dilemma situation. I simply move from there to challenge the distinct assumption that preferences for outcomes, abstractly considered, must be taken as controlling for preferences over actions and, hence, for choice. Moreover, while I have introduced the notion that a rational agent might prefer $40 to $30 and yet still prefer, within the context of a PD situation, to take the course of action leading to $30 rather than the course of action leading to $40, I have explicitly sought to do so in a manner that is not open to the charge of being *ad hoc*. My concern has been to offer an account that not only shows how that preference might come about, but also roots it precisely in the agent's concern to secure a larger rather than a smaller amount of money. That is, I explicitly suppose agents who are disposed to cooperate, not from any sense of a desire to help others but from a sense that failure to be so disposed will mean that they do not realize gains that are possible. I suppose that it is a sense of the coordination problem that they thus confront and a desire to achieve the gains that cooperation makes possible that leads them to prefer to take the cooperative option, given that they expect that others will do so as well. Such persons are motivated, not by concern for others, but from a sense that it is in their own self-interest to do so. Their preference for cooperation is rooted in a concern to maximize (albeit not parametrically) with respect to preferences for outcomes.

11.   ONE LAST OBJECTION CONSIDERED

Those who have opted for the more traditional view of utility maximizing will be unpersuaded, no doubt. They will insist that what counts against the model I have offered is a deeply rooted principle of rational choice. The notion is that rational choice is consequentially-oriented choice – choice shaped by reference to what lies in the future, what remains open to realization. The rational agent looks ahead, not behind. Call this the Principle of Consequences. It might seem that I have supposed (mistakenly, on this account) that the rational agent who faces a PD situation will, when it comes time to choose, look backward to the plan he adopted and not simply forward to the consequences of the actions still available.

I suggest in rebuttal that matters are more complicated than this. As I have already had occasion to observe, the dilemma that our agent faces is that on the standard account he fails to realize a consequence that is technically feasible and that he prefers to the one that he does realize. My objection to the standard view is fully consequentialist in spirit. Recall my remark at the end of Section 7: once again, the issue is not whether or not it is rational to look to consequences; the issue is the perspective from which the consideration of consequences is to be controlling for choice.

Again, it may be argued that what counts against my model is that the very concept of preference itself implies that the agent will be disposed, at each choice point in time, to choose an alternative that is maximally preferred and that the plan the agent adopts must have the property that it calls upon the agent to make choices at each choice point that are consistent with the preferences he has at that point in time. Call this the Principle of Dynamic Consistency. This principle is clearly one to which my proposed model is faithful. Indeed, it is precisely from a sense of the plausibility of this principle that I have argued for interpreting the disposition to behave as a CM in terms of context sensitive *ex post* preferences. If the concept of preference is to have any explanatory role in choice behavior, what must shape choice now is preference now – not preference that one had at some time in the past. Consequently, if anything like what Gauthier describes as constrained maximization is possible, it surely must be in virtue of the agent coming to view his *ex post* choice differently than he would have otherwise.

What works against my model is a third principle, altogether distinct from the two principles just discussed. This is a separability principle requiring that what determines preference at any point in a sequence of decisions to be made is what would govern preference at that point, were the agent to confront that choice *de novo*, as a new decision problem, i.e., not against the background of any previous decisions. According to this principle, preferences that figure in any sort of rational decision will not be sensitive to context. It requires that what might have happened under conditions that no longer obtain, other paths that could have been taken but were not, other events that might have taken place but did not, can have no influence on the choice that the agent now makes at some point within a decision tree, at least in so far as he is rational.[26]

---

[26] The qualifier "rational" is revealingly necessary. The phenomenon of contextually sensitive preferences that appear to qualify as irrational is well-documented. See, for example, A. Tversky and D. Kahneman, "The Framing of Decisions and the Psychology of Choice,"

I am happy to plead guilty to violating this principle. I see no reason to suppose that the preferences the agent has in a situation in which there is no coordination problem must be controlling for one in which he does face such a problem. On the contrary, it seems more plausible to suppose that, when faced with a coordinating with other rational agents, a person will be capable of disciplining future preferences to conform to a plan whose consequences he judges to be superior.[27]

12. CONCLUSION

The model I have proposed is distinct, I think, from the model proposed by Gauthier. As the discussion in the previous section is designed to suggest, while he is content to leave undisturbed the traditional theory of rational independent choice (for the single agent choosing against nature), and proposes only to modify the account offered for interdependent choice, I have suggested that a stronger argument for becoming a CM is to be found by carrying the critique back to principles governing independent, individual decision making. One can mark the difference in particular by reflecting that on my model the independent, and not just the interdependent, decision maker will have reason to constrain his disposition to reason, and to choose, parametrically. Robinson Crusoe, no less than the proverbial prisoners, will face dilemmas to which a resolute approach – adopting and then carrying through on plans – can provide an effective solution.

In the end, however, I am not so concerned with whether my argument is better seen as a reinterpretation of Gauthier's argument or as a distinct argument. This much I am happy to acknowledge: I see no conflict between what I have suggested here and the *spirit* of Gauthier's argument. What Gauthier seeks to establish is that the options available within certain types of interaction situations need to be reevaluated – that it is rational for the agent to come to view those options differently than *prima facie* he is disposed to view them. The disposition always to choose fewer years to more, and more money to less, in PD situations is just what must now seem unattractive to the agent: it costs him years in jail, and less by way of monetary payoff. It is just this disposition that the rational agent will want to leave behind. I have suggested that a useful way to conceptualize such a

---

Science, vol. 211 (1981), pp.453–458. My suggestion, of course, which runs counter to what most have been inclined to argue, is that in some situations having preferences that do in fact vary with the context turns out to be useful and hence rational.

[27] The distinctions developed in this Section are explored at much greater length in my book, *Rationality and Dynamic Choice: Foundational Explorations*.

problem is to think of the agent as being concerned that if and when the opportunity presents itself he will prefer to defect, even though here and now he prefers that he not do this. So also, then, a natural way to resolve this problem is to think of the agent as coming, as a result of reflection on the costs involved, to no longer have a preference for unilateral defection.

When Gauthier's notion of choosing a new dispositon is reinterpreted in terms of this sort of transformation of his preferences, his own remarks about human capabilities become all the more persuasive. Gauthier argues that it is reasonable to suppose that:

> . . . the capacity to make such choices is itself an essential part of human rationality. . . . At the core of our rational capacity is the ability to engage in self-critical reflection. The fully rational being is able to reflect on his standard of deliberation, and to change that standard in the light of reflection. Thus we suppose it possible for persons, who may initially assume that it is rational to extend straightforward maximization from parametric to strategic contexts, to reflect on the implications of this extension, and to reject it in favour of constrained maximization.[28]

This is a brief for rationality as a positive capacity, not a liability – as it must be on the standard account. But more to the point, it can be taken to express precisely what I have sought to press home, namely, that preferences need not be regarded as invariably fixed by something purely exogenous to the process of deliberation itself – that deliberation itself can result in a constructive and pragmatic transformation of one's preferences to meet the needs of a given situation.

Philosophy, Washington University in St. Louis

---

[28] *MA*, pp.183–184.

Social Philosophy & Policy 5:2 ISSN 0265–0525

THE RELATION BETWEEN SELF-INTEREST AND JUSTICE IN CONTRACTARIAN ETHICS*

CHRISTOPHER W. MORRIS

One of the most noteworthy features of David Gauthier's rational choice, contractarian theory of morality is its appeal to self-interested rationality. This appeal, however, will undoubtedly be the source of much controversy and criticism. For while self-interestedness is characteristic of much human behavior, it is not characteristic of all such behavior, much less of that which is most admirable. Yet contractarian ethics appears to assume that humans are entirely self-interested. It is not usually thought a virtue of a theory that its assumptions are literally false. What may be said on behalf of the contractarian?

I propose to discuss the rationales and functions of the assumption of self-interestedness in Gauthier's theory, only some of which are to be found in *Morals by Agreement*.[1] While initially I proposed to defend this assumption, finding its main rationale in the particular project that rational choice moralists assume, I now believe it to be indefensible. I therefore conclude that contractarian theorists, at least those working with a subjective account of value, cannot assume self-interestedness.

I. WHY FALSE ASSUMPTIONS IN CONTRACTARIAN ETHICS?

Humans often find themselves in situations where the outcome of individually rational actions is disadvantageous in relation to other outcomes. But the latter can only be attained through constraint imposed on the rational behavior of individuals. David Gauthier's theory of morals

* This essay makes extensive use of two unpublished papers: "Foundationalism and Contractarian Ethics", presented to the Canadian Philosophical Association in 1981; and "Justice and Self-Interest: the Function of False Assumptions in Contractarian Ethics," discussed in 1985 at the Université du Québec à Montréal and the UCLA Law & Philosophy Group. I am grateful to many individuals for comments on these papers. I am also very grateful to Peter Danielson and Jean Hampton for extensive comments on the first draft of this essay, as well to L.W. Sumner for useful discussions on these and other issues. For comments on the penultimate draft, I thank Jim Child, G.A. Cohen, Anthony Flew, Alon Harel, Alan Nelson, and the editors of this journal. My greatest debt is to David Gauthier for countless conversations on these and related issues over the last dozen or so years.

[1] David Gauthier, *Morals by Agreement* (Oxford: Oxford University Press, 1986). Hereafter *MA*.)

by agreement is an account of the constraints that rational individuals must accept to bring about the mutually advantageous outcomes not attainable by independent, rational action. These constraints Gauthier identifies with the requirements of justice. Thus, he says, "moral theory is essentially the theory of optimizing constraints on utility-maximization."[2]

The theory, "morals by agreement," is complex at first view. Gauthier begins with an account of rationality and of value. He then analyzes the problems that rational individuals face in interaction, problems typified by the well-known Prisoners' Dilemma (PD).[3] The core of Gauthier's moral theory consists in arguing that, under certain conditions, (1) rational agents faced with such problems will accept constraints on their individual actions, (2) they will rationally comply with these constraints, even in the absence of state or group enforcement, and (3) these constraints are those of morality, albeit an ideal, as opposed to a common-sense, morality. In addition, (4) Gauthier argues for two particular sets of constraints on interaction: (a) a principle that determines the division of the fruits of rational cooperation; and (b) a set of moral rights and duties that define the starting point or base line for cooperative interaction. The principle of (4)(a) is identified as one of distributive justice, while the rights and duties of (4)(b) are analogous to the fundamental rights and duties that many philosophers claim to be "natural."[4]

I think that (3) is the least important part of Gauthier's project. If his argument here does not succeed, so much the worse for morality, or so I believe.[5] The important parts, I would argue, are (1) and (2), and not so much the particular principles therein defended as the general approach

---

[2] *MA*, p.78. Gauthier's remark echoes that of John Rawls: "The theory of justice is a part, perhaps the most significant part, of the theory of rational choice." *A Theory of Justice* (Cambridge, MA: Harvard University Press, 1971), p.16. While Gauthier's theory concerns the internal constraints that rational individuals need to accept in order to bring about mutually beneficial outcomes, Thomas Hobbes's classic theory tries to make do with external constraints alone. James Buchanan's *Limits of Liberty* (Chicago: University of Chicago Press, 1975) tries to reach less drastic conclusions than Hobbes without requiring the internal constraints that Gauthier argues are necessary.

[3] A Prisoner's Dilemma is a type of situation where the outcome of individually rational choice is inefficient in the weak Pareto sense that another outcome would be better for each individual. Virtually any text in decision or game theory will discuss this dilemma.

[4] Gauthier exaggerates the "Lockean" nature of these rights. I have argued elsewhere that rights such as the ones he defends are best understood as "semi-natural," a notion I define along with that of a natural right. See my "Natural Rights and Public Goods," Thomas Attig, Donald Callen, & John Gray, eds., *The Restraint of Liberty, Bowling Green Studies in Applied Philosophy VII* (Bowling Green, OH: Bowling Green State University, 1985), pp.102–117.

[5] I also believe that (3), defended mainly in Chapter VIII of *MA*, should be distinguished more clearly from (1) and (2) than is actually done by Gauthier. The actual presentation of morals by agreement may lead many readers to confuse these very different stages of the argument.

and type of argument.[6] This said, and while I agree with Gauthier that the general project of deriving the constraints of justice from the choice of rational individuals is the correct methodology for fundamental moral theory, I shall argue that this rational choice cannot defensibly be construed as *self-interested*.

Morals by agreement is what I call, after Rawls's remark, a rational choice theory of ethics. Rational choice theory is the theory of rationality for individual and social choice, whether in contexts of independent or of interdependent choice. The conception of rationality invoked and developed is that of utility maximization, where an individual is rational insofar as she maximizes the satisfaction of her (coherent and considered) preferences. Rationality and justice are related thus. Rational individuals may often find themselves in situations where cooperative, nonmaximizing behavior is mutually beneficial, given their preferences. Yet in the absence of constraints on individually rational behavior, such cooperation may not be possible, for such individuals will act in maximizing ways that disadvantage others. Justice imposes the constraints necessary to make mutually beneficial cooperation possible, thereby stabilizing Pareto-efficient outcomes in situations analogous to n-person PDs.

Several cooperative outcomes may each be Pareto-efficient. Given that rational individuals will not be indifferent as to which is selected by the norms of justice, we may imagine the specific constraints of justice to be determined by a mutually advantageous agreement to select particular Pareto-efficient outcomes. Cooperation is advantageous to all, but there may be different cooperative arrangements, each distributing the benefits of cooperation differently. We may think of the agreement to select particular forms of cooperation as a type of bargain: each individual presses for the cooperative arrangement most beneficial to her, and all agree to some mutually acceptable cooperative arrangement. The theory of justice thus makes use of a particular part of the theory of rational choice, namely, bargaining theory.

The metaphor of the social contract serves – only, I would add – to express this particular conception of justice as an ideal convention, the terms of which may be thought of as the outcome of a rational bargain. The metaphor of the social contract is extremely misleading if it is taken, as

---

[6] I have been convinced of this in part by Peter Danielson. It is, of course, a theme of James Buchanan's writings, especially his essays on Rawls, that contractarians should not seek to establish particular principles for all times and places. See *The Limits of Liberty* and *Freedom in Constitutional Contract* (College Station, TX: Texas A & M Press, 1977). This is also a feature of Gilbert Harman's contractarianism. An accessible presentation of his views can be found in *The Nature of Morality* (New York: Oxford University Press, 1977). Indeterminateness may also be a feature of morals by agreement once the assumption of self-interest is dropped.

it often is, in any other way. Agreement here has only a heuristic value. As I understand contractarianism, justice and related parts of morality are conventions, and the purpose of hypothetical social "contract" is to determine the terms of the best (i.e., most rational) convention, at least for particular places and times. Accordingly, criticisms to the effect that hypothetical contract is no contract at all, or that nonmoral agreement does not bind, are misplaced.

How are we to conceive of these bargainers? First, they are rational, and Gauthier identifies rationality with the maximization of utility. Second, they are maximizers of subjective value, for Gauthier takes utility to be a measure of (coherent and considered) individual preference. This has the important consequence that values are relative to individuals and that "Each person's preferences determine her values quite independently of the values of others" (*MA*, p.25).[7]

For the purposes at hand, this may be thought to suffice as a characterization of rational bargainers. For such individuals, whatever their preferences, may find themselves in PD-like situations. All that is needed for such dilemmas is that the preferences of individuals have a certain structure, not that they be self-regarding. It is important to note that the introduction of a utility-maximization conception of rationality does not bring in self-interestedness. As Gauthier puts it, such a conception of rationality introduces a purely formal, not a material, selfishness (*MA*, p.73). Elsewhere he says that we may

> think of the egoist as maximizing whatever actor-relative value he pleases – perhaps his own happiness, perhaps not. He is then simply the person whose interests, whatever they may be, have no necessary link with the interests of his fellows, so that his values provide a measure of states of affairs quite independent of their values. This generic account affords a very weak characterization of an egoist, and indeed even an excessively weak one, since it admits to the egoistic ranks persons whose interests are other-directed, provided only that their other-directed interests are not simply dependent on others' interests. But that is all that our argument will require.[8]

Thus, Gauthier adds a third condition to the characterization of the

[7] It should be noted, as Gauthier does (*MA*, pp.51ff.), that morals by agreement doesn't require a subjectivist account of value, only a relativist (or individualist) one, and that some objectivist theories construe value as agent-relative. I shall come back to this point at the end of my essay when I conjecture that Gauthier can defensibly assume self-interestedness only by abandoning his subjectivism about value.

[8] David Gauthier, "The Incompleat Egoist," *The Tanner Lectures on Human Values*, Stanford University, May 10, 1983, p.73.

bargaining agents of morals by agreement, namely, self-interestedness. More precisely, he wishes to assume that their values are independent in another sense: utility functions are defined independently of one another (*MA*, p.86). The preferences of the rational bargainers do not include the preferences of others. Gauthier assumes that individuals do not take an interest in the interests of others,[9] or weaker yet, that they do not take an interest in the interests of those with whom they exchange. The latter condition is that of Wicksteed's "non-tuism," the former that of mutual unconcern.

The matter is actually more complicated than this, and Gauthier is insufficiently precise or careful. The first problem is that a variety of different motivational assumptions appear throughout the argument, the second that Gauthier is not always careful to distinguish these assumptions or to indicate which is being invoked at which stage of the argument. This is unfortunate given the importance of these motivational assumptions to the project.

I shall distinguish as carefully as I can between different motivational assumptions that appear in *MA*. Let us call an agent an *egoist* if his preferences are all self-regarding. Egoism thus conflates rationality and prudence. To be distinguished from egoism is *mutual unconcern* or *mutual disinterest*, which requires only that agents not take an interest in the preferences of others, to adapt Rawls's phrase.[10] Agents characterized by mutual unconcern need not be egoists, as they may take nonhumans to be the object of their concern. Next is *nontuism*, which only requires that agents not take an interest in the preferences of those with whom they exchange. Mutual unconcern and nontuism tend to be used interchangeably in *MA*.

In discussions of the theory of markets it is important to distinguish another motivational assumption, namely, that agents' utilities are functions only of "commodities." In certain markets (e.g., perfect competition), these are "private." I shall call this assumption that of *materialism* or *consumerism*, for want of a better label. We might make more determinate the character of "economic man" by characterizing his preferences as materialistic in this sense.[11] In any case, we should be careful to distinguish this assumption from the weaker condition of mutual unconcern.

Lastly, there is the general condition of asocial motivation or *asociality*

[9] The phrase, of course, is from Rawls, *A Theory of Justice*, p.13.
[10] *ibid.*
[11] This would accord with much of what Gauthier says about economic man in Chapters X–XI of *MA*, as well as in his earlier "The Social Contract as Ideology," *Philosophy & Public Affairs*, vol. 6 (1977), pp.130–164. It would not, however, be consistent with his characterization of "economic rationality" in "Economic Rationality and Moral Constraints", *Midwest Studies in Philosophy*, vol. 3 (1978), pp.75–96.

which Gauthier introduces late in *MA*. Borrowing an idea from Michael Laver,[12] Gauthier says that:

> we allow "only those assumptions about the motivations of individuals which can be precisely defined with reference to a single individual". Thus in accounting for the motivation of person *x*, we may refer only to those features of states of affairs that involve *x* and no one else (*MA*, p.311).

The condition of asociality, then, requires that descriptions of the preferences of individuals not make mention of other individuals. Other motivational conditions may be distinguished, but they are not necessary for my purposes.[13]

I have distinguished, then, several motivational assumptions: asociality, egoism, mutual unconcern, nontuism, and materialism. It is not always simple to determine which of these conditions is assumed at different stages of the argument of *MA*. Gauthier talks mainly of mutual unconcern and of nontuism, treating these more or less interchangeably. More importantly it is difficult to determine whether this condition (or these conditions) is (are) assumed throughout the argument. For while mutual unconcern is explicitly assumed in the discussions of the market and the base line for cooperation,[14] when discussing the "Archimedean point,"[15] Gauthier claims that the utilities of the ideal person "*may* be independent of the utilities of others; the Archimedean point is *compatible* with the supposition of mutual unconcern."[16] And in the discussion of bargaining, no explicit reference is made to mutual unconcern.

I shall simply presume that a condition like that of mutual unconcern is assumed throughout ("Throughout our argument, nontuism has served as an assumption . . ."; *MA*, p.329), although at least one knowledgeable reviewer has concluded otherwise.[17] Further, I shall only distinguish between particular motivational assumptions when necessary, and I shall refer indifferently to the conditions I distinguished, save that of

---

[12] Michael Laver, *The Politics of Private Desires* (Harmondsworth, Middlesex: Penguin, 1981), p.13.

[13] To be disguised from asociality is what I would call *asociability*. Someone is asociable if she takes no pleasure in the company of others. Someone takes an interest in another's interests or preferences only if the former cares about the latter's well-being or preferences. Sociability, by contrast, I think of as taking pleasure in another's company. (Gauthier uses the term more or less indifferently with the notion of taking an interest in others. See *MA*, pp.11, 19, 254). Someone may lack concern for others, yet be sociable. It may be that people are rarely asociable without also being self-regarding. Nonetheless, the concepts are not the same.

[14] For the latter see *MA*, pp.205, 220, 259.

[15] "In moral theory, the Archimedean point is that position one must occupy, if one's decisions are to possess the moral force needed to govern the moral realm" (*MA*, p.233).

[16] *MA*, p.235, emphasis added.

[17] Gregory Kavka, *Mind*, vol. XVCI (January 1987), pp.117–121.

materialism, with the term 'self-interestedness' (SI).[18]

Gauthier believes that "this conception, of persons as taking no interest in one another's interests, is fundamental not only to economics, but also to moral theory" (*MA*, p.100). Now self-interestedness is merely an assumption, albeit an important one. It is not meant literally to characterize humans, as Gauthier explicitly notes (*MA*, p.329). The question then arises as to the rationale of this assumption. Why assume that rational agents are entirely self-interested when in fact humans are not? It is this question that I wish to pursue.

II. SI AS SOMETIMES TRUE

Among "the circumstances of justice" is limited benevolence or a bias in favor of the self.[19] According to the contractarian tradition, a degree of self-interestedness is a feature of the human condition, one of those circumstances that jointly make cooperation beneficial and necessary. Perhaps the assumption of SI may be understood simply as an idealization of this bias in favor of the self. However, the "mutual unconcern presupposed by the market is an extreme form of self-bias" (*MA*, p.113), and we would want to know what allows us to idealize or, rather, to generalize this tendency.

The first possible justification for SI that comes to mind is simply that the assumption often is true. Most of our business interactions are with persons who take no interest in the interests of those with whom they interact. Indeed, often we do not even know the identity of the individuals with whom we interact, making it difficult to take an interest in their interests. Further, interaction between persons and groups in international contexts are also often disinterested. A moral theory that recognizes these features of our social life should be better placed than others to determine the constraints appropriate to justice.

That SI holds in some contexts is clearly a justification of the assumption, at least for those contexts. And no one can doubt that it would be desirable to have a conception of justice that would appeal to individuals who take no interest in one another's interests. The more we interact with

---

[18] My grouping of several different motivational assumptions under the umbrella term 'self-interest' does not, I believe, affect the argument of the essay. Nonetheless, the reader should be alert to potential problems here. (Ned McClennen has expressed worries to me on this point.)

[19] *MA*, pp.113–114. See David Hume, *A Treatise of Human Nature*, Book III, Part II, Sections II, and *An Enquiry Concerning the Principles of Morals*, Section III, Part I; H.L.A. Hart, *The Concept of Law* (Oxford: Clarendon Press, 1961), pp.189–195; Rawls, *A Theory of Justice*, pp.126–128.

such individuals, the more desirable such a conception becomes.

Some may object that the disinterestedness of such individuals is a form of false consciousness, that were they to pay attention to their actual interdependence and to the social nature of their nontuism, they would come to reject this standpoint. But this objection confuses genesis and motivation. "[W]e should begin by noting that in characterizing a being as asocial, we are concerned, not with her origins, but with her motivations and values" (*MA*, p.310).[20] Gauthier argues that no matter what our origins, insofar as we in fact are disinterested, SI may be justified as an assumption.

Important a consideration as this may be, it cannot be the whole story. SI is often true, but not always. It holds in some contexts, but clearly not in many others. Why favor some contexts over others? What is the justification for making it a general assumption, one which is to play such an important role in the determination of the norms of justice?

Morals by agreement, Gauthier notes, are the morals of economic man (*MA*, pp.315–316). Insofar as this is established, that such men have reason to have certain moral constraints govern their interactions, the edifice of morals by agreement is impressive. Perhaps SI is assumed only to allow the amoralism of economic men to be refuted?[21] But Gauthier wishes "to show that morals by agreement are more than the morals of economic man" (*MA*, p.329).[22] If morals by agreement are to be shown to be those of all, economic men and others, then it should be sufficient to drop SI. For this assumption *limits* the set of admissible preferences. Generality may be achieved by not imposing SI and thereby allowing people to have preferences that can, but need not, be self-interested. The resulting theory should then be able to appeal to economic men as well as to other individuals.

[20] But in fact the Sophists grasped, for the first time in human thought, the standpoint of a person who does stand outside social life, not in her capacities, not in being able to live without society, but in her motivations, in being able to view society as purely instrumental to goals that do not require social life for their formulation (*MA*, p.312). This line of argument will turn out to be problematic for Gauthier, for one of the main rationales for SI will turn on the matter of the *origins* of preferences. As I shall argue, preferences that have come about in certain ways may be ignored by rational choice reconstructions of justice in order to provide what I shall call a "fundamental evaluation" of morality.

[21] I owe this suggestion to Jean Hampton, who points out to me how much like Hobbes Gauthier would be in his desire to answer such an individual.

[22] "Morals by agreement have a non-tuistic rationale. . . . But it does not follow that [they] bind only non-tuists" (*MA*, pp.328, 329).

III. SI, MORALS, AND THE APPEAL TO REASON

The assumption of mutual unconcern is fundamental to moral theory, Gauthier claims, for he agrees "with Kant that moral constraints must apply in the absence of other-directed interests, that indeed they must apply whatever preferences individuals may happen to have" (*MA*, p.100).

> Hume believed the source of morality to lie in the sympathetic transmission of our feelings from one person to another. But Kant, rightly, insisted that morality cannot depend on such particular psychological phenomena, however benevolent and human their effect, and however universally they may be found (*MA*, p.103).

> Rejecting reason as the basis of morality, Hume saw no alternative but to find that basis in some feeling or effect (sic) that afforded a direct identification with others. Here we agree with Kant that morality makes demands on us that are and must be quite independent of any fellow-feelings we may have (*MA*, p.238).

> Morals by agreement have a non-tuistic rationale. Their constraints bind rationally, and independently of all particular preferences. . . . Throughout our argument, non-tuism has served as an assumption required to ensure that morality is not affectively dependent, so that it speaks directly to reason and not to particular, contingent emotions or feelings (*MA*, pp.328–329).

The references to Kant and to Kantian rejections of appeals to "contingent" feelings do not, however, constitute an *argument* for SI. Kant wished to avoid appealing to inclinations because, among other reasons, these are not universal (and necessary), and morality must, he believed, bind all persons.[23] There is, however, no Kantian argument for the necessity and universality of morality that is acceptable to Gauthier. For the latter, as for Hobbes, Hume, and all who accept the doctrine of the "circumstances of justice," morality is not necessary or universal in the ways in which Kant entertained. *Contra* Kant, our rationality is a necessary, not a sufficient, condition of moral obligation. Only if we find ourselves in the circumstances of justice are we rationally required to abide by the

---

[23] See *The Groundwork of the Metaphysics of Morals*, especially the Preface. Kantian conceptions of necessity and contingency are foreign to the enterprise of morals by agreement, as Gauthier notes:

> Rawls supposes that he follows Kant in treating the principles of justice in 'independence from the contingencies of nature'. In our view human individuality cannot be separated from these contingencies, and moral principles must not deny but reflect them (*MA*, p.237).

constraints of justice or, according to Gauthier, of morality *tout court*. In the world we live in, it is likely that morals by agreement will not accord moral standing to all rational humans.[24] It may turn out that there are reasons why non-Kantians will *want* moral judgments to be independent of sentiment, but these reasons are not expressed merely by noting agreement with Kant.

It should also be pointed out that Kantian concern over the "contingency" of particular preferences actually undermines the case for SI. For such an assumption requires that agents be motivated by a particular set of contingent preferences, namely, their self-regarding ones. It is not SI but its absence that would seem to be required by the desire that moral "constraints bind rationally, and independently of all particular preferences."[25]

IV. SI AS A SIMPLIFYING ASSUMPTION

Neoclassical economics assumes SI, albeit for explanatory purposes, and practitioners also have difficulties defending the assumption. One of the standard arguments is that SI is a "simplifying assumption," one which is made necessary by the complexity of the phenomena that economists wish to explain (or to describe). All theories, whether explanatory or normative, make simplifying assumptions. Without such assumptions, theories would be overwhelmed by the complexity of their objects, and, we may suppose, explanations would become (rich) descriptions. Further, simplification is a necessary part of isolating important from unimportant factors. So theoretical knowledge appears to require simplification. Similarly, we might argue that SI is a simplifying assumption required for the purposes of moral theorizing.

The particular interests that people actually take in one another's interests, it might be argued, are captured quite well by SI, for our actual concerns with others are partial. Gauthier seems to argue thus in favor of the assumption of nontuism.

> The assumption of mutual unconcern may be criticized because
> it is thought to be generally false, or because true or false, it is
> held to reflect an unduly nasty view of human nature, destructive
> not only of morality but of the ties that maintain any human

---

[24] I discuss issues having to do with moral standing in section XII. At least it should be clear that morals by agreement will not accord moral standing to, e.g., rational individuals who throw bombs into crowded restaurants and shops. For a further discussion of these issues, see my "Punishment and Moral Standing" (manuscript).

[25] I owe this point to L.W. Sumner.

society. But such criticism would misunderstand the role of the assumption. Of course persons exhibit concern for others, but their concern is usually and quite properly particular and partial. It is neither unrealistic or pessimistic to suppose that beyond the ties of blood and friendship, which are necessarily limited in their scope, human beings exhibit little positive fellow-feeling. Where personal relationships cease only a weak negative concern remains, manifesting itself perhaps in a general willingness to refrain from force and fraud if others do likewise, and in a particular willingness to offer assistance in extreme situations – for example, in the desire to aid victims of disasters, even at a greater cost than would have been needed to prevent the disaster. But this limited concern is fully compatible with the view that each person should look after herself in the ordinary affairs of life, with a helping hand to, and from, friends and kin (*MA*, pp.100–101).

I have quoted this paragraph completely because it is unclear what exactly is being defended. Gauthier does not appear to be denying that SI is false or nasty. I think that he can be read as arguing that given the partiality of mutual concern, we may simplify our assumptions and assume SI without adversely affecting our theory.

SI may be a simplifying assumption, and I accept the commonplace that such assumptions are necessary to theory. Yet this cannot be the justification of SI. For it might be argued that what SI simplifies – the complex and diverse interests that individuals take in one another's interests – is morally significant, and that it is surely no virtue of a moral theory to abstract away significant aspects of our moral lives in the interests of simplicity.

Further, the particular account of justice – its nature and its specific requirements – given by a rational choice theory of morality is likely to be very sensitive to changes in motivational assumptions. For instance, the outcome of the ideal rational bargain that defines the terms of justice will be very different if we allow parties to be mutually interested rather than exclusively self-interested. It will not suffice, then, to praise the virtues of simplicity. More must be said on behalf of SI.[26]

---

[26] It might be argued that SI is a simplification necessary for determinate conclusions. I have no doubt that this may be a *motivation* for assuming SI, especially in economics. However, it is not a rationale or justification for the assumption.

V. A PRAGMATIC DEFENSE OF SI

We may adapt to our ends another argument often made by economists. They, like other rational choice theorists, seek to explain or to predict human behavior and social phenomena by assuming that individuals are rational and self-interested. Milton Friedman, in a well-known essay, "The Methodology of Positive Economics,"[27] seeks to defend this assumption's "lack of realism." He argues that assumptions in a theory should be judged not by their veracity but by the truth of the propositions that may be derived by means of them. Noting that hypotheses simplify complex phenomena, Friedman argues that:

> the relevant question to ask about the "assumptions" of a theory is not whether they are descriptively "realistic", for they never are, but whether they are sufficiently good approximations for the purpose in hand. And this question can be answered only by seeing whether the theory works. . . . [28]

Friedman's argument has been very influential in economics. However dubious its merits for explanatory theory, we might adapt it to ethical theory and see whether it can provide a justification for assuming SI in the theory of justice. Friedman argues that true predictions are the only justification for a theory's assumptions. We might accordingly argue that we are warranted in assuming SI insofar as it enables us to derive true moral judgments from our moral theory.

Friedman's instrumentalist account of the assumptions of economics has been widely criticized by philosophers of science.[29] It is unlikely to do as a justification of the postulates of neoclassical economics. Independently of these difficulties, it is doubtful that the analogous argument will work for contractarian moral theory. For according to this account, the truth of moral judgments, especially those regarding justice, is not known independently of the plausibility of the moral theory. So we simply cannot test our theory by independently assessing the truth of its implications. Ordinary or intuitive moral judgments have no independent weight in Gauthier's enterprise.

We shall find no simple fit, or lack of fit, between our theory and

[27] Milton Friedman, *Essays in Positive Economics* (Chicago: University of Chicago Press, 1953), pp.3–43.
[28] ". . . which means whether it yields sufficiently accurate predictions." Friedman, *Essays*, p.15.
[29] One major problem is that Friedman's account conflates explanation with prediction. See Ernest Nagel, "Assumptions in Economic Theory", reprinted in *The Philosophy of Social Explanation*, A. Ryan, ed. (Oxford: Oxford University Press, 1973), pp.130–138; Alexander Rosenberg, *Microeconomic Laws* (London: University of Pittsburgh Press, 1976), pp.155–170.

the supposedly "plain duties" of conventional morality. . . . If the reader is tempted to object to some part of this view, on the ground that his moral intuitions are violated, then he should ask what weight such an objection can have, if morality is to fit within the domain of rational choice (*MA*, p.269).

The contractarian answer: they have no weight.[30] Contractarian moral theory stands or falls with the rational choice theory of which it is a part. We cannot defend the assumptions of the moral theory by an independent examination of its implications, for the veracity of these is contingent on that of the moral theory.

VI. SI AND MORAL SKEPTICISM

A more promising defense of SI might have to do with skepticism. We may conceive of contractarian moral theory as a reply to the moral skeptic who wonders, like Hobbes's Foole, "whether injustice, taking away the Feare of God . . . may not sometimes stand with that Reason, which dictateth to every man his own good."[31] The contractarian project thus understood attempts to refute the moral skeptic by way of a demonstration of the self-interested rationality of morals.

Need the moral skeptic be self-interested in the narrow sense of the term? Hobbes's Foole certainly is such a skeptic. But not all skeptical challenges to morality need be thus. For, as I have already claimed, the actual utility functions of most humans, genuine moral skeptics included, do not possess the independence that the assumption of nontuism requires. Indeed, the moral skeptics one actually meets often substitute the claims of party or tribe for the Foole's self-interest. Why, then, assume SI in the reply to the moral skeptic?

Perhaps we might understand the role of SI in contractarian ethics by analogy to that played by other assumptions in traditional philosophical replies to more general forms of skepticism. After all, the contractarian project was most popular in seventeenth- and eighteenth-century philosophy, a period especially concerned with skepticism.

---

[30] This may be too strong in several ways. First, intuitive moral judgments may have heuristic value for rational choice moral theory, pointing in the direction that contractarian theory might investigate. Also, insofar as moral conventions actually exist, for whatever reason, there may be good rational choice reasons for adopting (some of) these rather than seeking to establish new ones. The moral capital of past generations, however established, may be too valuable to do without. Lastly, insofar as morals by agreement is *explanatory*, positive fit between theory and ordinary moral judgments is confirmatory.

[31] Thomas Hobbes, *Leviathan*, ed. C.B. Macpherson (Harmondsworth, Middlesex: Penguin, 1968), Chapter 15, p.203.

Philosophers have often conceived of knowledge as an ordered, hierarchical system. Impressed with geometrical models, they have often thought of knowledge as a sort of building in which undubitable axioms, the data of the senses, or some other suitable entity, provide a firm foundation for the stories above, and in which chains of deductive reasoning provide the scaffolding and structure. Just as with actual houses, the moral of the analogy is to instruct us to pay attention to the foundations of knowledge, to avoid building or reconstructing the house of science on sand or mud. Such accounts of knowledge are "foundational," and we may compare and contrast them with alternative accounts which stress the coherence of our beliefs with one another.

Foundational models of knowledge have often been used as a means of refuting skepticism. Knowledge is foundational; the foundations are F; F is known with certainty; what the skeptic questions is derivable from F; therefore, the skeptic's doubts are unwarranted. The moral skeptic questions justice (and other moral notions). A strategy for answering the skeptic's doubts might be to show that the principles of justice are derivable from rational self-interest. By analogy to many modern theories about knowledge of the external world, such a strategy might accord an epistemically privileged status to the assumption of rational self-interest. Thus, we might have a type of moral foundationalism, which I have elsewhere[32] called *reductive moral foundationalism* and have characterized as follows:

(1) there exists a set of *basic* (non-moral) *facts* and a corresponding set of *basic* (non-moral) *judgments* or *propositions*,
(2) these basic judgments or propositions are self-warranting or self-justifying,
(3) all *moral* justification consists (ultimately) of logical deductions from the basic (non-moral) judgments or propositions.

The contractarian moralist, it may be thought, seeks to "ground" ethics in rational self-interest, much as other epistemologists once sought to "ground" knowledge on a bedrock of necessary truths or data of the senses. The contractarian thus takes the rational self-regarding preferences of nonmoral agents to be the *foundations* of morality.

While some may wish to defend SI thus, it is no more promising a strategy in ethics than in epistemology generally. There, certain criticisms of foundational models of knowledge are now commonplace. What are alleged as firm foundations are in fact shaky or lack the certainty of self-

---

[32] In "Foundationalism in Ethics", *Ethics: Foundations, Problems, and Applications*, E. Morscher & R. Stranziger, eds. (Vienna: Hölder-Pichler-Temsky, 1981), pp.134–136, and "Foundationalism and Contractarian Ethics."

warranting character they are supposed to possess. The foundations are not context- and theory-neutral, and so do not provide as claimed an independent basis for comparing and evaluating competing theories. In general, the contemporary dogma that all judgments or propositions are open to revision renders highly suspect the foundationalist's notions of epistemological primitives and a fixed, theory-independent order of epistemological priority.

VII. SI AS A "WEAK" ASSUMPTION

It might be argued that SI derives its rationale from its virtue as a weak assumption. If it can be shown, by appealing only to their self-regarding preferences, that it is rational for individuals to accept a morality, then it should be possible to show this given their full set of preferences, assuming that the former are a subset of the latter. If a given conclusion is derivable from weaker premises, that is a rationale for assuming these.

The paradigm for such an argument from weakness is proof in formal disciplines. If a theorem can be derived from weaker axioms, then that is a rationale for assuming the latter rather than the stronger set. Note, however, that this argument works only for proofs of the same theorem. If the theorem-analogue in morals by agreement is the conclusion "a morality is rational for agents in certain circumstances," then the weaker the premises, the better. But if the theorem-analogue is a specific principle of justice, then the conclusion of the argument may very well be altered by opting for the "weaker" premises. Thus, my point in section IV about the sensitivity of the conclusion of a rational choice theory of justice to changes in motivational assumptions.

Weakness may mean something else in this context. While the project of establishing knowledge on self-warranting and certain premises fails, the general strategy of arguing from weak, that is, widely accepted assumptions remains sound. We may agree with Rawls that "justification is argument addressed to those who disagree with us, or to ourselves when we are of two minds. . . . Being designed to reconcile by reason, justification proceeds from what all parties to the discussion hold in common."[33] Without claiming any special epistemic status for our premises, it is advisable to make them as weak and noncontroversial as possible.

A reason, then, for assuming SI is the desire to assume as little as possible at the outset, enabling one to appeal to as wide an audience as possible. Rawls defends SI in this way, and we may borrow his argument.

[33] Rawls, *A Theory of Justice*, p.580. See also his "Justice as Fairness: Political not Metaphysical", *Philosophy & Public Affairs*, vol. 14 (Summer 1985), pp.223–251.

Noting that individuals may find that they wish to advance the ends of others once the veil of ignorance is lifted, Rawls says:

> the postulate of mutual disinterest [SI] in the original position is made to insure that the principles of justice do not depend upon strong assumptions. Recall that the original position is meant to incorporate widely shared and yet weak conditions. A conception of justice should not presuppose, then, extensive ties of natural sentiment. At the basis of the theory, one tries to assume as little as possible.[34]

SI may be assumed simply because of its weakness as a theoretical assumption.

SI, however, is not merely a "weak" assumption. It is a nonmoral assumption, as are the other basic premises of moral contractarianism. Why base a conception of justice on nonmoral, albeit weak, assumptions? As I noted, an argument for a particular conclusion is made stronger by assuming as little as possible in the premises. An argument for justice, then, is stronger the less it assumes; in particular, an argument with nonmoral premises would be stronger than another with moral premises, other things being equal. However, by assuming a nonmoral base line for an account of the emergence of morality, one does more than merely strengthen the argument. By making only nonmoral assumptions, one avoids begging the important question "why morality?"

Deriving a morality from a set of moral premises may simply transfer the important questions about the conclusions to the premises. We may wish to know not only whether this or that act is right; we may wish to know why we should be just, why we should allow our interests to be overruled by moral constraints, or why the institution or morality is worth preserving. After all, we reject many traditional moralities, as well as many religious institutions. Why should morality not be shed as simply one of the many repressive forms of life inherited from primitive ancestors? What distinguishes morality from abandoned superstitions?[35] These questions and concerns can only be addressed and answered by an account of the whole of the institution of morality.

A theory that can generate a rationally acceptable morality from a set of nonmoral premises may more easily provide such an account since it does not assume any moral notions or principles. By assuming a nonmoral

---

[34] Rawls, *A Theory of Justice*, p.129.

[35] . . . we do not suppose that actual moral feelings represent the outcome of a prior valuing of participation and an awareness that voluntary participation requires the acceptance of moral constraints. Rather our argument is that, if we are to consider our moral affections to be more than dysfunctional feelings of which we should be well rid, we must be able to show how they would arise from such a valuing and awareness (*MA*, p.339).

starting point for the derivation of morality, contractarianism avoids problems of circularity or begging the question. Unless it turns out that the contractarian derivation is not possible, and unless there are disadvantages hitherto unknown, assuming a nonmoral base line is a clear theoretical advantage of contractarian theories. Such a derivation of a morality may provide an account of the relation between morals and reason, where others have failed.

As an argument for deriving moral constraints from nonmoral premises, this argument is good. However, as an argument for SI, it is not impressive. For SI is more than a weak, nonmoral assumption. It requires that morality be derived from the choices of disinterested individuals. If our concern is merely to ensure that morality is an institution worth preserving, then there is no need to assume nontuism, as long as no moral assumptions are introduced when the independence condition on utility functions is relaxed.

While the self-interested amoralist does resemble his sibling, the radical skeptic about knowledge, I argue against interpreting morals by agreement as a species of foundationalism. The matter of the "weakness" of the assumption of SI may suggest another rationale. It might be argued that the self-interested amoralist is the "worst-case" for morality and that addressing this individual's concerns will securely ground morality for all.[36] But is it the worst case for morality? A glance at the contemporary scene suggests alternatively that the worst-case, if there is just one, is that of a world of individuals who take an interest in the interests of others, albeit a particular kind of interest – for instance, envy, spite, hatred, intolerance. It is this world that threatens morality, and human welfare, more seriously than that of the self-interested amoralist.

VIII. SI, KINSHIP SYSTEMS, AND THE MARKET

The argument of classical and, especially, of neoclassical economists that the activities of rational individuals in markets that satisfy certain conditions – those of "perfect competition" – create extraordinary wealth or, more technically, have Pareto-efficient equilibria is one that rightfully impresses Gauthier.[37] Although the wealth produced by permitting the free

[36] I owe this suggestion to L.W. Sumner.

[37] Gauthier does not mention the significant result that the Pareto-efficient equilibria of perfectly competitive markets are in "the core" – that is, there are no other outcomes where some subset (or "coalition") of individuals could improve each member's position independently of that of nonmembers. The standard source is Kenneth Arrow & Frank Hahn, *General Competitive Analysis* (San Francisco: Holden-Day, 1971). For an accessible presentation of the two fundamental theorems of welfare economics, see Allan Feldman, *Welfare Economics and Social Choice Theory* (Dordrecht: Kluwer-Nijhoff, 1980), Chapters 3–4. These results may have interesting implications for determining the membership of the "cooperative ventures for mutual advantage" that constitute contractarian societies.

production of goods and the free provision of services is not a negligible benefit of markets, it is not the only one emphasized by Gauthier. Equally important is the liberation that the market makes possible.

> One of the problems facing most human societies is the absence of any form of effective and mutually beneficial interaction among persons not linked by some particular bond. Thus the fundamental importance of kinship systems. . . . The fundamental distinction between 'us' and 'them', between blood-brothers and strangers, has limited the scope of co-operation (and contributed to the subjection of women) among much of humankind. We invoke the assumption of mutual unconcern to determine if that limitation is an inescapable evil of the human condition.
>
> The superiority of market society over its predecessors and rivals is manifest in its capacity to overcome this limitation and direct mutual unconcern to mutual benefit. If human interaction is structured by the condition of perfect competition, then no bond is required among those engaged in it, save those bonds that they freely create as each pursues his own gain. The impersonality of market society, which has been the object of wide criticism, and at the root of charges of *anomie* and alienation in modern life, is indeed the basis of the fundamental liberation it affords. Men and women are freed from the need to establish more particular bonds, whether these be affective or coercive, in order to interact beneficially. The division between siblings and strangers disappears. . . (*MA*, pp.101–102).[38]

It is true that "liberation brings attendant dangers" (*MA*, p.102), ones which Gauthier, unlike other enthusiasts of competitive markets, does not neglect.[39] I wish, however, to reflect on the manner in which the assumption of SI might be defended by drawing attention to the enriching and liberating possibilities offered by market interaction.

It is actually one of the conditions of the welfare theorems of neoclassical economics that agents exhibit no concern for the interests of those with whom

[38] It should be noted that:
Against the market background of mutual unconcern, particular human relationships of trust and affection may flourish on a voluntary basis. Those who hanker after the close-knit relationships of other and earlier forms of human society are in effect seeking to flee from the freedom to choose the persons in whose interests they will take an interest (*MA* p.102).

[39] I put many economists of Chicago and UCLA persuasions, as well as some heads of government in the US, Britain, and France, in the camp of those who unduly neglect the dangers to which Gauthier refers. Amongst his colleagues, James Buchanan's work is notable for the emphasis he puts on the nonmarket conditions of markets.

they interact.[40] The Pareto-efficiency of the outcome of production and trade cannot be demonstrated in the absence of the assumption of non-tuism. This can be quickly shown thus. The proof of the Pareto-efficiency of perfectly competitive equilibria requires the absence of external economies.[41] But interdependence relations among utility functions are a type of external economy of consumption.[42] Thus, nontuism is required for the standard proof of the Pareto-efficiency of perfect competition.

Is the fact that the assumption of nontuism is necessary for the demonstration of the Pareto-efficiency of perfectly competitive markets, coupled with the liberating features of nontuistic market interaction, an argument for SI in morals by agreement? No. Rather, it is an argument against critics of the assumption, namely, those that claim that nontuistic social interaction is not possible or even desirable. As such, SI is a condition in a possibility proof.[43] But such an argument shows only that SI is not incompatible with outcomes having certain desirable properties. It does not show that it is a necessary feature for outcomes with these desirable properties.[44]

IX. SI AND FUNDAMENTAL EVALUATION

One reason to be careful about the assumptions of a theory of justice is the danger of begging the question by including moral notions amongst the basic premises. An account of justice which presupposes judgments of fairness or justice may simply transfer doubts about its conclusions to its premises, as I argued in section VII. I shall call this the "circularity problem."

[40] This, it should be noted, is Wicksteed's nontuism, which is weaker than other versions of SI. Given that agents, for the purposes of economic theory, can be households or other collectivities, it is this weaker assumption which is required. (Of course, it may not be possible to interpret the behavior of, e.g., households, as maximizing a single function, even those the members of which take an interest in each other's interests.)

[41] For the assumptions of the standard welfare arguments, see, in addition to the texts mentioned in note 37, D.M. Winch, *Analytical Welfare Economics* (Harmondsworth, Middlesex: Penguin Education, 1971), pp.34–35, 89. See also the discussion (pp.117ff.) relaxing the conditions of perfect competition and introducing externalities.

[42] "An 'externality' occurs if you care about my choice or my choice affects you." Thomas Schelling, "Hocky Helmets, Daylight Saving, and Other Binary Choices", in *Micromotives and Macrobehavior* (New York: W.W. Norton, 1978), p.213.

[43] The analogy to the possibility, or rather, existence proofs of general equilibrium theory I owe to Alan Nelson, who notes "the similarity between proving the existence of economic equilibrium and deriving a state from individual moral principles." See his "Explanation and Justification in Political Philosophy", *Ethics*, vol. 97 (October 1986), pp.170ff.

[44] This is fortunate since we would want to claim that individuals can and (often) should have (or develop) interests in one another's interests. Further, it is theoretically possible to achieve Pareto-efficient outcomes in noncompetitive, socialist economies under certain conditions. See Winch, *Welfare Economics*, p.94.

An argument for SI might be that this assumption is necessary in order to avoid another, but similar, mistake, that of "double-counting." Consider the following tale:

> Once upon a time two boys found a cake. One of them said, "Splendid! I will eat the cake." The other one said, "No, that is not fair! We found the cake together, and we should share and share alike, half for you and half for me." The first boy said, "No, I should have the whole cake!" Along came an adult who said, "Gentlemen, you shouldn't fight about this: you should *compromise*. Give him three quarters of the cake."[45]

If the adult's suggestion is intended as a basic account of just or fair division, then the problem is twofold: one, notions of fairness are included in the premises of the account (the circularity problem), and two, the first boy's interests are counted twice (double-counting).

It might be argued that SI is required in order to prevent "double-counting." For if some individuals are other-regarding, then the interests or preferences of some will count for more than those of others.[46] It is important to distinguish the problem of double-counting from that of circularity. For the two are not the same. The circularity problem is a reason for attempting to construct an account of justice from nonmoral elements. However, it is not clear how double-counting can be found objectionable, at least without appealling to fairness. Suppose that SI is not assumed and some people's interests count for more than others in contractarian justice. Why is this objectionable? The interests of the latter, after all, *are* the object of the coherent and considered preferences of others. Why should they not be counted twice or as often as they appear in the utility functions of others? We disapprove of "double-counting" in democratic elections, but only because we endorse a principle of fairness or justice requiring "one person, one vote." What objection could be made at the level of basic theory, prior to the introduction of moral principles?

I suspect that the worry about double-counting, when clearly distinguished from that about circularity, has to do with a concern for what I shall call fundamental evaluation. I shall consider, then, this concern as a possible defense of SI.

The notion of a fundamental evaluation I shall explain by reference to that of a fundamental explanation.[46] A *fundamental explanation* of a domain is an explanation of that domain in terms of something entirely outside of

[45] Raymond Smullyan, *This Book Needs No Title* (Englewood Cliffs, NJ: Prentice-Hall, 1980), p.56. Cited by Jon Elster, "The Market and the Forum", Elster & A. Hylland, eds., *Foundations of Social Choice* (Cambridge: Cambridge University Press, 1986), p.115.

[46] On several occasions in conversation, David Gauthier has given the worry about double-counting as a reason for SI.

it. For instance, an explanation of the color of the objects in terms of the noncolored microscopic elements of the objects, or that of macroeconomic phenomena entirely in terms of the preferences and choices of individual agents, are examples of fundamental explanations.

A *fundamental evaluation* (or *justification*) of a domain is an evaluation (or justification) of that domain by reference to values or standards entirely outside of the domain. For instance, a natural rights justification of a minimal state would be fundamental provided that the principles appealed to are in fact independent of that minimal state.[48] Fundamental evaluations or justifications need not be *moral*; indeed, the latter may be thought of as a species of the former.

Fundamental explanations and evaluations do not commit one to foundationalism of the sort discussed in section VI. For explanations and evaluations are fundamental only relative to some particular set of entities. No claims need be made with regard to the basic nature of the latter. Indeed, it may even be possible to have several compatible fundamental explanations or evaluations of a domain. Further, no claims need be made about the self-warranting nature of that by virtue of which the domain is explained or evaluated.[49]

Given contemporary controversies, it should not be surprising that we would want to have fundamental evaluations of our political institutions and social systems, of what Rawls calls the "basic structure of society."[50] Radical social critics raise questions about societies that cannot be answered by reference to values or principles that are themselves part of the social order at issue. For these critics raise questions about these norms or principles as well. Marxist critics of capitalism, for instance, will not be satisfied with a defense of market societies appealing to "bourgeois" conceptions of justice, for they grant the justice of capitalism thus understood. The Marxist critic raises questions that might be thought to be external to such standards of justice. Or the anarchist critic of the modern state will not be satisfied with a defense of the state in terms of people's

[47] See Robert Nozick, *Anarchy, State, and Utopia* (New York: Basic Books, 1974) pp.6–9; Laver, *Private Desires*, pp.13ff.; and Nelson, "Explanation," pp.157ff. See also Jean Hampton, "The Social Contract Explanation of the State" (manuscript, UCLA, 1985), as well as her *Hobbes and the Social Contract Tradition* (Cambridge: Cambridge University Press, 1986), Chapter 9.

[48] Marxist critics, among others, would surely be skeptical as to the requisite independence. We might think of fundamental evaluations or justifications with false principles or norms as "principle-defective" potential evaluations after Nozick's analogous notion of explanation. Insofar as Marxists attempt justifications of states, these may be nonfundamental as they would appeal to principles internal to that which is being evaluated, e.g., capitalism by references to bourgeois principles of justice.

[49] The suspicion may remain that without foundationalism, fundamental evaluations lose much of their interest.

[50] Rawls, *A Theory of Justice*, p.7.

needs and wants when these have been acquired by living in statist societies. The anarchist grants that the state makes itself necessary; what he or she does not grant is that this suffices to justify the state. To answer Marxist or anarchist critics requires some standard independent of the social system at issue.

We might also seek fundamental evaluations of our moralities. Very often the same radical critics of society claim that the moral values and principles of the society are corrupt as well. Or someone may raise the possibility that a particular morality, or even morality *tout court*, is exploitative. The doubts raised quite differently by Thrasymachus, Rousseau, and Nietzsche are familiar to us all.[51] We might wonder whether morality, like religion, can be an instrument of exploitation, one that we might be well rid of. Only fundamental evaluations can answer such doubts.

The fact that we want a fundamental evaluation of some domain does not, of course, entail that one is available. That remains to be determined. What I wish now to suggest is that we might use a single standpoint from which to make our fundamental evaluation of the basic structure of society and of our moral practices and principles. That standpoint is that of the rational choice of individuals who take no interest in the interests of others.

The appropriate basis for evaluation depends on the nature of value and hence on certain controversial questions of value theory. Let us follow Gauthier in understanding value to be determined by preference.[52] To be rational, then, is to maximize utility, which is to be understood as a measure of preference. Evaluation, then, takes considered preference as its standpoint; it is to be understood in terms of "rational choice." To show, then, that a social practice or system is justifiable is to show that it is mutually acceptable. A rational choice account of evaluation thus leads to a conception of society as "a cooperative venture for mutual advantage,"[53] given people's preferences.

What preferences should be used to determine rational choice? Some social theorists appeal only to people's *actual* preferences and argue that other appeals are not appropriate.[54] However, people's actual preferences may be inconsistent, or they may be uninformed, unconsidered, and inexperienced (*MA*, pp.29ff). So we may require that rational choice be made on the basis of coherent and considered preference.

People's *actual* coherent and considered preferences? That depends. For

---

[51] As perhaps are also the doubts of many contemporary economists when they suggest, as they so often do, that behind lofty appeals to moral virtue lies mere subjective utility maximization.

[52] See *MA*, Chapter II.

[53] Rawls, *A Theory of Justice*, p.4.

[54] Economists often argue that appeals to any other standard, including that of considered preference, would be "paternalistic" (in the economists', and not the philosophers' sense) and thus inappropriate.

instance, we often take the selection of a head of state as justified if it satisfies the accepted social choice rules that aggregate people's actual preferences, however ill-formed the latter may be. But then such a choice would not be a fundamental evaluation of the candidate or institution, for its standards are not independent of the domain of evaluation. For a rational choice evaluation of a social practice or system to be fundamental, the preferences are to be more than coherent and considered. They must also be independent of the practice or system. In the absence of such independence, all that can be shown by rational choice is that the preferences are, broadly speaking, consistent with the practice or system. But this, radical social critics may claim, may be due to socialization or habit.[55]

Let me illustrate this with some examples. Suppose that we wish to justify some institution. We might try to show that the institution serves the needs and wants of the people in question and that it does not violate the basic constraints imposed, for instance, by the legal system and by the basic moral rights of the people. For some purposes such a justification may be sufficient. But suppose that the institution in question is basic in the lives of the people and that it shapes much of their social interaction, as well as their preferences. Then someone might object to our justification by noting that it appeals to features of the individual's social life that are themselves products of the institution in question. Or consider another case, that of the debate between statists and anarchists. Defenders of the modern state cannot say to the anarchist that the state is justified because we have become the sort of person that cannot live without states. A fundamental rationale for heroin cannot be that one needs it, after one has started taking it. Similarly, a fundamental justification of the state cannot be that state junkies cannot get by without it.[56] We cannot attempt to justify the state by reference to values or principles that are themselves products of life in statist society.

We must, then, impose some constraints on the *content* of people's preferences. All preferences that are the products of the particular practices and systems that we wish to evaluate (fundamentally) are to be assumed away. Since we are interested in evaluating the "basic structure" of society, as well as its moralities, we must strip people of all of the relevant preferences.[57] Thus, the state of nature in traditional social contract theory.

[55] Recall the old debate on "consumer sovereignty." The fact that consumers freely buy the products they are offered did not impress critics who claimed that producers created much of that demand. The latter were implicitly calling for a fundamental evaluation. (On these matters, proponents of Say's Law may not find much interest in fundamental explanations.)

[56] A point made essentially by Michael Taylor in *Anarchy, Community, and Liberty* (Cambridge: Cambridge University Press, 1982).

[57] I do not claim originality in requiring that our protagonists be stripped of their social attributes. I am following Rousseau here in his criticism of Hobbes' account of human beings

Are the requirements for a fundamental evaluation a rationale for SI? No. The constraints on the content of preferences required for fundamental evaluation do not introduce SI. It is certainly not the case that all, or even most, concern for others is determined by social practices and systems, including moralities. Indeed, it would appear to be the case that the dominant form of other-regarding interest, the concern humans have for their offspring and kin, is independent of political system. All that the quest for fundamental evaluation requires so far is that we eliminate all preferences induced or formed by the institutions we wish to evaluate, namely, morality and the basic structure of society. No additional worry about the possible objects of preferences is warranted by the argument thus far.[58] The rationale for SI remains to be found.

X. SI, FUNDAMENTAL EVALUATION, AND EXPLOITATION

Not only might we wish for a fundamental evaluation of our moral sentiments, we might want a similar account of tuistic feelings generally. Perhaps it is here that we will find the rationale for SI. Gauthier argues thus:

> The contractarian need not claim that actual persons take no interest in their fellows; indeed, we suppose that some degree of sociability is characteristic of human beings. But the contractarian sees sociability as enriching human life; for him, it becomes a source of exploitation if it induces persons to acquiesce in institutions and practices that but for their fellow-feelings would be costly to them. Feminist thought has surely made this, perhaps the core form of human exploitation, clear to us (*MA*, p.11).

Relations between family, friends, and lovers may often hide relations of domination. Fundamental evaluations are called for here as well.[59] SI may

in the state of nature. Rousseau's alleged "noble savage" should not be understood as some ideal man to be contrasted with our fallen, modern selves. Rather, the human being in the early stages of Rousseau's hypothetical state of nature is merely the product of stripping ordinary individuals of all of their social attributes. Since Rousseau believed, *contra* Hobbes, that essential human attributes are largely a product of socialization, stripping individuals of their social attributes turns them into the naked scarecrows that we find in the *Second Discourse*.

[58] We may thus eliminate preferences that have been formed in certain ways that threaten a fundamental evaluation. It may not be completely true, then, "that in characterizing a being as asocial, we are concerned, not with her origins, but with her motivations and values" (*MA*, p.310).

[59] Suppose that humans are genetically predisposed, for instance, to have concerns for their relative standing. See Robert Frank, *Finding the Right Pond* (New York: Oxford University Press, 1985), Chapter 2. We might then want a fundamental evaluation of our actual utility functions. See also Frank, "If Homo Economicus could choose his own Utility Function, would he want one with a Conscience?", *American Economic Review* (forthcoming).

be introduced by our interest in determining a standpoint from which we can evaluate (fundamentally) our other-regarding interests, both moral and nonmoral.[60] An evaluation of tuistic sentiments, moral or nonmoral, must be from a standpoint independent of these if it is to be fundamental.

A rational choice evaluation which presupposes SI, then, should enable us to evaluate fundamentally the basic structure of society, our moral practices, and our tuistic sentiments. Why evaluate all of these, especially our moral and nonmoral interest in others, from the same standpoint? We could construct a fundamental evaluation of our moral sentiments from a standpoint which abstracted away only these, leaving in place our nonmoral interests in others. However, that fundamental evaluation would not answer some questions or allay some worries we have about morality, namely, that it presupposes an antecedent concern for others and that people with such a concern may be taken advantage of by moral practices. We may wish to ensure that we be not worsened or disadvantaged by our tuistic concerns (MA, p.329). And this we may only be able to do by presupposing SI.[61]

It should not be supposed that contractarians are thereby committed to understanding human beings or human nature as fundamentally nontuistic, asociable, or asocial. The standpoint constructed here is hypothetical and counterfactual. The priority it has over that of our normal tuistic – that is, altruistic and envious – selves is for purposes of fundamental evaluation (or explanation) alone. We appeal to such a standpoint because it is one that is independent of those practices and states of society that we wish to evaluate (fundamentally).

Further, the construction of such a standpoint in no way commits us to any claims about the genesis of human sociability or tuism. We need not claim, for instance, that humans "start off" as asocial and "become" tuistic, either individually or as a species. The assumption of SI and asociability is made only for the purposes of evaluation and does not commit us to any claims about what is most fundamental to human nature.

There may be something to this argument. (See the appendix.) However, it is not available to Gauthier or to any contractarian who invokes a subjective account of value. Note that while fundamental evaluation need not be construed as foundationalist in the sense explicated earlier, such

---

[60] "The assurance that interaction is subject to the constraints of justice [which are determined by self-regarding rational choice] meets the concern emphasized in feminist thought, that sociability not be a basis for exploitation" (MA, p.351).

[61] Recall the distinctions I drew earlier in note 13 between asociability and egoism, as well as Laver's notion of asociality. For an even more fundamental evaluation of our practices and sentiments, then, we may impose the further condition of asociability. A more radical position yet may be achieved by assuming asocial motivation or asociality. From this position we may evaluate (fundamentally) our moral and non-moral tuistic sentiments, as well as our characteristic sociability.

evaluation does presuppose a certain relation of priority between the premises and conclusion of the evaluation. Specifically, anyone for whom a fundamental evaluation succeeds must assume that the premises have an evaluative priority over the conclusion (a relation which is asymmetric). But it is not possible to hold this if one also subscribes to a subjective account of value of the sort to be found in *MA*. For such an account of value denies any such (asymmetric) relations of priority amongst the preferences of an individual. No claim can be made that the self-regarding preferences of a person have an evaluative priority over her other-regarding ones. They are, after all, her considered and coherent preferences. Without appealing to prudence or to an objectivist account of value, no priority relation can be sustained. Ironically, Gauthier's subjective account of value blocks this possible defense of SI.

XI. THE VIRTUE OF JUSTICE

Suppose that we have an evaluative standpoint, that of self-interested rational choice, from which to make fundamental evaluations of our social practices and systems, including our tuistic sentiments. The values and principles that we are able to derive from this standpoint we may call *fundamental values* and *principles*. We might defend SI by arguing that these fundamental values have certain properties and functions that are sufficiently similar to the properties and functions of ordinary notions of justice that we may identify the two. Thus, we conclude, these fundamental values *are* those of (ideal) justice.

Justice is the virtue we normally appeal to when evaluating distributions of benefits, social institutions, political practices, and the like. Further, it is one of the main values used for the evaluation of social systems and entire societies and civilizations. As Rawls notes, "Justice is the first virtue of social institutions." It is a value that applies first of all to the "basic structure of society, or more exactly, the way in which the major social institutions distribute fundamental rights and duties and determine the division of advantages from social cooperation."[62] Justice is the moral standard that enables us to judge a society as a whole or as a system. To do so requires evaluating the basic structure of the society from afar, as it were. The standpoint of fundamental evaluation can provide one with such a perspective.

This, however, will not get us SI, for the fundamental evaluation of society need not abstract away, as I have already argued, our other-regarding preferences.

[62] Rawls, *A Theory of Justice*, pp.3, 7.

Let us reflect on other traditional features of the virtue of justice. Where benevolence or charity attach themselves to the good or well-being others, justice is that "cautious, jealous virtue"[63] that speaks of rights and duties, not of welfare, and that binds independently of the interest we may take in others. These features of justice, its independence of benevolence and the priority it accords to rights and duties, is what makes utilitarian and related moralists antithetical to the virtue. Justice, it is often said, is what is *due* or *owed* to someone, where these notions are independent of appeals to the individual's welfare.[64]

It might be argued that these features of traditional notions of justice may enable us to identify (ideal) justice with choice from the standpoint of fundamental evaluation. Justice would then be a fundamental value. Be that as it may, such an argument provides no rationale for SI. Suppose that benevolence is thought of as a *moral* virtue. Then SI would be too strong. Given that not all other-regarding preferences are moral, SI would abstract away more than our benevolent sentiments. Suppose instead that benevolence is not thought of thus, as a moral virtue. In this case, the separation of justice from benevolence (in this broader sense) would be question-begging. SI remains without rationale.

XII. OBJECTIONS TO SI

Consider what I shall call *pure charity*, namely, giving which is not reciprocal. That is, such charity is not motivated by any expectation of the donor that the gesture be reciprocated, even in the long term. I shall not claim that such charity is a common feature of human societies, only that the concept is coherent and the practice possible. A fundamental evaluation of pure charity that assumed SI would, however, find it irrational or

[63] Hume, *Enquiry Concerning the Principles of Morals*, Section III, Part I.

[64] It is perhaps this feature of justice that makes many social theorists long for a society "beyond justice" or claim that the virtue is inappropriate for realms, e.g., the family, where people do take interests in others. The first position is often attributed to Karl Marx. Hegel finds the

  ethical aspect of marriage [to consist] in the parties' consciousness of this unity as their substantive aim, and so in their love, trust, and common sharing of their entire existence as individuals . . .

  [Thus] marriage, so far as its essential basis is concerned, is not a contractual relation. On the contrary, though marriage begins in contract, it is precisely a contract to transcend the standpoint of contract, the standpoint from which persons are regarded in their individuality as self-subsistent unity.

The Philosophy of Right, trans. T.M. Knox (Oxford: Oxford University Press, 1967), paragraph 163. Aristotle is well-known for his view that "when men are friends they have no need of justice", *Nicomachean Ethics*, trans. W.D. Ross, Book VIII, 1155a.

unacceptable.[65] That seems absurd. At the very least, such fundamental evaluations would have no force to one actually motivated by charitable sentiments of this sort.

If one reflects on what I would think to be the most common other-regarding preferences, namely, kin-altruism, the radical and dubious nature of SI becomes even clearer. The regard that humans characteristically have for, e.g., their offspring, is rather deep. Given the extraordinary sacrifices that people make for their children, without expectation of care in their old age, it would not be surprising were such concern to fail the test of fundamental evaluation if SI is assumed. However, given how deep are such sentiments, it is hard to see how such an evaluation would have any force in the absence of an independent standard of prudence.

The way in which SI is actually foreign to the conception of rational agents that is central to morals by agreement may be brought out by a more elaborate case, to which I shall turn. Consider the case of Adolf, Bécassine, and Charles. Adolf, although rational, exploits Bécassine. He does this because he is able to do so and it is to his advantage. Adolf and Bécassine do not find themselves in the circumstances of justice, perhaps due to the former's superior strength.[66] While Charles does not find himself in the circumstances of justice with regard to Bécassine, he does with regard to Adolf.

According to morals by agreement, poor Bécassine stands outside of the protection of morality, or at least of justice. She finds herself in a Hobbesian state of nature, where she and others are at liberty to do as they please with one another. Adolf and Charles, however, are in a different situation. They are morally bound to one another insofar as rational cooperation is mutually advantageous.

While Adolf is a purely self-interested fellow, Charles is not. Indeed, the latter is most upset by the former's treatment of Bécassine. Charles does not consider Bécassine's virtual slavery to be *unjust*, for it is neither just nor

---

[65] I owe basis for this objection to SI to G.A. Cohen and L.W. Sumner. In a different context, that of the prebargaining situation, Gauthier claims that:

> it would be irrational for an individual to dispose herself voluntarily to make unproductive transfers to others. An unproductive transfer brings no new goods into being and involves no exchange of existing goods. . . . Thus it involves a utility cost for which no benefit is received, and a utility gain for which no service is provided (*MA*, p.197).

[66] This case is explicitly considered by Hume:

> Were there a species of creatures intermingled with men, which, though rational, were possessed of such inferior strength, both of body and mind, that they were incapable of all resistance, and could never, upon the highest provocation, make us feel the effects of their resentment; the necessary consequence, I think, is that we should not, properly speaking, lie under any restraint of justice with regard to them, nor could they possess any right or property. . . .

Enquiry Concerning the Principles of Morals, Section I, Part I.

unjust according to morals by agreement. It is, rather, that he simply takes an interest in her interests. He would like to liberate Bécassine from her plight, by force if necessary. However, morals by agreement will not permit him to do so. For Charles is morally obliged to respect Adolf's life, liberty, and possessions, as well as to accord him the distribution of the social surplus afforded him by the principle of minimax relative concession.[67]

Suppose Charles were to consider himself in a Hobbesian state of nature with regard to Adolf and thus be able to liberate Bécassine? This would be irrational, according to Gauthier's account of morals by agreement, for he is not in such a state of nature *given his nontuistic preferences*. Indeed, it would actually be unjust for Charles to come to Bécassine's aid!

This situation may seem contrived unless one substitutes for our characters some of the parties in the contemporary debate over South Africa, or even that over nineteenth-century American slavery. If the rights and duties of justice are determined by nontuistic and asocial rational choice, then it may be morally wrong for, e.g., North Americans to assist in certain ways the liberation of black South Africans. If we wish to avoid such implications, our options would seem only to be to forgo SI, to abandon the subjective account of value, or to reject the whole rational choice, contractarian enterprise.

It is true that part of the counterintuitive implication of morals by agreement in cases such as these stems from the manner in which the account accords individuals moral standing. To have *moral standing* is to be owed (some) moral consideration. Someone to whom one has a moral duty has moral standing. In order for two or more individuals to possess moral standing with regard to one another, two conditions must be satisfied. First, the individuals must find themselves in the circumstances of justice, and second, they must be capable of constraining their behavior toward one another in accordance with whatever constraints justice imposes on their interactions. These conditions are individually necessary and jointly sufficient for possession of moral standing.

According to Gauthier, the preferences that determine whether one finds oneself in the circumstances of justice with regard to another are nontuistic (and even asocial). But this is bound to come into conflict with the interests that we actually do take in one another's interests. Our tuism, Gauthier notes, is characteristically particular and partial (*MA*, pp.100–101). We care especially for kin, friends, cooperators, and victims of disasters. On Gauthier's account of morals by agreement, obligations of justice are generated by relations of self-interested mutual advantage

---

[67] This principle governs the distribution of the benefits of cooperation and requires that these be distributed so that the greatest relative concession required of any individual be as small as possible. See *MA*, Chapter 5.

between individuals. Actual individuals, with the tuistic concerns noted above, may very well find themselves forbidden by justice from acting in defense of others for whom they care. (If you will, suppose that Bécassine is Charles' handicapped daughter.) It should be clear that morals by agreement will have little hold on such individuals.[68]

Note that the objection here is not the standard sort of criticism made of morals by agreement, that it violates one of our intuitive moral judgments or "moral intuitions." I do not deny that this is the case; it is morally unintuitive that morals by agreement has these implications. But that is not the objection. (Nor is it an objection, given the rational choice methodology.) Rather it is that rational tuistic individuals, with utility functions like ours, will not be moved by justice in cases such as these. The problem is not (merely) one of compliance; it is not that we would refuse to comply with norms that we would otherwise endorse. It is that we would find the norms themselves unacceptable in such situations.

XIII. RATIONALITY, PRUDENCE, AND RATIONAL CHOICE ETHICS

I have considered a variety of rationales for the assumption of SI in Gauthier's development of morals by agreement, and I have found them all wanting. The irony of my conclusion will not be lost on David Gauthier, for I have sought for years to persuade him that his theory needed SI. I shall conclude by considering the implications of the argument of this essay for rational choice ethics.

I have argued that the subjective account of value that is part of Gauthier's version of morals by agreement ultimately denies him a rationale for SI. For such an account of value accords no priority to self-regarding preferences, much less to prudence. One possibility, then, would be to retain the framework of morals by agreement but to abandon SI. This is the approach I currently favor. It is, of course, possible that dropping SI would deny the theory the determinate conclusions that Gauthier wishes to derive.[69] For instance, it is not clear that agents with complicated other-

---

[68] In discussion David Gauthier suggested that a troublesome variant of this case is where Charles's tuistic preferences are such that in the hypothetical bargaining situation, he would insist that Becassine be given moral standing.

Wayne Sumner has argued that the range of beings accorded moral standing by contractarian theory is determined in part by the range of the concerns of the agents. I failed to understand his point at the time, but it now seems correct to me. See Sumner, "Subjectivity and Moral Standing," Morris, "Value Subjectivism, Individualism, and Moral Standing: Reply to Sumner," and Sumner, "A Response to Morris," Wayne Sumner, Donald Callen, & Thomas Attig, eds., *Values and Moral Standing, Bowling Green Studies in Applied Philosophy VIII* (Bowling Green, OH: Bowling Green State University, 1987), pp.1–15, 16–21, 22–23.

[69] James Buchanan and Gilbert Harman, perhaps for different reasons, will both urge that determinate conclusions were never to be expected from this enterprise.

regarding preferences would bargain from a unique base line or initial position in the manner argued in *MA*. More significantly, it is not clear that such agents, depending on the nature of their other-regarding preferences, would regard bargaining as the most appropriate manner in which to resolve disagreement about the division of the social surplus. I do not know.[70]

Another possibility would be to retain SI but to drop the subjective account of value. As Gauthier notes (*MA*, pp.51ff.), it should not be supposed that objectivist accounts of value must construe reasons as "agent-neutral." And it is the agent-relativity of value that pushes in the direction of contractarianism, or so I would argue.[71] It could then be argued that *prudence* is the appropriate value for fundamental evaluations of morality. Given that the assumption of a subjective account of value seems to play no significant role in the argument of *MA*, aside from entailing an agent-relative conception of reasons, it is possible that this option will be attractive to some defenders of contractarian ethics.

A last possibility would be to abandon the whole enterprise of a rational choice, contractarian account of morality or of justice. This option is too heretical to be considered.

XIV. APPENDIX

The contractarian moralist, Gauthier believes,

> sees sociability as enriching human life; for him, it becomes a source of exploitation if it induces persons to acquiesce in institutions and practices that but for their fellow-feelings would be costly to them. Feminist thought has surely made this, perhaps the core form of human exploitation, clear to us. Thus the contractarian insists that a society could not command the willing allegiance of a rational person if, without appealing to her feelings

[70] In the event that we drop SI, we are faced with Gregory Kavka's case of the Inequality Glutton, an individual whose preferences are, in varying ways, for more than others. See the review mentioned in note 17. Kavka's purpose is to show how counterintuitive Gauthier's principle of minimax relative concession will be given certain preference profiles, a standard by which Gauthier does not intend morals by agreement to be judged. I suspect that others will not find it beneficial to allow such Gluttons to join in their cooperative ventures for mutual advantage. People with certain sorts of concerns for relative standing may not be attractive partners for cooperative endeavors until they forgo those concerns.

[71] Philippa Foot suggests that we "ask awkward questions about who is supposed to *have* the end which morality is supposed to be in aid of. . . . Perhaps no such shared end appears in the foundations of ethics, where we may rather find individual ends and rational compromises between those who have them." "Utilitarianism and the Virtues," *Mind*, vol. XCIV (April 1985), p.209.

for others, it afforded her no expectation of net benefit. (*MA*, p.11).

In this appendix I shall illustrate the suggestion considered in section X that self-interested rational choice might be thought to make such exploitation apparent. Taking a cue from the feminist criticisms to which Gauthier refers, I shall analyze a case which raises issues of exploitation between the sexes. These, it might be argued, cannot be adequately addressed without appealing to a standard of evaluation that is independent in a certain manner of the preferences of the individuals in question.

Consider the case of Annabel and Bertie who have been living together for several years and who one evening face a collective choice problem. Annabel is a sociable person; she enjoys the company of others. She especially enjoys Bertie's company, though as the story unfolds the reader may come to doubt Annabel's capacity for critical judgment. Bertie, by contrast, is indifferent to the company of others; he does not care one way or the other about being with others. We may think that Annabel would be better off without Bertie. The economist quickly denies this; were she worse off with Bertie, she would leave him. Without invoking revealed preference theory, the economist tells us that Annabel enjoys the company of others, where Bertie does not. Given these preferences, she is not "worse off" with Bertie than she would be without him. I disagree. Without supposing that Bertie coerces Annabel into staying with him, or that she suffers from weakness of the will or some other conflict between intention and volition, I shall argue that she gets a bad deal from the relation, even though she does not *want* to leave Bertie.

The decision problem that confronts our couple is the following. The two wish to go out. Bertie most wants to go to the ballet, Annabel to a boxing match. While Annable is not especially concerned that Bertie enjoy himself – I have not yet made her other-regarding in her preferences – it is important to her that they go together. Going to the match alone is a bore – better to go to *Swan Lake* with Bertie for the *n*th time. Bertie, however, cares much more about going to the ballet than about Annabel's company. Simplifying the range of possibilities, we shall suppose that their preferences are as follows:

TABLE 1

Annabel	*Bertie*
1. boxing, boxing	1. ballet, ballet
2. ballet, ballet	2. boxing, ballet
3. boxing, ballet	3. boxing, boxing
4. ballet, boxing	4. ballet, boxing

where 'boxing, ballet' should read 'Annabel goes to the boxing match, Bertie goes to the ballet'. These ordinal preferences map onto a 2×2 matrix as follows:

MATRIX 1

		Bertie	
		ballet	boxing
Annabel	ballet	2,1	4,4
	boxing	3,2	1,3

where $1 > 2 > 3 > 4$ ('>' reading 'is preferred to').

What should our friends do? Consider their reasoning, starting with Bertie. Annabel either goes to the boxing event or to the ballet. If the first, he is better off going to the ballet $(2 > 3)$; if the second, he is still better off going to the ballet $(1 > 4)$. Whatever Annabel does, Bertie is better off going to the ballet; going to the ballet *dominates* going to the boxing match. Consider Annabel's situation. Should Bertie go to the ballet, she is better off accompanying him $(2 > 3)$; but should he go to the boxing match, she should also go $(1 > 4)$. Whatever she decides, Bertie will go to the ballet. Thus, she should decide to go to the ballet.

During the performance Annabel has time to reflect on her situation. Given their preferences, she always gets her second choice while Bertie always secures his first.[72] Something is amiss. Given Bertie's asociability she would be better off were she also asociable (in terms of the preferences she would then have). Her sociability disadvantages her in her relations with asociable people.

Further, it can be argued that Annabel is worse off still should she, in addition to being sociable, take an interest in Bertie's interests. To be sociable is to enjoy the company of others. Most people who are sociable also take an interest in the interests of (at least) those whose company they enjoy. But I have treated sociability as being distinct from taking an interest in others. Now let us suppose that Annabel takes an interest in Bertie's interests, while the latter remains indifferent to her interests. To take an interest in the interests of others is to include (some of) their preferences as values of one's utility function.

[72] Interpersonal comparisons need not be made here.

Annabel takes an interest in Bertie's interests. Her utility function ranges over his preferences as well as her interests. Her function has the following form: $U_A = f(P_a{'} P_b)$, where P_a and P_b are Annabel and Bertie's respective benefits.[73] Let us assign cardinal and interpersonally comparable utilities to Annabel and Bertie's first preferences as follows:

MATRIX 2

Bertie

		ballet	boxing
	ballet	8,10	2,1
Annabel			
	boxing	5,9	10,3

Including Annabel's other-regarding preferences, we assign new cardinal values:

MATRIX 3

Bertie

		ballet	boxing
	ballet	10,10	1,1
Annabel			
	boxing	7,9	7,3

Annabel's decision problem is now even simpler. Bertie's first choice is now her first choice. The cardinal utility of (ballet, ballet) for her now is $f(P_a, P_b) = 8 + 2 = 10$.

Annabel is sociable. She takes pleasure in the company of others (Table 1 and Matrices 1–2). Further, she takes an interest in the interests

[73] More precisely, Annabel maximizes a weighted sum of P_a and P_b:
$$U_a = w_a P + y_a P_b$$
where $-1 < w_a < 1$ and $-1 < y_a < 1$.
When $y_a = 0$ (and $w_a \neq 0$), Annabel is a pure egoist. When $w_a = 0$ (and $y_a \neq 0$), Annabel is a pure altruist. (When $y_a < 0$, Annabel's "altruism" is negative, i.e., she suffers from envy.)

of others (Matrix 3). Given her sociability, she and Bertie go to the ballet, and she is left with her second choice. Given her interest in his interests, this turns out to be her best alternative. We are now in a position to understand the sense in which Annabel would be better off without Bertie, although it would not be rational for her to leave him given her sociability and other-regarding interests.

In terms of their self-regarding preferences, Annabel's relationship with Bertie is costly. Her sociability saddles her with her second choice in Matrices 1 and 2, and her other-regarding interests make her most "prefer" this in Matrix 3. Without Bertie, Annabel would be better off, *in terms of her self-regarding preferences*. In terms of her *actual* preferences, Annabel is "doing what she wants." The problem lies in large part with her preferences. In relations with asociable and self-regarding individuals, Annabel does less well than she would do were she also asociable and non-tuistic.

A fundamental evaluation of Annabel's relationship with Bertie cannot just examine Matrix 3 and assess her situation by reference to her sociable and other-regarding nature. To do that would be to miss the way in which Annabel is disadvantaged by her sociability and tuistic sentiments, at least in her interactions with asociable and self-regarding individuals. A fundamental evaluation of her relationship must assess how well off she is, given her sociability and tuistic preferences, compared to how well off she would be were she asociable and self-regarding. In this case she would say that she would be better off were she not involved with Bertie. Thus her relationship with him fails the test.

Philosophy, Bowling Green State University

Social Philosophy & Policy 5:2 ISSN 0265–0525

RATIONALITY AND AFFECTIVITY:
THE METAPHYSICS OF THE MORAL SELF*

LAURENCE THOMAS

INTRODUCTION

There is a way of doing moral philosophy which goes something like this: If it can be shown that it is rational for perfectly selfish people to accept the constraints of morality, then it will follow, *a fortiori*, that it is rational for people capable of affective bonds, and thus less selfish, to do so. On this way of proceeding the real argument – that is, the argument for the actual constraints (theory or principles) to be adopted – proceeds with only fully rational individuals who have no other concern than to maximize their nontuistic (selfish) preferences. Then it is noted that the affective capacities of human beings actually make quite palatable the constraints that the fully rational persons with wholly nontuistic preferences have agreed upon.

David Gauthier's latest work, *Morals by Agreement,*[1] exemplifies this approach. In this very important and seminal work, Gauthier explicitly claims that morality cannot be founded upon any affective bonds, writing:

> But Kant, rightly, insisted that morality cannot depend upon such particular psychological phenomena [that is, affective capacities], however benevolent and humane their effect, and however universally they may be found (*MA*, p.103).

Yet, towards the end of the book, we find the following passage:

* In writing this essay, my greatest debt is to Annette Baier for her recent essay "Trust and Anti-Trust," *Ethics*, vol. 96 (1986), which crystallized my thinking about a number of issues. I am also indebted to: David Copp, who persuaded me of a more charitable reading of Gauthier, let me see his forthcoming "Contractarianism and Moral Skepticism," and commented extensively on the penultimate draft of this essay; Bernard Boxill, who forced me to rethink what was involved in choosing to be a moral person; Geoffrey Sayre McCord, who was ever so patient, instructive, and encouraging through numerous versions of the paper that I shared with him; and Alfred MacKay, for many instructive comments on the very first draft of this paper. For years, Terrence McConnell has been a tremendous source of philosophical common sense; so he was with this paper.

[1] David Gauthier, *Morals by Agreement* (Oxford: Oxford University Press, 1986). Further references to this work are indicated parenthetically in the text by *MA* followed by a page number.

Persons rationally recognize the constraints of morality as conditions of mutually beneficial co-operation. They then come to value participation in co-operative and shared activities that meet these constraints, and to take an interest in their fellow participants. And finally they come to value the morality that first appeared to them only as a rational constraint (*MA*, p.338).

On Gauthier's argument, it is important that the claims of this latter passage be true, and it is because of the affective capacities of human beings that they are true. If it is important that they be true, how can it be irrelevant whether the affective capacities are deeply constitutive of the human self? More precisely the question is this: How can it be irrelevant to moral theory construction whether or not the affective capacities are deeply constitutive of the human self if, at the same time, it is of the utmost importance to show that these very same capacities enhance the possibility that human beings will abide by the constraints agreed upon by wholly rational and selfish beings?

According to Gauthier, it is important to show that "morality binds independently of the nature and content of our affections" (*MA*, p.103). But is it true that how we morally ought to behave, assuming that is what he means here, is independent of the nature of our affections? Can it be that we morally ought to comfort one another from time to time if we are altogether lacking in the capacity for empathy and sympathy? Can we even know how? Can it be that we morally ought to take notice that our actions do not harm others if we have only nontuistic preferences? How can we even be moved by the thought that our actions might cause harm to others if we are capable of being moved only by the satisfaction of our own preferences? More generally, we may ask: If a nonegoistic conception of morality requires a nonnegligible measure of altruism, what reason would people with only nontuistic preferences to maximize have to abide by such a conception of morality in the absence of some coercive-like structure?

Kant identified our true nature with a conception of the self called the noumenal self, which is purely rational and devoid of emotions, sentiments, and the desires which are expressive of these things. Further, he held that reasons can motivate independently of desires. Given these starting points, to show that morality is a requirement of rationality is to show that it is expressive of what it is to conceive of ourselves as rational beings; accordingly, assenting to the requirements of morality is no more coercive than assenting to the truths of mathematics.[2] More to the point, the thesis that morality is binding independently of the content of our affective

---

[2] Cf. Immanuel Kant, *Groundwork of the Metaphysic of Morals*, trans. H.J. Paton (New York: Harper and Row, 1964).

capacities is a logical consequence of Kant's metaphysics of the moral self. But Gauthier, far from severing the connection between motivation and desire, wholeheartedly embraces the view that the two are inextricably connected, writing:

> Hume reminds us, 'Reason is, and ought only to be the slave of the passions', and while Hume's dictum has been widely disputed, we shall defend it. Desire, not thought, and volition, not cognition, are the springs of good and evil (*MA*, p.21).

I can now state with some precision the difficulty that I have with the arguments of *Morals by Agreement* and the approach to moral theory of which it is representative.

The Kantian ideal that morality is expressive of our true nature, and so the way in which we are motivated to behave, is indeed a noble one. Kant had the metaphysics of the moral self which enabled him to say that this holds independently of the content of our desires. However, Gauthier subscribes to a desire-based conception of motivation. And no one who subscribes to such a conception of motivation and who also has it as his aim to offer a moral theory which is true to this Kantian ideal can rightly hold that morality should be binding independently of the content of our desires. For given a desire-based conception of motivation, a person could have no reason, in the absence of some coercive-like structure, to abide by a moral theory which was not congruent with her desires. It is thus unacceptable to proceed as if the real argument can take place quite independently of the nature of our affective capacities, and then to note that one has argued well because, as it turns out, given their affective capacities, persons are (or could come to be) motivated to abide by the theory. If one rejects a Kantian metaphysics of the moral self in favor of a desire-based conception of motivation while holding to the Kantian ideal of congruence between the requirements of morality and the motivation to follow them, then the nature of our affective sentiments has to have a central place in one's moral theory.

I have suggested that otherwise the result is a moral theory the compliance with which is reasonable only in the face of some coercive structure. I shall use *Morals by Agreement* to illustrate this point. Given my aim, Gauthier's work is especially suitable. For rather than attempting to forge the link between rationality, nontuistic preferences, and morality at the level of each individual choice of action, he attempts to do so at the level of the choice of dispositions. In a word, his thesis is that it is rational for persons to have a morally virtuous disposition because in this way they can best maximize their nontuistic (selfish) preferences. As Gauthier's own previous work shows,[3] when the attempt is made to forge the link between morality, rationality, and nontuistic preferences at the level of each individual choice of action, there will be many instances when it will be eminently rational to act contrary to morality. Accordingly, in the absence of some coercive structure, a rational person will be disposed to act contrary to morality.

The move to dispositions would seem to circumvent this difficulty very nicely: for there can be no doubt that in terms of maximizing one's nontuistic preferences it can be rational to have a certain disposition, though it is false that as a result of having that disposition one thereby maximizes one nontuistic preferences with every behavioral manifestation of that disposition. For example, since consuming food is generally a necessary condition for staying alive, the disposition to eat is a rational one, though obviously not all behavior which is a manifestation of that disposition is rational. A person can eat too much or the wrong sorts of foods, either of which can be inimical to his health. So, with one stroke, Gauthier would seem to have resolved one of the deep problems in the history of moral philosophy. For if, to begin with, the disposition which it is rational to have is a moral one, then on some occasions, at any rate, the fact that a rational person does not act contrary to morality though he could thereby maximize his nontuistic preferences can be explained without reference to some coercive structure. But as I hope to show, this is not so in Gauthier's case.

In the section which immediately follows, I develop the notion of what I shall call coercive rationality. In the next section, I argue that Gauthier, and others who argue for morality in a similar vein, fail to take persons seriously. This is not a sloppy statement of the now fashionable charge which has been made against utilitarianism, namely, that it fails to take seriously the separateness of persons. I shall develop a different point, which can be put roughly as follows. If there is a set of moral principles which people capable of affective capacities have reason to accept, the explanation for this cannot be that persons with nontuistic preferences would find such principles rationally acceptable.[4] Finally, I argue, in

---

[3] See David Gauthier, "Morality and Advantage," *Philosophical Review*, vol. 76 (1967), where he criticizes the central argument of Kurt Baier's *The Moral Point of View* (Ithaca, NY: Cornell University Press, 1958), who attempts to make the argument at the level of each individual choice.

[4] The argument which I shall develop echoes themes found in Alasdair MacIntyre, *After Virtue* (Notre Dame, IN: University of Notre Dame, 1981); see chapters 3–5, especially 3. The argument of this essay is somewhat anticipated by Adrian M.S. Piper in her "Instrumentalism, Objectivity, and Moral Justification," *American Philosophical Quarterly*, vol. 23 (1985). She makes a sweeping argument to the effect that no instrumentalist moral theory, which she takes Gauthier's to be, can yield an objective justification of morality.

Section III, that on Gauthier's view morality turns out to be coercively rational.

Throughout this essay, I shall, as Gauthier does not, use the terms 'desire' and 'preference' interchangeably. Further, I shall assume what is no doubt questionable, namely, that it makes sense to say that a person can have a genuinely moral disposition – that is, the set of dispositions which make up a moral one – though it is not for moral reasons that he came either to have or, in any case, to maintain that disposition.

I. COERCIVE RATIONALITY

Suppose that the lives of a person's children are made contingent upon his performing some base deed such as violating the trust of a close friend. Or suppose that a captain must abandon his ship's precious cargo if both he and the ship are to survive a fierce storm.[5] In either case, there can be little doubt that the person involved will perform the act in question; indeed, it will be eminently rational to do so, though it is manifestly clear that in neither case would the agent so act but for the predicament in which he has found himself. The first person desires that his children should live; the second desires that he should live (and that his ship should not sink).

Understandably, these are very deep desires which are rather unlikely to vary depending on the circumstances in which a person finds himself. In order to secure the satisfaction of his respective desire, each has to perform an action that is incompatible with another deep, but understandably, and no doubt justifiably, less deep desire of his. Given this ordering of desires, each acts rationally. But the rationality is coercive precisely because the person is forced to forgo satisfying a very important desire in order that a deeper one may not go unsatisfied. It is one thing to forgo movie entertainment so that one's children may live; it is quite another to have to violate the trust of a dear friend. Again, to have a few precious personal items lost to a bad storm at sea is in no way on a par with having the effort which defines one's livelihood and with which one deeply identifies, namely, being able to transport cargo safely, be lost to the seas on account of a storm.

[5] The account of coercive rationality offered here owes its inspiration to Aristotle (*Nicomachean Ethics* 1110a; *Eudemian Ethics* 1225a). My thinking about this matter owes much to T.H. Irwin, "Reason and Responsibility in Aristotle," Amelie Rorty, ed., *Essays on Aristotle's Ethics* (Berkeley: University of California Press, 1980), esp. pp.133–137. I have also profited from Robert Nozick, "Coercion," Peter Laslett, et al., eds., *Philosophy, Politics, and Society*, 4th series (Oxford: Basil Blackwell, 1972), and Harry G. Frankfurt, "Freedom of the Will and the Concept of a Person," *Journal of Philosophy*, vol. 68 (1971).

A self is comprised of a number of very deep desires, which admit of an ordering. We have an instance of coercive rationality (a) whenever it is rational for a person to sacrifice the satisfaction of a deep desire in order that a deeper desire does not have to go unsatisfied or (b) whenever it is rational for a person to do something that he otherwise would not desire to do, and so would not do, but for his endeavor to satisfy a deep desire of his. Regarding (b), the idea is that the person attaches no positive worth whatsoever to the activity apart from its being a means to the satisfaction of the deep desire in question, and thus deeply prefers not to engage in it. The agent is not indifferent to engaging in it; he strongly prefers not to do so. The hope, of course, is that one never has to sacrifice the satisfaction of one of these desires for the sake of another. However, sometimes the rational thing to do is just that. We have in such cases what I have called coercive rationality. Coercive rationality is to be contrasted with intrinsic rationality. We have an instance of the latter whenever it is the case that one is able to satisfy a desire that is deeply constitutive of oneself, and in order to do so one does not have to sacrifice the satisfaction of another desire that is deeply constitutive of oneself.

Being moral in one's behavior can be a matter of coercive rationality. This is so whenever it is the case that (i) one acts morally and there is a desire which is deeply constitutive of oneself the satisfaction of which is incompatible with one's acting morally, and (ii) the desire as a result of which one acts morally is less deeply constitutive of oneself than is the desire whose satisfaction is incompatible with one's acting morally. A case in point would be a person who abhors the demands of morality and wishes he could act contrary to them, but who nonetheless always does what is morally right in order to avoid the deep pangs of guilt which he cannot help but feel whenever he does what is wrong.[6] Indeed, it can be coercively rational for a person to be moral even if he has a moral disposition, if under the circumstances having a moral disposition is the only thing that it is rational for the person to do, and the desire which gives rise to that disposition is less deeply constitutive of the person than some other desire whose satisfaction is incompatible with his acting morally.

Finally, but very importantly, I should point out that the account of coercive rationality offered here is compatible with a person satisfying his primary deep desire to a far greater extent than he would have had he not forgone the satisfaction of a subordinate deep desire. Suppose that Smith, who finds racism morally abhorrent, most deeply desires to become a

---

[6] Cf. Sigmund Freud, *Civilization and Its Discontents*, trans. James Strachey (New York: W.W. Norton and Company, 1961). The idea that a person need not always act in accordance with his deepest desire is powerfully developed by Frankfurt in "Freedom of the Will and the Concept of a Person."

successful and morally decent politician. However, without the backing of a certain club, which embraces racist views ever so warmly, she has no chance of succeeding in politics. Assuming that Smith will not herself succumb to the racist views of the club's members and that she will in fact make a good faith effort to advance the cause of equality, then it is rationally coercive for Smith to join the club. And this is no less so because, as a result of doing so, she goes far beyond her wildest dreams in her political ambitions.

If we start with the assumption that nontuistic desires or preferences are most deeply constitutive of the self, meaning that none other are more deeply constitutive of the self, and then proceed to argue that it is rational to have a morally virtuous disposition because and only because we are thereby best able to maximize nontuistic preferences, then acquiring a morally virtuous disposition will be the rational thing to do, but only coercively and not intrinsically so. As I hope to show, such is the case with Gauthier's argument. But first, I wish to comment upon the general strategy of Gauthier-like contractarian arguments.

II. REASONS FOR ACTING

Contractarian arguments for morality generally proceed under the following assumption: if a set of altruistic moral principles can be shown to be rationally acceptable to mutually disinterested persons, then, *a fortiori*, the principles will be rationally acceptable to persons capable of affective capacities, or as I shall often say, altruistically-capable persons. Supposing that this is right, would the reason, *cum* motivational explanation, why altruistically-capable persons would find a set of altruistic moral principles rationally acceptable be that such principles were agreed upon by entirely nontuistic persons? And if not, is there not something wrong with arguing in this way?

Consider an example. Two wealthy individuals, Smith and Jones, move into a very posh community. A week after they have moved in, they learn that this quite well-off community very much prides itself in its yearly project which helps the poor of another community, and that any member of the community who does not participate is looked upon with great disdain by its other members and is ostracized. Upon learning of the project, Smith is delighted to participate, thinking that it is a good thing for a well-off community to have such a project. Jones, being quite stingy, despises the idea, but since he very much wants to be on good terms with the members of the community, because of the enormous benefits which that brings, he begrudgingly participates. Smith, obviously, is aware of the drawbacks which would stem from not participating in the community project, and is not indifferent to receiving the benefits of the community. However, these matters do not figure into the explanation of why he is motivated to participate in the project. Finally, imagine that in terms of location, status, and so on, there is no other community in which either Smith or Jones would rather live.

Given all of these considerations, is it the case that the reason, *cum* motivational explanation, why Smith participates in the project is the same as the reason, *cum* motivational explanation, why Jones does so? Of course, the answer would be affirmative if Smith were like Jones. But she is not. Imagine someone speaking as follows to Smith: "We know that in spite of his selfish spirit it is rational for Jones to participate because if he did not he would forgo the benefits of the community. And since you, too, would forgo these benefits if you did not participate, it is also rational for you to do so. Moreover, we assume that, as with Jones, your desire not to forgo these benefits is the reason why you participate; thus as an explanation of your behavior in this regard, we consider as irrelevant the fact that you sincerely believe that the community project is a wonderful idea." What I take this example to show conclusively is this: From the premises that (1) it would be rational for S to do A for reason R, and (2) the circumstances which make R a reason to do A obtain, it does not follow that (3) S does A for reason R.[7]

An example involving coercion lends support to this point. Suppose Jones says to Smith that he will divulge some dark information about Smith unless she contributes to the community project, not realizing that Smith is absolutely delighted to contribute and was going to do so anyway.[8] Seeing that Jones would not believe this, Smith says nothing. Despite how things appear to Jones, he does not coerce Smith. What is more, Smith does not contribute in order to prevent Jones from divulging that information, although it would be rational for Smith to comply with Jones's command in order to prevent that information from becoming public. So, we have here another case where (1) and (2) are true, but (3) is false.

It may, in the abstract, be tempting to think that (3) follows from (1) and (2), but as these examples make clear, it does not. And the first example involving Smith and Jones (the one about the community project) shows that although a reason R for doing A may obtain for two individuals, it does not thereby follow that both will do A for reason R.

---

[7] Thus, contra Bernard Williams, there is a clear sense in which a person can be said to have an external reason for doing A, though that is not her reason for doing A. Cf. Bernard Williams, "Internal and External Reasons," *Moral Luck* (New York: Cambridge University press, 1981).

[8] This example was inspired by Robert Nozick, "Coercion," p.103; and Harry G. Frankfurt, "Alternative Possibilities and Moral Responsibility," *Journal of Philosophy*, vol. 66 (1969).

Now, if R^* is S's reason for doing something and S sincerely avows this, but one insists (in the absence of any reasonable considerations) that he did it for reason R, instead, then one fails to take S seriously. For treating a person as an autonomous being involves treating him as one who is capable of regarding himself as having reasons for acting. And one cannot do that if (in the absence of any reasonable considerations) one maintains that a person's reasons for doing something are other than what he avows them to be.[9] When treating a person (or groups of persons) in this way is embedded in the basic structure of society, then the result is social death.[10]

Bearing the preceding discussion in mind, suppose that there is a set of moral principles which both nontuistic persons and persons with affective capacities would find rational to accept. What should be clear is that these two types of individuals will not be moved to accept these principles for the same reason *cum* motivational explanation. This is so if, as I hope to show with Gauthier's work, it can only be coercively rational for nontuistic persons to accept a set of altruistic moral principles. As I have said, we have an instance of coercive rationality (a) whenever it is rational for a person to sacrifice the satisfaction of a deep desire in order that a deeper desire does not have to go unsatisfied or (b) whenever it is rational for a person to do something that he otherwise would not desire to do, and so would not do, but for his endeavor to satisfy a deep desire of his. That is, the person attaches no positive worth to the particular activity apart from its being a means to the satisfaction of the deep desire in question.

Now, by hypothesis a nontuistic person would not of his own accord be moved to accept altruistic constraints on his behavior. Having no concern for others, he is not disposed to take their well-being into account except insofar as it bears upon the satisfaction of his own desires. To be sure, a nontuistic person may see the benefits of cooperation, and for that reason may cooperate to the extent necessary. However, he attaches no intrinsic value to cooperation. In effect, he regards it as a necessary evil. His benefiting others through cooperation has no worth to him independently of the gain that accrues to him.

There is, then, an unbridgeable gulf between the motivational structure

[9] For this way of thinking about avowals, I am indebted to Raziel Abelson, *Persons: A Study in Philosophical Psychology* (New York: St. Martin's Press, 1977), chapter 2.

[10] I came across the term "social death" in John Rawls, "Justice as Fairness: Political as Metaphysical," *Philosophy and Public Affairs*, vol. 14 (1985). Rawls borrows the term from Orlando Patterson, *Slavery and Social Death* (Cambridge, MA: Harvard University Press, 1982). Patterson writes: "Everything has a past, including sticks and stones. Slaves differed from other human beings in that they were not allowed freely to integrate the experience of their ancestors into their lives, to inform their understanding of social reality with the inherited meaning of their natural forebears, or to anchor the living present in any conscious community of memory" (p.5). One cannot do this without routinely treating a person as if his avowed reasons for doing something are other than he claims them to be.

of a nontuistic person and that of a person capable of affective capacities. It is enough to say that the latter, unlike the former, has the capacity for love, since to love another is to be concerned about her well-being without regard for whatever benefits might accrue to one in virtue of displaying such concern. Thus, an altruistically-capable person would be moved to accept a set of altruistic moral principles for reasons that have nothing whatsoever to do with maximizing his nontuistic preferences, quite unlike a nontuistic person. Construction of altruistic moral theories which ignore this fail to take seriously what it means to be an altruistically-capable person.

The fact of the matter just is that human beings have a considerable capacity for affection.[11] If we did not, life as we know it simply could not be. Romantic loves, friendships, and the parent–child relationship would be radically different in the absence of the capacity for affection.[12] Trust is essential to the flourishing of these relationships, and cannot abound among individuals who are incapable of altruistic concerns. It is not coercive interaction which gives rise to trust, whether we have one person being coerced by another or a group of individuals cooperating only because it is coercively rational for them to so interact.[13]

Now, if a theory can be defective because it requires that persons identify more closely with the good of one another than we actually do, then it would seem that a theory can also be defective if it is grounded in the assumption that persons do not at all identify with the good of others when in fact we do. Presumably, the problem with theories of the former type is that they make requirements in terms of behavior and attitudes towards others which are deemed to be unacceptable, given our

[11] I have developed this point at length in my "Love and Morality: The Possibility of Altruism," James Fetzer, ed., *Epistemology and Sociobiology* (Norwall, MA: D. Reidel, 1985). Perhaps support for this view can be found in the idea of an evolutionary stable strategy: "a strategy which, if most members of a population adopt it, cannot be bettered by an alternative strategy." Richard Dawkins, *The Selfish Gene* (Fairlawn, NJ: Oxford University Press, 1976), p.74. Dawkins argues that a population of hawks, who fight without restraint until seriously injured, is not an evolutionary stable strategy, since this strategy would favor the spread of dove genes should a mutant dove, who is understood never to fight, arise in the population. For although doves would win no fights, they would also sustain no injuries (pp.75–77). A mixture of doves and hawks is shown to yield an evolutionary stable strategy as well. For a population consisting only of doves would favor the spread of hawk genes should a mutant hawk arise, since a hawk would win every fight in such a population. The suggestion here is that a population of nontuistic persons would not yield an evolutionary stable strategy from the standpoint of social interaction, since up to a point at least, it would favor the spread of altruistic genes should a mutant altruist arise in the population. Gauthier is not altogether unaware of considerations of this sort; see chapter 6, section 2.3.

[12] Cf. P.F. Strawson, "Freedom and Resentment," *Freedom and Resentment and Other Essays* (New York: Methuen, 1974).

[13] To my mind, this is one of the deep, deep insights of A. Baier's essay "Trust and Anti-Trust." See especially the section entitled the "Male Fixation on Contract."

psychological make-up.[14] The problem with theories of the latter type is that the justification for their principles does not speak to what is essential in the way that we conceive of ourselves and social interaction. In view of our psychological make-up, they give a false account of what makes morality attractive to us. To insist that this is irrelevant, since necessarily a set of principles grounded in nontuistic preferences demands no more of altruistically-capable persons than they are able to give, is to ignore motivations in a way that has been characteristically thought unacceptable, by those favoring deontological theories, in the evaluation of persons and their behavior.

One reason why deontological theories are said to be superior to utilitarianism is that they are not goal-based theories and, therefore, do not make the nature of the motivations of individuals ontologically subordinate to the attainment of some end, as is the case with utilitarianism.[15] Contractarian arguments give ontological priority to the rational and unanimous acceptance of a set of moral principles. If they are not to be unacceptable on account of ignoring the motivational character of human beings, then the motivational structure of the idealized rational contractors cannot be radically at odds with what that structure is like in reality. If human beings are best characterized as having nontuistic preferences, as Hobbes no doubt thought, that is one thing. But if, instead, the capacity for affection is a deep feature of persons, then it is simply a mistake to suppose that the motivational structure of altruistically-capable persons has not been ignored just because the assumption of nontuistic preferences means that a theory so grounded requires no more of such individuals than they are capable of giving. Such a theory requires less, and sometimes that can be morally offensive, as the exclamation "You don't trust me" makes clear. The offense here is that the hearer of these words expected much less of the speaker (of these words) than was warranted given the history of the speaker's behavior (which it is assumed that the hearer of these words is sufficiently familiar with).

The difference between coercive and intrinsic rationality serves to crystallize this point. As I have said, my thesis is that it can only be coercively rational for nontuistic persons to accept an altruistic morality. Whatever else is true, it has to be less coercively, and more intrinsically, rational for altruistically-capable persons to accept an altruistic morality.

---

[14] Surely, this is the force of Williams's now famous "one thought too many" critique of impartialist moral theories in his "Persons, Character, and Morality," *Moral Luck*. It is simply unreasonable to expect someone to adopt the impartial perspective about saving her spouse. See also Lawrence Blum, *Friendship, Altruism, and Morality* (Boston: Routledge and Kegan Paul, 1981).

[15] See Ronald Dworkin's masterful development of this point in *Taking Rights Seriously* (Cambridge, MA: Harvard University Press, 1977), chapter 6, "Justice and Rights."

This is because there is a congruence between the demands of an altruistic morality and the deep desires of altruistically-capable persons which does not and cannot obtain between such a conception of morality and nontuistic persons. To ignore this congruence is not to take seriously the motivational structure of altrustically-capable persons, not in the sense that utilitarianism is thought not to take the separateness of persons seriously, but in the sense that the theory takes the class of creatures called human beings and then ignores what it is like to be a human being from the standpoint of motivation with regard to the good of others. Whereas utilitarianism gives short shrift to the desires which are the embodiment of particular individuals, contract theory grounded in nontuistic preferences goes one step beyond that and ignores what it means even to be a human being, treating our affective capacities rather like an appendix.

Recall Gauthier's remarks:

> But Kant, rightly, insisted that morality cannot depend upon such particular psychological phenomena [that is, affective capacities], however benevolent and humane their effect, and however universally they may be found (*MA*, p.103).

I realize that he wants to say that it is a feature of morality that it binds independently of the affections of persons. As I have said, I do not believe that sense can be made of this claim unless one subscribes to the Kantian view that reasons can motivate in and of themselves, which Gauthier does not do. But even if one could make sense of this claim without appealing to this Kantian view, the concern I have raised would still remain. The reason, *cum* motivational explanation, would differ between nontuistic and altruistically-capable persons. In particular, the altruistic morality would remain only coercively rational for nontuistic persons. That it is rational to accept principles which fail to be congruent with desires which are deeply constitutive of the self does not make it the case that one's acceptance of them is other than coercively rational, as coercion makes abundantly clear.

III. GAUTHIER'S ARGUMENT

The principle argument of *Morals by Agreement* can be briefly summarized as follows:

(1) Each person is concerned to maximize her or his nontuistic preferences.

(2) Cooperation is possible only among individuals (at least a sufficient number of them) who are constrained maximizers as opposed to straightforward maximizers.

(3) Constrained maximizers are better able to maximize their nontuistic preferences by cooperating than by not doing so. ["We have insisted that the co-operative outcome afford one a utility greater than non-co-operation . . . " (*MA*, p.177).]

(4) Therefore, as a way of maximizing her or his nontuistic preferences it is rational (a) for each person to become a constrained maximizer and (b) for each person to adhere to that choice.

(5) But a constrained maximizer just is a person who has chosen to have a morally virtuous disposition because and only because she believes that she can thereby best maximize her nontuistic preferences.

(6) Therefore, if (4)(b) is true, then it follows that as a way of maximizing her nontuistic preferences, it is rational for a person to continue with the choice of having a morally virtuous disposition.

Some points of clarification are in order. A constrained maximizer is Gauthier's technical term for a person who is "conditionally disposed to co-operate in ways that, followed by all, would yield nearly optimal and fair outcomes, and does co-operate in such ways *when* she may actually expect to benefit" (*MA*, p.177, emphasis added). In other words, a constrained maximizer maintains a morally virtuous disposition when (because) and only when (because) she believes that she can thereby best maximize her nontuistic preferences. It might be thought that, in due course, a constrained maximizer is one who comes to value having a morally virtuous disposition as an end in itself. But this reading of Gauthier should be resisted, though admittedly he seems to unintentionally invite this reading in claiming that honesty is best treated as a disposition rather than a policy (*MA*, p.182). I return to this point in Section IV below.

Now, a constrained maximizer is to be contrasted with a straightforward maximizer, a person whose is concerned to maximize his nontuistic preferences with each choice that he makes. It is to be understood that a person is either a constrained maximizer (a person with a morally virtuous disposition) or a straightforward maximizer and that we are talking about the kind of cooperation that exemplifies moral behavior, moral cooperation let us call it.

Finally, let me say a word about premise (3), specifically. As Gauthier himself has persuasively argued,[16] it is, first of all, important to distinguish between (i) a nontuistic person's being better off with, rather than without, there being widespread cooperation among the members of his society and (ii) such a person's always being better off if he acts in accordance with the cooperative rules of morality *whenever* it is his turn to do so; second, (i) hardly entails (ii). In particular, it is possible that a person should be better

---

[16] Gauthier, "Morality and Advantage."

off for not acting in accordance with the cooperative rules of morality when it is his turn to do so. Now, to be sure, when Gauthier advanced this argument he was talking specifically about rational choice with respect to individual action; however, the point is no less sound when the object of rational choice is dispositions rather than actions. It does not follow from (i) that a nontuistic person is always better off, in circumstances of widespread cooperation, if he has a disposition as a result of which he will always act in accordance with the cooperative rules of morality *whenever* it is his turn to do so, since a person's disposition can get in the way of his maximizing his nontuistic preferences. There is little difference, however. If a person has a disposition to follow the cooperative rules of morality, then a relevant variable in calculating the utility of his not doing so or his giving up that disposition altogether is the utility expended in doing either one of these things. I shall return to this point momentarily.

In developing his argument, Gauthier distinguishes between transparency and translucency as follows:[17] A person is transparent if it is directly known to others whether or not he has a morally virtuous disposition or the disposition of a straightforward maximizer. A person is translucent if the nature of his disposition cannot be directly known to others, but ascertaining it is not simply a matter of guess work. Presumably, this does not mean that in every instance a correct determination will be made as to the nature of a translucent person's disposition. For Gauthier maintains that the argument is about "beings as translucent as we may reasonably consider ourselves to be" (*MA*, p.174); and a correct determination is not always made as to the nature of the disposition of such beings.

Regarding transparency, he writes: "But to assume transparency may seem to rob our argument of much of its interest. . . . We shall have refuted the Foole [whose ultimate argument is that the "truly prudent person, the fully rational utility-maximizer, must seek to appear trustworthy . . . " (*MA*, p.173)] but at the price of robbing our refutation of all practical import" (*MA*, p.174). Thus, rather than assuming that all individuals are transparent, Gauthier assumes that most are translucent. His reason for not assuming transparency is that it is an assumption which is not true to the facts, in that most individuals are not transparent.

However, there is another drawback to the assumption of transparency. If (i) all constrained maximizers have a morally virtuous disposition because and only because they can best maximize their nontuistic preferences as a result of being able to enter into cooperative arrangements, and (ii) people will cooperate only with individuals who have a morally virtuous disposition, because it is known that cooperation is impossible with anyone

---

[17] My thinking here owes much to Geoffrey Sayre McCord, "Deception and Reasons to be Moral," *American Philosophical Quarterly*, vol. 25 (1988).

who has an sm-disposition (that is, the disposition of a straightforward maximizer), then the assumption of transparency makes it utterly irrational for a constrained maximizer even to attempt give up her morally virtuous dispositon for an sm-disposition. Accordingly, having a morally virtuous disposition turns out to be coercively rational.

We may liken the assumption of transparency to a community of mutated individuals each of whom has a Pinocchio gene, and so each of whose nose grows whenever she prevaricates. Hence, for this very reason and only for this reason, we can imagine that each person has an honest disposition. But needless to say, it can hardly be inferred from this that any member of this community values the disposition of honesty as an end in itself. On the contrary, it is clear that, as I have told the story, each person would prefer not to have this disposition. Their mutated biological trait makes honesty a necessity of life; and that is precisely the way in which each views this virtue. In a word, then, their mutated biological trait has made being honest coercively rational for them.

With the assumption of transparency we have a parallel situation. Gauthier's focus upon one truth, namely, that the assumption is unrealistic, has obscured another, namely, that the assumption makes being moral coercively rational. My suspicions are that Gauthier is on to the problem of morality being coercively rational and wishes to avoid it, and that the move to translucency is meant to aid in his doing just that. This reading of Gauthier finds support from his discussion in Chapters X and XI, where he acknowledges (in X) that "*Morals by agreement can speak only to [economic man's] intellect, but not to his feelings*" (*MA*, p.327, emphasis added), and then proceeds to argue that the theory is compatible with individuals having and valuing affective bonds. Before turning to argue that morality is coercively rational, given translucency, I should first say a word about choosing dispositions.

Gauthier does not give either an account of dispositions or an account of what choosing to acquire a disposition comes to. Here are some intuitive remarks. Actions are performed; dispositions are acquired. The difference is not merely verbal. Rather, it bespeaks the fact that psychological states are constitutive of dispositions and that a change from one disposition to another requires a change in the relevant psychological states. That change is generally not thought to constitute an action even if it is the outcome of one or more actions. Moreover, a change in dispositions is invariably thought to be one that takes place gradually. Hence, no one save the schizophrenic is thought to be able to move back and forth between polar dispositions.[18]

[18] I have developed the substance of this line of thought in my "Ethical Egoism and Psychological Dispositions," *American Philosophical Quarterly*, vol. 17 (1980), where I talk about polar dispositions (e.g., honesty and dishonesty) and dispositional fits (e.g., honesty and integrity).

Acquiring a disposition, then, may be thought of as psychologically setting oneself (or one's future self) up to performing the actions over which the disposition ranges even when, in a particular instance, it is contrary to one's self-interest to do so. Thus, a person who has acquired a particular disposition has given up the option of being able to perform without a considerable struggle actions contrary to actions covered by this disposition whenever it suits her; that is, she has made it the case that being able to perform these contrary actions comes significantly less easy to her.

These considerations would suggest that acquiring a disposition is rather like executing a long-range plan, such as getting a college degree or running for political office or planning for a new kind of space flight maneuver, all of which generally require performing a series of actions over several years in order to achieve the desired end. Since the execution of long-range plans involve a considerable investment in terms of both time and effort, the extent to which they are rationally choiceworthy is, naturally, tied to whether or not they are worth the investment of time and effort required to execute them. The relevance of these considerations to translucent constrained maximizers with a morally virtuous disposition are as follows.

With respect to the rationality of changing from a morally virtuous disposition to an sm-disposition, a constrained maximizer must take three things into account: (a) whether or not she is translucent enough that she could pass herself off as having a morally virtuous disposition, though in reality she has an sm-disposition; (b) whether or not replacing her morally virtuous disposition with an sm-disposition would be worth the effort, given the entrenchedness of the former disposition; and (c) whether, given the content of the person's nontuistic preferences, having such a disposition, would significantly enhance the likelihood of her satisfying them. Now, the myth of Gyges' ring (*Republic*, 359c–360c) makes it ever so clear that (c) would receive an affirmative answer for all but a very few constrained maximizers. On the other hand, we can assume that for most translucent constrained maximizers an affirmative answer will not be forthcoming for both (a) and (b), in which case it will not be rational for them to attempt to change from having a morally virtuous disposition to having an sm-disposition. But, alas, given an affirmative answer to (c), the explanation for why it is not rational for them to make the attempt renders morality coercively rational for them.

To take consideration (a), if a constrained maximizer's translucency borders on being transparent, then her continuing to have a morally virtuous dispositon is to be explained by the risk she runs of being discovered were she to acquire an sm-disposition. And if, to take consideration (b), a person's morally virtuous disposition is so entrenched that she cannot rid herself of it although she wishes to, then in that case her having a morally virtuous disposition is rather like the psychological baggage of guilt for the person who unsuccessfully attempts to avoid feeling deep pangs of guilt whenever he does something morally wrong. Given an affirmative response to (c), it turns out in either case that it is coercively rational for the constrained maximizer to continue maintaining a morally virtuous disposition. For, to begin with, such a disposition is something that a constrained maximizer would not have acquired but for the fact that it is a means to the satisfaction of his desires (preferences). And his continuing to maintain that disposition is not to be explained primarily in terms of the desire that is most deeply constitutive of himself, namely, that of maximizing his nontuistic preferences. Rather, it is to be explained in terms of either his belief that he cannot appear to have a morally virtuous disposition while actually maintaining an sm-disposition or the fact that his psychological structure does, contrary to his wishes, not permit the change from a morally virtuous disposition to an sm-disposition because the former is too entrenched. And as the case of guilt shows, from the fact that a dispositon is deeply entrenched, it in no way follows that a person delights in having that disposition or identifies with it in some fundamentally important way. One can very much want to be rid of a deeply entrenched disposition, as the case of an addict makes manifestly clear.[19]

IV. CONCLUSION: THE APPEAL TO AFFECTIVE CAPACITIES

In Chapters X and XI of *Morals by Agreement*, we find a moving account of the importance of the affective capacities in the lives of human beings. The force of this account is, I believe, to temper significantly the nontuistic content of the preferences of persons. Thus, in terms of the argument of preceding section, this means that most people will give a negative rather than an affirmative answer to (c). Gauthier is all too aware of the fact that if we start with a wholly nontuistic individual (Gauthier's economic man [*MA*, p.316]) and make no changes along the way, then we will end up with none other than a wholly nontuistic individual. This would suggest that Gauthier does not for a moment think that in the absence of the affective capacities a constrained maximizer can come to value morality as an end in itself, as if the desire to be moral wins an endurance test. To put the matter in another and perhaps more forceful way, he seems to realize that in the absence of these capacities, the problem of defection from the ranks of the

[19] Cf. Frankfurt, "Freedom of the Will and the Concept of a Person."

morally cooperative remains an insuperable one (*MA*, pp.172–177).

This is not to deny that time can make a difference in how we are constituted, but just that it can make that difference only if it is given something to work with. And one does not do that if one insists throughout, as Gauthier does, that persons be characterized as wholly nontuistic with respect to their preferences. For it will be remembered that on Gauthier's view a constrained maximizer maintains a morally virtuous disposition when (because) and only when (because) she believes that she can thereby best maximize her nontuistic preferences. She is not to be understood as an individual who aspires to maintain a morally virtuous disposition come what may; nor is she to be understood simply as one whose virtuous disposition needs reinforcement.[20] Rather, her commitment to morality is quite explicitly contingent upon those with whom she interacts having a like commitment.

It should come as no surprise that Gauthier appeals to the affective capacities. A moral person, if there be any, is one who identifies with the aims of morality in a deep way. One may say that her desire to be moral resounds from a desire that is most deeply constitutive of the self.[21] Because there can be no such resounding in the absence of the affective capacities, the wholly nontuistic (selfish) are constitutionally unable to experience this sort of identification with morality. If morality has any deep hold on our lives, it is surely in virtue of our affective capacities. *Morals by Agreement*, which advances our understanding in so many ways, serves only to underscore this point. For even if the theory should show that agreement is possible, it does not, because it cannot, show that the agreement is intrinsically desirable. Thus, the morality it gives us is very much a shadow of the moral ideal that Plato, and many since him, have sought. Perhaps we can have no more than that. *Morals by Agreement* may very well offer as much as anyone can ask for in a moral theory. That, however, is no reason to suppose that it offers as much as many have wanted.

APPENDIX: GAUTHIER AND RAWLS

In *A Theory of Justice*,[22] John Rawls aims to show that the parties in the original positon would choose the principles of justice as fairness. These

[20] This, I have argued in "Beliefs and the Motivation to be Just," *American Philosophical Quarterly*, vol. 22 (1985), is indeed the case for morally virtuous people.

[21] In "Freedom of the Will and the Concept of a Person," Frankfurt writes: "When a person identifies himself *decisively* with one of his first-order desires, this commitment 'resounds' throughout the potentially endless array of higher orders" (p.16, emphasis in original).

[22] John Rawls, *A Theory of Justice* (Cambridge, MA: Harvard University Press, 1971). I shall not here be concerned with developments in John Rawls's thinking since the publication of this work.

individuals "are conceived as not taking an interest in one another's interests" (*ATJ*, p.13); and Rawls makes the following motivational assumption: "they [the parties in the original position] assume that they would prefer more primary social goods rather than less" (*ATJ*, p.141). Thus, it might seem that insofar as the arguments of this essay are telling against Gauthier, they are just as telling against Rawls. I think not, however.

One of the most powerful arguments in Rawls's work is the argument from psychological stability.[23] He writes: "But a decision in the original position depends on a comparison: other things equal, the preferred conception of justice is the most stable one" (*ATJ*, p.498).[24] Notwithstanding their nontuistic characterization, then, the parties in the original position are to choose with the aim of enhancing psychological stability in society: hence the tremendous importance which Rawls attaches to a well-ordered society. That is a concern of theirs from the start. Herein lies the difference between Rawls and Gauthier.

For Rawls, psychological stability is an important consideration to be taken into account at the very outset in the choice of principles of justice; this is not so for Gauthier. Rawls maintains that the parties in the original position know, among other things, the laws of human psychology (*ATJ*, p.138); and the two principles of justice as fairness are chosen over utilitarianism because, among other things, the parties realize that given the laws of psychology utilitarianism is less successful than the two principles in generating psychological stability. As I trust is clear, this is not the character of Gauthier's argument at all.

In *Morals by Agreement*, we have nontuistic individuals choosing principles of morality for nontuistic individuals, namely, themselves. In *A Theory of Justice*, we have nontuistic individuals choosing principles of morality (justice) for altrustically-capable individuals. This is a stark, but nonetheless accurate, characterization of the difference between these two works. If I am right in this difference, then Rawls's work is relatively unaffected by the arguments of this essay.

Philosophy, Oberlin College

In writing this appendix, I am indebted to conversations with David Copp and, especially, Norman Care.

[23] Indeed, in *The Liberal Theory of Justice* (Fairlawn, NJ: Oxford University Press, 1973), Brian Barry writes: "Unfortunately, this argument is so powerful that it seems to be in imminent danger of short-circuiting the whole elaborate argument in favour of the 'two principles'. For if (as Rawls sometimes appears to imply) they are the only principles capable of satisfying the demands of stability, that would seem to end the matter then and there" (pp.14–15).

[24] See also Rawls, *A Theory of Justice*, p.138 and section 29, "The Main Grounds for the Two Principles of Justice," where Rawls writes: "A second consideration invokes the condition of publicity as well as that of the constraints on agreements. I shall present the argument in terms of the question of psychological stability. . . . [A] strong point in favor of a conception of justice is that it generates its own supports."

Social Philosophy & Policy 5:2 ISSN 0265–0525

MORALITY, RATIONAL CHOICE, AND SEMANTIC REPRESENTATION
A Reply to My Critics

DAVID GAUTHIER

I

(1) In his recent paper, "Justice as Fairness: Political not Metaphysical," John Rawls makes use of a footnote to disown what to many readers must have seemed one of the most striking and original underlying ideas of his theory of justice, that it "is a part, perhaps the most significant part, of the theory of rational choice."[1] That Rawls should issue this disclaimer indicates, at least in my view, that he has a much clearer understanding of his theory, and its relationship to rational choice than he did at the time that he wrote *A Theory of Justice*. As I note in *Morals by Agreement* (pp.4–5), Rawls does not show that principles of justice are principles of rational choice. Hence, in appropriating the idea, I can claim that I am undertaking a pioneering enterprise. No doubt Thomas Hobbes would have undertaken it had the resources of the theory of rational choice been at his disposal, but I do not intend to pursue counterfactuals in a search for historical antecedents. Moral theory as rational choice theory is, I claim, a new venture.

The underlying ideas are simple and, I believe, natural. What distinguishes human beings from other animals, and provides the basis for rationality, is the capacity for semantic representation. You can, as your dog on the whole cannot, represent a state of affairs to yourself, and consider in particular whether or not it is the case, and whether or not you would want it to be the case. You can represent to yourself the contents of your beliefs, and your desires. But in representing them, you bring them into relation with one another. You represent to yourself that the Blue Jays will win the World Series, and that a National League team will win the World Series, and that the Blue Jays are not a National League team. And in recognizing a conflict among those beliefs, you find rationality thrust upon you. Note that the first two beliefs could be replaced by desires, with the same effect.

[1] John Rawls, *A Theory of Justice* (Cambridge, MA: Harvard University Press, 1971), p.16. The footnote is in *Philosophy & Public Affairs*, vol. 14 (1985), p.237, n.20.

It is perhaps just conceivable that the capacity for semantic representation could be motivationally inert. This is not to say that what is represented could be motivationally inert. Desires are necessarily motivating. But it does not follow from this that in representing the desire, some further motivation arises. However, no plausible evolutionary story could be told that would yield beings whose representations have no motivational role. The step from represented desire to conscious action governed by such representation is a short one, and the only one needed to make sense of acting for a reason. How the physiological mechanisms work that establish a capacity for semantic representation and link it motivationally to action is a story that I cannot, and need not, tell, but that story, whatever it is, shows how reasons are causes.

Since in representing our desires we become aware of conflict among them, the step from representation to decision becomes complicated. We must, somehow, bring our conflicting desires into some sort of coherence. And it is widely supposed that there is only one plausible candidate for a principle of coherence – a maximizing principle. We order our desires, in relation to decision and action, so that we may choose to maximize our expectation of desire-fulfillment. And in so doing, we show ourselves to be rational agents. I shall not question this maximizing view here, agreeing with economists and others that there is simply nothing else for practical rationality to be.[2]

This is not the whole story, of course. The capacity to represent our desires enables us – I should rather say, requires us – not only to embark on the task of rendering our behavior practically coherent, but also to reflect on the very desires themselves, both in their relations one with another and simply in themselves. You and your dog can both desire a piece of meat, but you can, in ways in which your dog cannot, wonder whether you truly desire that meat. To be sure, the meat may not smell right, and this may give your dog pause as well as you. But nothing in your dog's behavior needs to be explained by attributing to it a capacity to reflect on its desires, so that it can act on them in the assurance that they are fully considered. And this reflection, arising also out of the capacity for semantic representation, is an essential dimension of practical rationality.

Reflection and maximization both have costs. But it is not germane to my present concerns to consider how those costs complicate the simple account I have sketched. I want, rather, to move directly to morality. The conception of human beings as having a capacity for semantic representation that brings with it a reflective and maximizing rationality has deep implications for moral theory. One option open to the moral theorist is, of

---

[2] I should, however, note that I am increasingly aware that the case for incorporating maximization into practical rationality needs to be argued, and not simply assumed. But I cannot argue it here.

course, to suppose that the introduction of morality requires a supplementation to this account of human beings. Thus, we might suppose that morality arises as a constraint on the objects of desire imposed by our awareness of an objective goodness in the world. On such a view, rationality and morality would be independent. A rational and moral person would seek to maximize the fulfillment of her morally constrained desires; a rational but immoral person would seek to maximize the fulfillment of her desires without regard to their moral appropriateness; a moral but irrational person would fail to seek to maximize the fulfillment of desires that were morally constrained. But there are, it seems to me, grave difficulties in the way of such a view of morality, and these make it more attractive, at least in an initial attempt, to seek an account of morality that will require no supplementation in the conception of human beings as semantic representers. Can we introduce morality without postulating any features either of the world or of persons over and above those which naturally suggest themselves if we think of human beings as animals with this one peculiar and distinctive capacity – a capacity that brings with it, on the surface, only the apparatus of rationality?

Morals by Agreement answers this question affirmatively. And in doing so, it offers us the only plausible way of defending morality against what I consider to be the fate of religion. Religious practice and religious language are, or until recently have been, ubiquitous in human life. But if we take religion at face value, and ask ourselves what must be the case if the claims of religion, literally construed so that they possess ordinary truth-value, are some of them to be true, then we find ourselves driven to an account of the world that is prodigal in admitting into its ontology entities that play no role in our best explanations and justifications. The best explanation we can give of claims about a god does not make reference to such a being. The only theory of religion that, to my mind, has the least credibility, is an error theory.

Unlike some, I am not easy about the practical consequences of the incredibility of religious claims. I am not persuaded that the evil men do in the name of religion is greater than what they do in their liberation from religion. But I should be even more uneasy were I to suppose that morality would share the fate of religion, so that our moral claims, literally construed, would, to be true, require us to accept a prodigal and ultimately incredible ontology. Now it may be the case that, as heretofore understood, moral claims do presuppose an objective value that we have no good epistemic reason to embrace. But just as we may look on the Newtonian and Einsteinean revolutions in physics as reconstructionist, in enabling us to reinterpret our earlier talk about the world in a way that can be made to conform with the demands of the new theories, so we may seek a reconstruction of morality that will enable us to reinterpret our moral claims in a way that conforms with the picture of human beings and the world that is suggested if we distinguish ourselves from our fellow animals primarily by our capacity for representation.

We begin, then, by thinking of human beings as seeking to maximize the fulfillment of their reflectively held desires.[3] And we ask what might lead, not us, but the persons themselves, each seeking to maximize her reflectively held desires, to be uneasy or discontent. To be sure, the world does not assure success, but that would not lead persons to doubt that they were doing the best they could. Now if we take persons in isolation, considering only the individual agent, nothing may seem to cause unease. (This claim is overly optimistic, as recent work on preference change and dynamic choice shows. I shall return to this in my discussion of Edward F. McClennen's paper in Section V.) But when we bring in the idea of interaction, and suppose that the outcome, the effect on each person's desires, will be determined not simply by her own behavior given the state of the world, but rather by her behavior in conjunction with the behavior of some one or more of her fellows, then we find, in the structural problem represented most clearly by the Prisoner's Dilemma, a clear source for unease. For in Dilemma-structured situations, each maximizer will confront the uncomfortable truth that the outcome of the apparently rational, maximizing behavior of herself and every other person, leaves her, and indeed each person, worse off than need be, given where it leaves the others. Each does best for himself, yet everyone could do better.

Anyone who recognizes this can make sense of a constraining factor in human interaction. For she can understand, not just that she would benefit, but that she and everyone else would benefit, were some constraining device to enable them to achieve one of the mutually better outcomes to that resulting from unconstrained, straightforward utility-maximization. In understanding this, she has taken the first step needed to reinterpret moral claims in a way that does not leave them vulnerable to elimination by an error theory. And essential to this step is the recognition that whatever force moral claims have derives, and derives entirely, from their role in overcoming the structural problem of interaction represented by the Prisoner's Dilemma, the problem of reconciling individual maximizing action with Pareto-optimality. Anything else would only be a mythical addendum that, when understood, would leave morality as impotent as religion.

It is clearly not enough to show that some form of constraint would be beneficial. We must show, on the one hand, that the constraint would itself

---

[3] I am using 'desire' here, although in *Morals by Agreement* I speak of 'preference'. I don't think this matters for my present purpose.

be effective. We must show that, given the constraint, each person would be rational to act in a way that would yield an outcome that would be mutually advantageous in relation to the outcome of unconstrained individual maximization. And we must show, on the other hand, that the constraint captures at least something of our intuitive or pre-analytic understanding of morality. Failure here would not deprive our argument of interest and significance, but it would disqualify it as a rational reconstruction of morality. If Hobbes were right in supposing that an absolute sovereign were the necessary and sufficient condition of overcoming the natural Prisoner's Dilemma-like condition of humankind, and if such a sovereign could be instituted, then we should indeed have a solution to the problem of interaction posed by Dilemma-like structures, but it would not be a solution that we could identify with morality. A Hobbesian sovereign is a replacement for, and not part of a reconstruction of, a moral system.

(2) I shall say that a moral constraint is characterized by two features – it is internal, in operating through the will, or decision making, of the agent, and it operates in a manner that satisfies some standard of impartiality among persons. This is enough for my reconstructive purpose. The question, then, is whether such a constraint can be shown to be a part of rational choice procedures. And of course, I argue that it can. Now here we may distinguish three levels of increasing specificity. First, we may think simply of a defence of the claim that an internal, impartial constraint on directly maximizing actions can be established within the framework of rational choice. Second, we may introduce a particular procedure by which, we argue, this claim may be defended. In my theory, this procedure requires us to show that rational persons would agree on a constraint that would obtain each person's compliance. Third, we may specify a particular principle, or set of principles, as the content of rational agreement, and a particular argument, addressed to each individual, that would elicit her rational compliance. In my theory, minimax relative concession, the revised Lockean proviso, and the argument for disposing oneself to constrained maximization, together constitute this third level of specification.

Although the third level receives the most extensive treatment in *Morals by Agreement*, it, or its parts, are the most expendable. In saying this I am not proposing, nor shall I propose, that any of these should be abandoned, and I shall be defending them against my penetrating critics, but I want first to focus, more clearly than I do in the book, on the first and second levels, since I am more concerned with defending the idea of a contractarian moral theory than with upholding the particular variant of such a theory that I have developed.

What delimits contractarian theory is the step from the first to the second level of specificity. At the first level we simply require that morality be developed as part of rational choice. At the second level we specify a particular way of developing morality, involving rational choice in two very distinct ways, in agreement and in compliance. On the one hand, we argue that moral principles are those to which persons would rationally agree. On the other hand, we argue that moral principles afford a rational basis for individual choice. And this will immediately indicate a problem. Moral principles constrain straightforwardly maximizing behavior. Now if we ask, what constraints would it be rational to agree to, then, provided we can appropriately demarcate the context of agreement, we may find an answer. And if we ask, what constraints would it be rational to adhere to, then again, given appropriate demarcation of context, we may find an answer. But why should these answers coincide – why should the same principles be the object of both rational agreement and rational compliance? And this question will seem especially pressing if we suppose, as I do, that the context of agreement differs from that of compliance, so that the rationality of agreement is established in relation to a hypothetical presocial or premoral situation, whereas the rationality of compliance is and must be determined in the actual situation of the agent. In considering this question in the present context, I have in mind especially, although not exclusively, Gilbert Harman's claim that I do "not show that rational agents will dispose themselves to adhere only to arrangements that offer them at least as much as would be provided by minimax relative concession plus the proviso" (*Supra*, p.15), a claim that Harman defends at length in his paper.

Given the suboptimality of straightforwardly maximizing behavior, someone might argue that it would be rational, in suitable circumstances, for an individual to accept certain constraints on her choices, provided she could expect others also to accept constraints. Some form of constrained maximization may thus be rational. But this constraint need have no relation to agreement, rational or irrational, actual or hypothetical. An individual may find herself in a society in which certain forms of constraint are generally practiced; she may find it rational to accept them. But the constraining principles that she adopts may not satisfy the requirement of impartiality. And their validity may be thought to derive, not from any agreement, but from divine command, or natural rights, or overall well-being, or established practice, or existing authority.

Again, given the suboptimality of straightforwardly maximizing behavior, someone might argue that it would be rational for persons to agree to certain principles mutual adherence to which would yield the expectation of an optimal outcome. And actual agreement might yield principles with which it would be rational for each individual to comply. But they need not satisfy any requirement of impartiality. And hypothetical agreement –

consideration of what one would rationally agree to in an appropriate state of nature such that impartiality would be ensured – need not yield principles with which it would be actually rational to comply. To suppose that such principles nevertheless constitute morality would then be to abandon the attempt to develop morality within the framework of rational choice. Rawls, as I have noted, has recognized that it was a mistake for him to suppose that his theory of justice was a part of the theory of rational choice, and the nature of the mistake should now be apparent. Although he makes some use of rational choice arguments in considering what principles persons in an appropriate initial situation would agree to, he does not show, or attempt to show, the rationality of their compliance with the agreed principles.

I am thus pointing to what may seem a gap between the idea of morals by agreement – morality as a set of principles that would elicit our rational agreement, and morality as part of rational choice – morality as a set of constraints with which it would be rational for each of us to comply. But of course, I want to deny that there is a real gap here.

The claim that there is a gap is present, not only in Harman's discussion, but in two other critiques to which I am replying – those of James Buchanan and James Fishkin. Each is suspicious of the appeal to a hypothetical agreement. Buchanan is explicitly critical of the attempt to ground "a liberal social order, including the place that individual principles of morality hold in such an order . . . in the rational choice behavior of persons" (*Supra*, p.75). Harman believes that I show "that it can be rational to dispose oneself to cooperate" but that I do not demonstrate that rational cooperators "will agree to distribute their cooperative surpluses in accordance" with the terms of an ideal or hypothetical bargain (*Supra*, p.15). Fishkin argues "that once we depart from actual life, we can appeal to any number of counterfactual situations," so that the appeal to a hypothetical bargain proves indeterminate (*Supra*, p.58). I can begin to meet each of these challenges if I can close the apparent gap between rational compliance and rational agreement.

Begin, then, *in medias res*; assume an ongoing society in which individuals accept, more or less, a given set of moral principles as constraining their choices in relation to what they would be taking only their nonmoral desires, aims, and interests directly into account. Perhaps they have internalized the values inherent in these principles as preferences; perhaps they regard the principles as specifying duties that override preferences. In any case, their behavior is constrained in relation to what it would be in the absence of the principles. Suppose that a disposition to conform to the existing moral principles is *prima facie* advantageous; suppose that persons who are not so disposed may expect to be excluded from desirable opportunities by their fellows. However, the principles themselves have, or at least need have, no basis in agreement. They need satisfy no intuitive standard of fairness or impartiality. They are simply principles constraining individual behavior in a mutually advantageous way.

Suppose now that our persons, as rational maximizers of individual utility, come to reflect on the principles constituting their morality. They will, of course, assess the principles in relation to their own utility, but with the awareness that their fellows will be doing the same. And one question that must arise is: why *these* principles? For they will recognize that the set of actual moral principles is not the only possible set of constraining principles that would yield mutually advantageous, optimal outcomes. (Indeed, the existing set may yield outcomes that, while mutually advantageous in relation to the absence of constraint, are suboptimal.) They will recognize the possibility of alternative moral orders. At this point it will not be enough to say that as a matter of fact, each person can expect to benefit from a disposition to comply with existing principles. For persons will also ask themselves: can I benefit more, not from simply abandoning morality, and recognizing no constraint, but from a partial rejection of existing constraints in favor of an alternative set? Once this question is asked, the situation is transformed: the existing moral order must be assessed, not only against simple noncompliance, but also against what we may call alternative compliance.

Now I suggest that to make this assessment, each will compare her prospects under the existing principles with those she would anticipate from a set that, in the existing circumstances, she would expect to result from bargaining with her fellows. If her prospects would be improved by such negotiation, then she will have a real, although not necessarily sufficient, incentive to demand a change in the established moral order. More generally, if there are persons whose prospects would be improved by renegotiation, then the existing order will be recognizably unstable. No doubt those whose prospects would be worsened by renegotiation will have a clear incentive to resist, to appeal to the status quo. But their appeal will be a weak one, especially among persons who are not taken in by spurious ideological considerations, but focus on individual utility-maximization. Thus, although in the real world we begin with an existing set of moral principles as constraints on our maximizing behavior, yet we are lead by reflection to the idea of an amended set that would obtain the agreement of everyone, and this amended set has, and will be recognized to have, a stability lacking in existing morality.

But how does agreement come in? We began with a set of moral principles. We offered no story about their basis. We assumed simply that they were entrenched in social practices and institutions in such a way that each person found it rational to be disposed to conform to them. We then supposed that persons would be aware of alternative possible principles, and evaluate existing ones in relation to them. Why do I claim that the relevant evaluation is based on a consideration of what would result from agreement? To simplify discussion, let us suppose for the moment that there is no problem of compliance, so that each person may reasonably expect that agreement on a set of constraining principles would be effective. Now we ask, if the existing set of principles would not result from agreement, then why is it as a matter of fact effective? Why do those persons, who would not agree to it, nevertheless comply with it? There seem to be two main possibilities. The first appeals to the costs of reaching agreement, given that it is not embodied in the status quo. The second appeals to the interest some persons have in preserving the status quo, since they would expect to do less well given agreement. But what is the basis of this expectation? Why should they expect to lose, given that they must be parties to the agreement, and so must find the set of principles that would emerge from agreement acceptable in some sense?

Here again the answer seems to be twofold. First, as we noted previously, some persons may recognize that the status quo simply offers them benefits that agreement would not sustain. But if this is all, then they are really powerless to block the changes that agreement would bring about. To the extent to which it is generally recognized that these persons, although they would lose in terms of their present position, would nevertheless find a negotiated set of principles acceptable, they are left without any effective defense against such a set. But there is a second possibility. Agreement is not without conditions. In particular, although we may speak of forced agreement, agreement itself is unforced. I may force you to agree by constraining your set of options, but within that set you must be free to choose, if the outcome is to be an agreed one. The status quo may, then, be maintained coercively, in a manner incompatible with agreement. This is, indeed, the point of my reference to the South African situation in *Morals by Agreement*. If the South African government, recognizing the suboptimality of the present situation, were to offer to make a mutually advantageous deal with the Blacks, the immediately obvious problem is that present arrangements are coercively maintained, and any alternative that could be said to be agreed, and that could possibly be stable as the result of agreement, would require the abandonment of much of the existing coercive apparatus, with the result that the agreed outcome would leave the Whites worse off, or so they suppose, than the present suboptimal coercively maintained arrangements. The conditions for reaching and maintaining agreement are incompatible with the coercive apparatus that permits the Whites to maintain their present advantages.

Recognition of this last possibility requires me to modify my argument. In some circumstances the gap between existing constraining principles and those that would emerge from agreement can not be treated merely as the effect of the costs in moving from the status quo. But of course, in such circumstances, although it may be rational for some persons to dispose themselves to acquiesce in the existing principles, it would be a misrepresentation to identify their disposition with one of unforced compliance. And the existing principles could not plausibly be identified with morality.

Recall at this point that my discussion assumes rational, utility-maximizing individuals, who are not mistaken about the nature of morality or, more generally, who recognize that the sole rationale for constraint must be ultimately a utility-maximizing one. In the real world a set of constraining principles that, among rational persons, could be maintained, if at all, only coercively, may be sustained in a manner that I call ideological. Belief in hellfire may do the work of a repressive police or military force. But I am simply not concerned, in *Morals by Agreement*, with such situations. I am not attempting to construct an account of morality, and its relation to rationality, that will be directly applicable to persons who have false or mistaken beliefs, and who would, of course, reject the theory as inadequate to their (mis)understanding of morality. That my theory would invite this sort of rejection is not itself an argument against it, as comparison with theories of religion that reject the truth of any positive first-order religious claims should make clear.

Returning now to situations involving rational persons, and leaving aside those situations that are structured in such a way that some persons would suffer long-term overall costs were they to give up the existing coercive apparatus, we may suppose that each person recognizes the benefit, to her and to her fellows, of an effective set of mutual constraints. Each then must consider it rational to agree to some set or sets of constraints, provided others will do likewise, and provided also, as we have been assuming, that she may expect their agreement to be effective. And each must believe that everyone else will consider such agreement rational. Indeed, we may reasonably suppose that there will be some set or sets of principles, such that everyone would prefer agreement on the set, both to no agreement and to continued negotiation, given the costs and risks of such negotiation. And when such a set is identified, no alternative that would not emerge from agreement can be stably maintained.

(3) To this point I have argued only the relevance of actual agreement to constraining principles, and that only under the simplifying assumption that compliance poses no independent problem – that agreement on a set of principles carries with it, in some manner, adherence to those principles.

Can we go further? Consider first the compliance problem. As a rational utility-maximizer, I should comply with and only with those constraints for which I can give myself a utility-maximizing rationale. Now a direct rationale is obviously impossible; in a particular situation I cannot have a maximizing rationale for constraining my maximizing activity. An indirect rationale can in principle work in a number of ways. I could, for example, suppose that fate rewards those who constrain themselves in certain ways, the reward being in terms of the degree of success they achieve in fulfilling their preferences. Or I could simply prefer to be the sort of person who constrains the fulfillment of certain of his preferences. But these rationales require assumptions or suppositions quite independent of those provided by the idea of human beings, characterized by their capacity for semantic representation, interacting in a normally structured world. Only the fact that, given the structure of interaction, others benefit from 'my constraints, and benefit in ways such that they can profitably make me better off if I am willing to constrain myself than I would be were I not so willing, can provide us with a rationale that does not require us to go beyond the suppositions we have already made. So what we suppose is that I find reason to comply with constraining principles in the benefits that accrue to me through the response of my fellows – a response that, obviously, cannot simply be the effect of compliance, since that would provide me with a direct maximizing rationale for compliance that would eliminate constraint, but that operates indirectly, in terms of the expectations others form about me on the basis of their judgment of whether or not I am disposed to compliance, and the opportunities they then give me or deny me.

So it is rational for me to acquire those dispositions to comply with constraining principles that others find it advantageous to reward. What form of compliance should you reward? In general, you cannot expect to benefit from an idiosyncratic practice of rewarding and punishing, in part because you could not expect others to divine your practice, in part because, even if they could, they would have to balance the rewards they would receive from you with the very different rewards others would offer. Provided the existing pattern of constraint is one from which you benefit, you will, other things equal, do well to seek to uphold it. And we may now run an argument parallel to that which we have already presented, beginning with the status quo and leading to what would result from agreement. Indeed, we may suppose that, in considering the rationality of agreeing to a set of constraining principles, an individual will take into account the benefits of others' compliance, the costs of his own, and the effects, whether benefits or costs, of his own enforcing activity, in the opportunities he extends to others based on their assumed willingness to comply. The agreed principles are then the ones with which compliance will be expected, and consequently those with which each person, other things equal, will find an indirect rationale for complying herself.

If I were then to identify morality with what would be agreed, I should have an account that would have strong affinities with the views of Buchanan, Fishkin, and Harman. To be sure, I should want, with Fishkin, to focus on preference formation in a way that seems absent from both Buchanan and Harman. And I should want, with Buchanan and Harman, to defend a more substantive content than that which seems acceptable to Fishkin. And my concern with rational compliance is not paralleled in the argument of any of them. But I should have rejected the distinctively hypothetical character of agreement, which is central to the theory presented in *Morals by Agreement*, and that I claim is essential if one is to have reason to identify morality with rational constraining principles. This identification is of little moment to Buchanan, but it cannot, I think, be ignored by Fishkin or Harman.

The reflective capacity of rational agents leads them from the given to the agreed, from existing principles and practices of constraint to those that would receive each person's assent. The same reflective capacity, I claim, leads from those principles that would be agreed to, in existing social circumstances, to those that would receive *ex ante* agreement, prior to all society. Fishkin worries about the determinacy of this move. Buchanan and, especially, Harman worry about its relevance. Why should rational utility-maximizers, outcome-oriented as they are, concern themselves with a merely hypothetical agreement?

Now it is not my concern at this point in the argument to defend the particular hypothetical agreement that I present in *Morals by Agreement*. Neither the principle of minimax relative concession nor, more relevant here, the revised proviso, is at issue. I shall turn to these in Section III. Rather, I am concerned with the underlying question – why appeal to hypothetical agreement at all? If morality is to be related to rational choice, then surely, given the arguments I have just presented, an actual-agreement theory, rather than a hypothetical-agreement theory, affords the linkage.

But as the status quo proves unstable when it comes into conflict with what would be agreed to, so what would be agreed to proves unstable when it comes into conflict with what would have been agreed to in an appropriate presocial context. For as existing principles must seem arbitrary insofar as they do not correspond to what a rational person would accept, so what such a person would accept in existing circumstances must seem arbitrary in relation to what she would accept in a presocial condition.

Think of moral principles as constituting that part of the structure of practices and institutions, constitutive of a society, that requires individual constraint. Now in an ongoing society, the principles, and more generally the structure of institutions and practices, that would obtain agreement will reflect the existing character of the society, insofar as this affects, as it does and must, the negotiating powers of the individual members. But the existing character of the society is not itself the product of rational agreement. Thus, if the principles resulting from agreement differ from those previously accepted, as we may suppose they will, each person will view the choice of constraining principles as itself determined in part by the very principles supplanted by the choice, and so by principles whose rationality, as constraints, has been called into question and found wanting. And this now calls the rationality of the agreed principles into question. In undermining the moral status quo, the newly agreed moral constraints undermine themselves. Finding good reason to reject constraints that do not command their agreement, the members of society find equally good reason to reject constraints that command their agreement only because of the effect of other constraints that they have good reason to reject.

To escape this self-undermining process, rational persons will revert from actual to hypothetical agreement, considering what principles they would have agreed to from an initial position not structured by arbitrary constraints. To be sure, the implementation of such agreement may be expected to meet with greater obstacles than the implementation of actually agreed principles. For in abstracting from the actual situation of persons, we must expect that hypothetical agreement will yield principles that have even greater adverse effects, on some individuals, than actual agreement, and we must also expect that such persons will have greater resources to protect themselves. For they have those resources that they would retain in the outcome of actual agreement but lose in hypothetical agreement. Nevertheless, I suggest that, once awareness of what persons would have agreed to, apart from the arbitrary contingencies of actual society, becomes known, existing institutions and practices in contravention of those agreements will be destabilized, so that society will move in the direction of those constraints that are not self-undermining.

(4) But have I really answered the objection, that my argument assumes a concern that forward-looking utility-maximizers will not or, at least, need not have? Am I not importing into the argument certain widely held moral assumptions that would, at least plausibly, be effective in destabilizing con-travening arrangements among those who subscribed to the assumptions, but which my theory would lead rational persons to reject? Is not my attempt to bootstrap our way from rational choice to morality itself vitiated by the use of moral bootstraps?

To answer this objection, and to reinforce the move from actual to hypothetical agreement, I need to defend the admissibility of appealing to equal rationality in arguing from rational choice to morality. Harman in particular has found this appeal unconvincing. And I should admit, at the outset of my discussion, that were I to become convinced that an appeal to equal rationality was either a concealed moral appeal, or inadmissible on some other ground, then I should have to abandon much of the core argument of *Morals by Agreement*.

Let me try to motivate an appeal to equal rationality initially by a discussion of the apparent indeterminacy of rationality in bargaining situations in which equilibrium considerations do not decide among the members of a range of Pareto-optimal outcomes. Pareto-optimality is the property possessed by an outcome if no feasible alternative is better for some persons and no worse for any person. In bargaining situations, agents select from a range of Pareto-optimal outcomes, and are not constrained in their selection by a compliance requirement that would make it necessary for the chosen outcome to be in prior equilibrium, i.e., the outcome of best reply strategies available to the agents in advance of the bargaining. (In some treatments of bargaining, it is assumed that any outcome is enforceable in the sense that, once it is selected, strategies will then, in virtue of its selection, be available to the agents that are mutual best replies. But for me, compliance with bargaining outcomes gives rise to a problem since I do not assume this; I assume that persons may rationally agree to an outcome even though some may be able profitably to defect from the outcome given compliance by the others.) How are rational persons, each seeking to maximize her own utility, to select from such an unconstrained range? Each will no doubt propose an outcome favorable to herself, and each proposal will, on the face of it, seem to have as much and as little to be said for it as any other – i.e., that agreement on it would leave each person as well-off as possible, given the payoffs to the others.[4]

The bargaining problem can be solved, in my view, only by introducing an equal rationality assumption. Given a no-agreement outcome, each person recognizes that she would be better off at any strictly superior Pareto-optimal outcome. But it is not therefore rational for her to agree to any such outcome. Call those outcomes in the Pareto-optimal range that are strictly superior to the no-agreement point *admissible*. And suppose that there is an admissible outcome that is enormously profitable to some individual. Then it is not rational for her to agree to another outcome, even though it is admissible, if it is only marginally profitable to her but enormously profitable to one or more of her fellow bargainers. For

---

[4] This problem seems to plague social choice, in which the attempt to impose plausible conditions on a choice set, given that these conditions are to define a non-empty choice set for any finite set of individual preference orderings over any finite number of alternatives, leads to including the entire range of Pareto-optimal outcomes in the choice set.

intuitively, this divides the proceeds from bargaining in a way that is more advantageous to those fellows than to her, and it is not rational for her to accept less advantage.

Why not? Well, suppose it were. Suppose that it is rational for Jane to accept less advantage from a bargain (where advantage is related in some manner to the outcome of no agreement) than John. Then it is not rational for John to accept less advantage than Jane. Again, why not? Given that John is a utility-maximizer, it is not rational for him to accept less than he can get, assuming that others are rational, and since he can get more advantage than Jane, even though Jane is rational, and since the greater his advantage the more favorable to him the outcome, then it is not rational for him to accept less. So (by hypothesis) it is rational for Jane to accept less advantage than John, but (given this hypothesis) not rational for John to accept less advantage than Jane. What difference is there, between Jane and John, that would permit this? Jane and John are similarly characterized as semantic representers and utility-maximizers. Nothing in this characterization enables us to distinguish Jane from John in the way needed by the hypothesis. So the hypothesis fails. It is not rational for Jane to accept less advantage than John.

Here I have appealed to equal rationality. Since Jane and John are similarly characterized in those respects relevant to rationality, what is rational for Jane must, other things equal, be rational for John. Now this is not to say that, as actual persons, Jane and John need be equally rational in their behavior. Jane may have been brought up to believe that, like it or not, women should always defer to men. And so she may think that it is rational for her to accept less advantage than John, but not vice versa. But her thinking this does not make it so. Jane's impaired rationality does not affect what is rational for her, but only what she thinks rational. John could be less rational than Jane in a quite different way, in being less able to ascertain his best course of action; thus, Jane might be able to impose less advantage on him by persuading him that he will benefit from what is in fact a poor bargain. But this does not affect what is rational for him, but only his ability to ascertain and act on what is rational. What is rational for Jane and John alike is to accept a bargain that is no less advantageous than it is for the other.

Now determining the comparative degree of advantage in a bargain without treating individual utilities as themselves interpersonally comparable is a matter I treat in *Morals by Agreement* by introducing the ideas of relative concession and relative benefit. I shall not repeat that here, since it would take us into that third level of specification of contractarian moral theory that I am leaving aside in this part of my reply. For our present purpose, all we need note is that an equal rationality requirement enables us to select from the many admissible outcomes one that, in being equally advantageous to each bargainer, is rational for each to accept. If anyone had reason to accept a less than equally advantageous outcome, then some other person would have no reason to accept anything short of a more than equally advantageous outcome, and equal rationality would be violated.

How does an appeal to equal rationality move us from actual to hypothetical agreement? Rational persons will accept an agreement only insofar as they perceive it to be equally advantageous to each. To be sure, each would be happy to accept an agreement more advantageous to herself than to her fellows, but since no one will accept an agreement perceived to be less advantageous, agents whose rationality is a matter of common knowledge will recognize the futility of aiming at or holding out for more, and minimize their bargaining costs by coordinating at the point of equal advantage. Now the extent of advantage is determined in a twofold way. First, there is advantage internal to the agreement. In this respect, the expectation of equal advantage is assured by procedural fairness. The step from existing moral principles to those resulting from actual agreement takes rational persons to a procedurally fair situation, in which each perceives the agreed principles to be ones which it is equally rational for all to accept, given the circumstances in which agreement is reached. But those circumstances themselves may be called into question insofar as they are perceived to be arbitrary – the result, in part, of compliance with constraining principles that do not themselves ensure the expectation of equal advantage, and so do not reflect the equal rationality of the complying parties. To neutralize this arbitrary element, moral principles, to be fully acceptable, must be conceived as constituting a possible outcome of a hypothetical agreement under circumstances that are unaffected by principles that themselves lack full acceptability. Equal advantage demands consideration of external circumstances as well as internal procedures.

But what is the practical import of this argument? It would be absurd to claim that it has magical efficacy, overturning the established moral and social order at one blow. It would be irrational for anyone to abandon resources, or to give up principles, simply because he comes to realize that they afford him more than he could expect from pure rational agreement with his fellows. And it would be irrational for anyone to accept a long-term utility loss, simply because she comes to realize that disposing herself to comply with existing constraining principles would afford her less than she could expect from pure rational agreement. Nevertheless, I want to argue that these realizations do transform, or perhaps bring to the surface, the character of the relationships between persons that are maintained by the existing constraints, so that they become recognized as coercive. These realizations constitute, if you like, the elimination of false consciousness, and they result from a process of rational reflection that brings persons into what, in my theory, is the parallel of Jürgen Habermas's ideal speech situation.[5] Without an argument to defend themselves in open dialogue with their fellows, those who are more than equally advantaged can hope to maintain their privileged position only if they can coerce their fellows into accepting it. And this may of course be possible. But coercion is not agreement, and it lacks any inherent stability.

Stability plays a key role in linking rational choice to contractarian morality. Aware of the benefits to be gained from constraining principles, rational persons will seek principles that invite stable compliance. Now compliance with agreed principles is stable if each person considers both that the terms of agreement are sufficiently favorable to herself that it is rational for her to accept them, and that they are not so favorable to others that it would be rational for them to accept terms less favorable to them and more favorable to herself. An agreement affording equally favorable terms to all thus invites, as no other can, stable compliance.

My discussion here is intended to answer the objections that Harman and others have raised to my use of equal rationality. I have offered only an oblique answer to Harman, since his particular arguments move between two of the levels of specificity that I have distinguished – between a general worry about the relevance of equal rationality, and so ultimately of agreement, to rational choice, and more specific and, for all I have yet said, possibly valid worries about my particular appeals to equal rationality, to defend the principle of minimax relative concession and the revised Lockean proviso. I shall return to these appeals in due course. But here I want to conclude my general examination of the relation between rational choice and contractarian morality.

Moral principles constrain straightforwardly maximizing behavior. The only general rationale such principles can be given turns on their role in making interaction mutually more beneficial, and the consequent possibility that each person may find her opportunities for individually beneficial interaction improved by being disposed to comply with them. Once the role and rationale of moral principles come to be fully recognized, stable and unforced compliance with them is possible only insofar as they can be considered to be objects of an agreement that it would be equally rational for each person to make. Thus, to provide principles for rational choice – principles with which rational persons comply in their choices – morality must be itself the object of a rational agreement. The two

---

[5] As Raymond Geuss characterizes it, the ideal speech situation is one "of absolutely uncoerced and unlimited discussion between completely free and equal human agents." See Raymond Geuss, *The Idea of a Critical Theory: Habermas & the Frankfurt School* (Cambridge: Cambridge University Press, 1981), p.65.

seemingly conflicting ways in which rational choice enters our theory of morality are thus linked.

II

(1) The papers in this volume range very widely over the issues I discuss in *Morals by Agreement*. To do full justice to such a wealth of critical comments far exceeds my powers, and even if it did not, would exceed the patience of any reader, since my reply would easily grow to the length of the combined critiques. I begin more detailed discussion, then, by recognizing the selectivity and brevity of my treatment.

Let me consider first, the idea that utility, the quantity to be maximized by rational agents, is to be understood as a measure of considered preference. Without challenging the underlying maximizing conception of practical rationality, both Kurt Baier and James Fishkin raise questions about my account of what is to be maximized.

Consider two states of affairs (types), instantiations of which might be alternatives one to the other, and might be within the power of some agent to bring about. Observing the agent's choice behavior in situations in which instantiations of the two states of affairs are alternatives, we infer his preference for one over the other. Equally, listening to the agent's remarks about the two states of affairs, we infer his preference for one over the other. We infer, in each case, an ordering to the states of affairs. If the two orderings coincide, well and good. If not, we have yet to discern his preference.

If we observe only the agent's choices, then we normally assume that the ordering we infer from it represents his preference. We may of course be mistaken; the agent may, as Baier recognizes, be a victim of weakness of will. Again, if we observe only the agent's remarks, we normally assume that the ordering we infer represents his preference. And we may be mistaken; the agent may be insincere, or may deceive himself. We can guard against these errors by observing both the agent's choices and his remarks – although, of course, if he prefers to mislead us about his preference over the two states of affairs to acting in accordance with that preference he can do so. But in many cases we have no ground to suspect that our limited evidence is misleading.

Baier supposes that what matters, from the agent's point of view, is to settle his preference (and so to be in a positon to express it), and then to choose in accordance with it. Insofar as he is rational, deciding his attitude determines his behavior. It would be irrational, Baier thinks, for the agent to proceed in the reverse direction, to bring the determination of his attitudinal preference into line with his past or anticipated choice. Why so?

John expresses a preference for blondes but consistently chooses brunettes. Here we may think that actions speak louder than words. And John, brought to awareness of his choices, may agree. Whether we say that he revises his attitudes, or that he corrects his previously mistaken judgment of his attitudes, John decides in favor of his behavioral preference. The agent is also an observer, and indeed, he could not be a rational agent without the capacity to reflect on his own behavior, and so to be aware of it as an observer. And from this perspective, an agent, finding his choices and attitudes in conflict, may find either or both in need of revision or reformulation. But the resolution reached by the agent, reflecting on his initial attitudes and past choices, is of course itself primarily attitudinal, so that Baier is right to defend "the dependence of the rationality of choices on their conformity with attitudes" (*Supra*, p.33), if this is understood as a defense of *considered* preference as the basis of rational choice.

Baier distinguishes between prima facie preferences and enacted concrete preferences. But I am not persuaded that this affords a perspicuous mode of classification. Suppose I prefer eating an apple to eating a pear. How shall I classify my preference? I understand it as a preference for any concrete state of affairs in which I eat an apple to any concrete state of affairs in which I eat a pear, given that the world remains relatively unchanged except in those respects necessary for the states of affairs to come about (so that, for example, I do not acquire an allergy to apples), and the two states of affairs are normal (so that, for example, the apple is not poisoned), and similar except in those respects necessary for the different characterizations to apply (so that, for example, the comparison is not between eating an apple when sated and eating a pear when hungry). The preference need not be stable nor long-lived, as with Baier's prima facie preferences, but it is not restricted to a particular occasion, as with his enacted concrete preferences.

If preferences are conceived in the way I have very loosely sketched, is their measure a plausible candidate for what the rational person endeavors to maximize? Baier argues that if "preference is contrary to what I regard as a compelling reason, I act irrationally" (*Supra*, p.38). Practical reasoning, he insists, enters into our reflection on preferences: "Instead of determining what is rational and what irrational choice on the basis of what we prefer, we have to say that rational choice is the maximization of the measure of rational preference, which involves reflecting on the preferences we have, which in turn involves asking ourselves what we have the best reason for doing, which requires us to operate with and according to what we regard as the best reasons, quite irrespective of what we *find* ourselves preferring after reflection, and it may require us to change or ignore these preferences" (*Supra*, p.38).

But what is involved in asking ourselves what we have the best reason for doing? In my view reasons must be preferentially derived, so that we typically find, by reflecting on our preferences, what our reasons are. Other things equal, I have best reason to do what I most prefer. Of course other things may not be equal, and a person may have reasons to act counterpreferentially; I insist that moral constraint rests on such reasons. But it is a central tenet of my moral theory that these reasons are themselves preferentially derived; constraints on maximizing activity require a maximizing justification. That all reasons are preferentially based, directly or indirectly, is implicit in my insistence that the rational person acts to maximize her utility, treated as the measure of her considered preference. That preference must, as I mentioned above, be considered indicates another way in which one can have reason to act counterpreferentially; one may have reason to act contrary to one's actual occurrent preferences given that, were one adequately to reflect, one would change those preferences. I may unthinkingly prefer to go to a film tonight rather than to cogitate on Baier's arguments, whereas were I to reflect, I should come to prefer the latter; I have, then, reason to choose contrary to my present preference.

But Baier supposes that I may have reasons of a different kind. For someone may believe "that it is *contrary to reason* to do anything that seriously harms . . . health" (*Supra*, p.37). And this reason does not seem to be preference-based. She may initially prefer to smoke, but reflecting on her preference, she asks herself what she has best reason for doing, and judges that it is contrary to reason to do anything, such as smoking, that seriously harms her health. If her preference is to be rational, or a basis for rational action, she must revise it. But Baier seems to me to get things the wrong way round, in supposing that in reflecting on our preferences we ask ourselves what we have best reason for doing. Rather, as I have said, in reflecting on our preferences we find what we have best reason for doing, i.e., what we prefer in an appropriately considered manner. Reflecting on her preference to smoke, she realizes that it is harmful to her health, and this affects her attitude, so that she does not in a considered way prefer what is harmful to health, even though her craving for a cigarette is undiminished. She may still smoke, but her smoking now simply reveals a behavioral preference that is not only unconsidered, but contrary to her considered attitudinal preference, and so one that she recognizes as irrational, a manifestation of weakness of will. If, after full and informed reflection, she retains a favorable attitude overall towards smoking, then although she may agree that she has *a* reason not to smoke, she may correctly deny that she has best or sufficient reason.

Baier rightly rejects the view that "Rationality does not consist in those concrete preferences, whatever they may be, that one happens to end up with after sufficient reflection" (*Supra*, p.40). For concrete preferences, to use Baier's terminology, are revealed in one's behavior, and this may be determined by inclinations that reflection proves powerless to affect. Inclinations may be physiologically based in a way that quite escapes one's conscious or deliberate control. Thus, after full consideration, one may come to a preference on which one fails to act, revealing one's weakness of will, and so one's practical irrationality. But the alternative to the view that a rational preference is not what emerges after reflection in one's *inclinations* and so in one's actual choices, need not be the view that a rational preference is what accords "*with the judgmental outcome of these reflections*" (*Supra*, p.40), where this is understood to involve a judgment about one's reasons for acting. Rather, a rational preference is what emerges in one's *attitudes* after reflection.

To be sure, there are no doubt persons who do ask themselves, in reflecting on their preferences, what they have reason to prefer. But I know no plausible account of what such reasons could be, if we suppose that they are to be discerned independently of reflective preferences and serve as a guide for them, save where, as I have already mentioned, they are preferentially-based constraints on preference-fulfillment of the kind that I identify with morality. Baier endeavors, at the end of his very rich paper, to begin to offer an account of these preference-independent reasons, by introducing the commonsense suggestion "that it is rational to follow what are generally regarded as reasons and how weighty they are, rather than ignore this and judge the matter on the basis of one's own independent reflections, because the public system of reasons has the backing of the experience and wisdom of many generations" (*Supra*, p.44). Now the possibility of public advice, which a person will normally want to take into account in reflecting on her preferences, need not be doubted. But that this advice directly provides reasons for acting seems to me mistaken. Rather, it takes the form of judgments about those things that persons, given the aims they commonly have, come to find fulfilling, and so to prefer. I reflect on such advice, and what I then prefer constitutes a more adequately considered preference, and so more a fully rational basis, for my choices. But it is only insofar as it becomes incorporated into my preferences that the advice actually provides practical reasons. To insist that such advice provides reasons for acting, and provides *me* with reasons for acting, whether or not on reflection it informs my preferences, seems to require an appeal to some objective good, or some objectively rational end, which Baier sensibly does not defend, and which I reject as mystifying, rather than clarifying, our understanding of rationality and morality.

(2) Recognizing that my remarks are at best only the beginning of a reply

to Baier, I turn to Fishkin's objections, which in part take up where Baier's leave off. Fishkin is concerned with preferences as the basis of rational, or more explicitly of moral, action because of what he calls the indoctrination problem. He does not discuss this problem at length, but claims that my insistence that preferences be considered is insufficient to prevent preferences from being the effect of indoctrination, and then argues that indoctrinated preferences do not provide a moral or rational basis for choice. Thus Fishkin wants to lay down requirements on the conditions for preference formation to rule out the fact that "some preferences seem morally suspect as the basis for choice" (*Supra*, p.54).

I agree with Fishkin that some preferences are indeed suspect. And I agree that it is possible to interpret my requirement that preferences be considered in such a way that it does not rule out these suspect cases, for it may be that the bizarre preferences held by the brainwashed members of some sect might well prove stable under experience and reflection, as these might be understood. But not as I understand them. And Fishkin clearly misrepresents my position in claiming that "The criteria for considered preferences . . . are only given . . . for preference maintenance (stability) and consistency with behavior – provided that those preferences survive whatever questioning or scrutiny the person cares to engage in" (*Supra*, p.54). I insist that the preferences be held in a considered way, and this is not a matter of what consideration the person cares to give, but what would in fact survive adequate experience and sufficient reflection – admittedly vague standards but not dependent on individual whim.

Furthermore, I insist on the self-critical dimension of practical rationality, so that rational persons must have a capacity for reflection, which I characterize as "a full self-critical capacity, so that they may subject their preferences to reflective assessment, and alter them . . . in the light of that assessment" (*Morals by Agreement*, p.324). Now this is characteristically lacking in the brainwashed or indoctrinated individuals described by Fishkin. They have failed to develop, or have been deprived of, a capacity for self-critical reflection. They are not autonomous, and are therefore not fully rational.

Hence, I do not think that my account is vulnerable to the indoctrination problem. It is true that I do not lay down conditions on the process of preference formation, but this process does not seem to me what is important. How I came by my preferences does not matter, as long as I am free self-critically to examine and revise them. To be sure, some processes of preference formation may eliminate any self-critical capacity; they would then be ruled out but ruled out not in themselves but for their effects. I do not need further conditions, over and above the requirement of self-critical reflection, to escape Fishkin's worry about indoctrination.

I agree, then, that "The first question to raise about the state is . . . whether . . . it is possible for *us*, in some reasonable fashion, to evaluate *it*" (*Supra*, p.61). Fishkin insists that authority is legitimate only in a "*self-reflective political culture* . . . that . . . subjects its supporting rationales to widespread, conscientious criticism" (*Supra*, pp.61–2). Now this, I believe, is fully captured by the essentially just society, as I sketch it. For it ensures the autonomy of its members, and its institutions and practices are designed to accommodate themselves to all persons, whatever their particular capacities and preferences may be. Such a society provides for its own continual reshaping in the light of the changing concerns of its members. Thus, it opens itself not merely to their evaluations, but to any consequent demands for redirection.

A fully rational individual will choose essential justice, for she will realize that without it, she can never be sure that her social environment will be fairly responsive to the preferences that emerge from her self-critical reflection. And an essentially just society can allow and indeed encourage individuals to develop a fully self-critical capacity, because in setting no aims beyond those set by the preferences of its members, and in being fully and fairly responsive to those aims, its existence is in no way threatened by the needs for social change that emerge from their reflection.

Fishkin does not claim that a self-reflective political culture is sufficient for solving the legitimacy problem. For the existence of such a culture does not ensure responsiveness to the demands that emerge from individual reflection. But the essentially just society adds, to Fishkin's requirement of self-reflection, the capacity to change in accordance with the demands generated by self-reflection, and thus proves sufficient, and not merely necessary, to ensure legitimacy.

(3) Fishkin raises a second problem for my argument, and more generally for contemporary liberal theory, the jurisdiction problem. This "is the issue of which hypothetical starting point is the morally relevant status quo from which to evaluate rival [social] principles" (*Supra*, p.54). To avoid what he considers an undecidable conflict among different proposals for the starting point, Fishkin himself defends actual against hypothetical agreement, in the context of his self-reflective political culture. His intention is not to derive a principle or set of principles as fully determinate as those proposed by such defenders of hypothetical agreement as Rawls and myself. Rather, his aim is to entrench those requirements of liberty that constitute the core of liberal theory, by showing, not that they would be objects of agreement, actual or hypothetical, but rather that they are necessary conditions for the ongoing process of agreement (or perhaps of acceptance) required in a self-reflective culture.

But Fishkin's conception of actual agreement is an unorthodox one. He says, "When the situation for choosing principles is the one in which those who must abide by the principles live together as an ongoing enterprise, I will classify it as an 'actual' choice situation" (*Supra*, p.55). But what seems relevant to Fishkin's proposed solution to the jurisdiction problem is not that the choice situation is the one in which the choosers actually live, but that the choice situation is one in which the choosers are free to engage, and to continue to engage, in "continuing, collective self-evaluation at the level of fundamental principles" (*Supra*, p.61), because they live in a self-reflective political culture. Such a situation is, of course, free from the biasing or coercive features of most actual choice situations. In effect, Fishkin argues that social principles are legitimate only if they are agreed to under certain highly ideal conditions. Now this is not strictly to propose a hypothetical contractarian theory, since Fishkin does not claim that social principles are legitimate for us if we would agree to them under the ideal conditions of a self-reflective political culture. Legitimacy, properly speaking, exists only within such a culture. But if we are to suppose that Fishkin's analysis has any application to our concern with legitimacy in our society, then surely we shall treat him as proposing a hypothetical contractarianism – our social principles are legitimate to the extent to which they would be required as conditions of or accepted in a self-reflective political culture.

Fishkin's position seems to me essentially akin to that of Jürgen Habermas. His appeal to a self-reflective political culture parallels Habermas's appeal to the ideal speech situation (see note 5 *supra*). And just as Habermas has a transcendental justification of those conditions needed to maintain the ideal speech situation, so Fishkin has a transcendental justification of those conditions needed to maintain a self-reflective political culture. A legitimate society can only be one that maintains the conditions under which its legitimacy can be assessed.

Although the parallel to Habermas's ideal speech situation is one that I applaud, and believe to be present in my own theory, yet I think that Fishkin's – and Habermas's – attempt to provide a transcendental deduction is a mistake. I do not deny the substantive claim that a legitimate society will indeed maintain the conditions under which its legitimacy can be assessed. But legitimacy derives from agreement; a legitimate society is one that would result from a fully voluntary agreement among rational persons. Of course, we may find that the best test for legitimacy is to appeal to a noncoercively based agreement among actual persons, and, knowing this, rational persons would agree to social arrangements that permitted, and indeed encouraged, this test. But maintaining such arrangements is not itself the basis of legitimacy.

In my theory, the requirement that a self-reflective political culture be maintained derives, not only or perhaps even primarily from the concern of each person to engage in continuing assessment of the principles, practices, and institutions of her society, but especially from her concern that her considered preferences be satisfied as she, her fellows, and their environment all continue to change. The need for continuing adaptation, rather than continuing assessment, is foremost.

III

(1) I shall return to Fishkin's concern with the adequacy of the revised Lockean proviso to eliminate coercion from bargaining or agreement. I want first to examine my account of the bargaining process itself, and my defense of the principle of minimax relative concession. Bargainers find themselves faced with a range of possible outcomes, any one of which they may attain by agreeing on it. The strategy of my account is to show how, given a well-defined initial positon, bargainers can use their common knowledge of their rationality to select a unique member of this range which is Pareto-optimal and Pareto-superior to that initial position. But the principle of minimax relative concession is only one of several proposals to resolve the bargaining problem, and Gilbert Harman insists that there is no distinctively salient principle for resolving it (*Supra*, p.8).

Consider, then, this defense of minimax relative concession. Suppose that the solution is to depend on the initial positon and the ideal point – the point determined by each person's maximum claim. Consider then a bargaining situation in which, for each individual, the utility of the initial position is 0, and the utility of his claim is 1. Then the agreed outcome must afford each individual the same utility, since the individuals are, for the purposes of the bargain, in indistinguishable positons. But given that the solution also passes the basic tests in the preceding paragraph, so that it is Pareto-optimal and invariant with respect to positive linear transformations of the bargainers' utility functions, then the solution is easily shown to be that yielded by minimax relative concession.

Now this is of course not the last word on the matter. For one might challenge the supposition that the solution be determined by the initial position and the ideal point. One might, that is, challenge the assumption that the solution depends on each bargainer focusing on what she has at stake in the situation, as measured by her possible gain from her initial bargaining positon. But such a challenge does not seem plausible to me. For a rational utility-maximizer lacks comparative concerns, and there seems then nothing other than her possible gain for her to consider.

Another way of reaching this conclusion, closer to the line of argument developed in *Morals by Agreement*, is this. Consider the range of outcomes that are Pareto-optimal and strictly superior to the initial bargaining positon. And suppose that there is no problem of compliance, so that agreement on some member of this range suffices to bring it about. Then if it were not rational for each person to agree on some member of the range, we should have to conclude that it was rational for persons to end up at the initial position, the residual outcome of nonagreement, or at some nonoptimal outcome, in either case leaving every person worse off than need be. But this is absurd; everyone can see the cost of nonoptimality. Hence, there must be at least one member of the range on which it is rational for everyone to agree; let such a member be X. It cannot, then, be rational for any person to agree on any member of the range affording him less than he gets from X, since he can not consider it rational to agree to less than he could get from the rational agreement of the others. But since the range contains only Pareto-optimal outcomes, every alternative to X affords some person less than he would get from X. And so no alternative to X can be rationally agreed to by everyone. Hence, there cannot be more than one outcome on which it is rational for everyone to agree. X must be the unique object of rational agreement; how is it to be determined? Suppose each person assigns a utility of 1 to her preferred outcome in the range, and 0 to her initial position. Then, since there is nothing to distinguish the persons, we must suppose that it is rational for them to agree on that outcome which, given these utility assignments, yields each the same numerical utility. But then, given the invariance of rational agreement under transformations of each individual's utilities, it must be rational for them to agree on the outcome yielded by minimax relative concession.

In I.4 *supra*, I defended in a general way the appeal to equal rationality. Here I have been concerned with the particular appeal that grounds the principle of minimax relative concession. One could agree that the bargaining problem was to be solved in terms of the equal rationality of the bargainers without supposing that minimax relative concession provided the solution. But if one also agrees that the outcome must depend on the initial bargaining positon and the ideal point, then equal rationality immediately yields my solution.

(2) Minimax relative concession (MRC) is intended to be applicable, at least in principle, to any bargaining situation. But in *Morals by Agreement* my primary concern is to propose it as a test of the fairness and rationality of moral and social institutions and practices. A just society affords its members the benefits of social cooperation, the net social product, shared among them according to principles and procedures that would have gained their agreement in an *ex ante* bargain conforming to minimax

relative concession. I agree with Russell Hardin that "A Hayekian would blanch at the very notion of the required data collection" for a literal application of the principle (*Supra*, p.7). But this does not prevent us from considering whether an actual society can plausibly be judged to approximate to its requirements.

Hardin claims that, where side payments are possible (or utility is fully transferable), "MRC produces egalitarianism. As any reader must recognize, this does not seem to be Gauthier's sense of his own theory" (*Supra*, p.68). And of course it is not, since, as he notes, I suppose that each person's claim to the net social product "is bounded by the extent of his participation" (*Morals by Agreement*, p.134), and different persons participate unequally. Can Hardin be right that I am nevertheless committed by MRC to egalitarianism? I think not.

Consider this simple situation. A, B, and C are potential partners in cooperative interactions that yield fully transferable utilities as their products. We may then assign each such interaction a value, representing its total utility, which may be divided in any way between those involved. Let the value to each of independent action be 0; we represent this as $v\{A\} = v\{B\} = v\{C\} = 0$. Let the values of the possible paired interactions be as follows: $v\{A,B\} = 2$, $v\{A,C\} = 1$, $v\{B,C\} = 3$. And let the value if all three work together be: $v\{A,B,C\} = 5$. We assume that each person can be involved in only one interaction. Thus, overall there are five possibilities: (i) no cooperation, with a total value of 0; (ii)–(iv) cooperation involving any two persons who share the value of their particular interaction; (v) cooperation among all three, who share the total value of 5.

To apply MRC, we determine each person's base point utility, evidently 0, and each person's claim. Now determining claims in interactions involving more than two persons does not prove to be as straightforward a matter as I once believed. But it seems clear that each may claim at least what is added to the social product by his presence. Thus A claims $v\{A,B,C\} - v\{B,C\} = 2$; similarly, B claims 4, and C, 3. MRC then divides the 5 possible units of transferable utility, 1.11 to A, 2.22 to B, and 1.67 to C.

A second example will illustrate my hestitation in pronouncing on the way to determine claims. As before, let $v\{A\} = v\{B\} = v\{C\} = 0$. But now let $v\{A,B\} = 0$, and $v\{A,C\} = v\{B,C\} = v\{A,B,C\} = 1$. If A claims $v\{A,B,C\} - v\{B,C\}$, then his claim is 0, as is B's; C claims, and MRC gives her, the full unit of transferable utility. Yet C needs the cooperation of either A or B, and indeed would be required by MRC to divide the unit of transferable utility equally with either of them, were the other absent. A promising, but let me emphasize, very tentative proposal, would be to treat the three ways of capturing the cooperative surplus (interaction between A

and *C*, between *B* and *C*, and among all three) as equal likely, and take each person's overall claim as the sum of her probability-weighted claims for each interaction. *A* and *B* would then each claim 1/3; *C* would claim 1. MRC would divide the unit of transferable utility .2 to each of *A* and *B*, and .6 to *C*.

However this may be, the essential point is that the claims of the agents differ markedly in these situations, and the claims affect the outcome determined by MRC. Fully transferable utility does not entail egalitarianism. Furthermore, if we take each person's contribution to be proportional to what her presence adds to the net social product, then it is evident that MRC divides the social product in a way that reflects individual contributions.

This is unfortunately obscured by two-person situations. For if there are only two persons, then the presence of each is equally necessary for the total net social product, since it is simply what their joint interaction adds to what each could achieve alone. And so each claims the entire net product, and insofar as it is transferable, MRC divides it equally between them. If we then attempt to measure individual contributions in ways that reflect, not what the presence of each adds, in the given circumstances, to the net social product, but in ways that would be appropriate were alternative partners for cooperation available, then such equal division may *seem* unfair.

(3) At the beginning of his paper, Hardin claims that I present "a partial theory of distributive justice . . . because it applies only to the distribution of gains from joint endeavors" (*Supra*, p.65). And at the end he notes that if my theory "is to be applied continually at the margin to various social cooperations as we go along, it wants some justification for the status quo from which we begin" (*Supra*, p.74). But this is exactly what I endeavor to provide in offering the other component of a full solution to the bargaining problem, which is a specification of the initial bargaining positon. Minimax relative concession is only part of my theory of distributive justice; I turn now to the other part.

In appealing to a revised form of the Lockean proviso to constrain the initial bargaining position in relation to what, in Buchanan's terminology, would be the natural distribution, I have, at least in my own view, ventured on a far more precarious construction than in developing minimax relative concession or in arguing for constrained maximization. Buchanan, in characterizing his own enterprise, states that "I commence from the status quo distribution of rights and I do not apply criteria of justice to this distribution. My emphasis is almost exclusively placed on the *process* through which potential changes may be made, rather than on either the starting point or the end point of change" (*Supra*, p.85). I agree, of course, that the end point does not provide an independent basis for introducing considerations of justice. But how are we to understand Buchanan's view "that the contractarian exercise does not require rectification of prior injustices before application to relevant forward-looking questions" (*Supra*, p.87)? What is the status of prior injustices in Buchanan's theory? He insists that any process, historical or prospective, may be evaluated in terms of contractarian criteria of fairness. Hence, it would seem that we can identify prior injustices. But the evaluation of past processes would seem normatively idle, for Buchanan insists that were one to apply such an evaluation in rectificatory redistribution, then, viewed as a process, it would "involve violation of the contractarian . . . criteria for fairness," which apply to "potential changes from *that which exists*" (*Supra*, p.87). Is it, then, unjust to remedy injustice?

I shall not repeat my previous argument, which is in effect that failure to rectify past injustice destabilizes present arrangements. If I am right, then the evaluation of past processes in terms of justice is not normatively idle. My concern here is to defend the particular characterization of past injustice required by the revised proviso. Why is it that interactions are unjust if one person has bettered himself by worsening the position of another, where both bettering and worsening are to be judged against a no-interaction base line? And why, in the absence of prior agreement, are no other interactions unjust?

Fishkin considers the proviso too weak, in failing to eliminate what he calls "coercively structured bargaining situations" in which one party agrees to benefit the other only to avoid "*what both know to be reasonably expectable disaster*" (*Supra*, p.48). But why are such bargains morally suspect, unless the expectable disaster results from the actions of the other party, in which case the revised Lockean proviso will be violated? It would seem that the second party could have no reason to refrain from accepting benefits in return for what enables the first party to avoid disaster. It may be pure good luck on her part that she is able to provide the needed aid, and pure bad luck on the other party's part that he needs the aid that she can provide. But why is this morally objectionable?

There is, it seems to me, an answer to this question, but not one that will help Fishkin. Each of us may expect, *ex ante*, to do better in a society in which everyone aids those faced with disaster in ways that offer only moderate benefit to the parties giving aid. Hence, an obligation to afford aid on such terms may reasonably be expected to be one of the practices that constitutes social morality. Baier seems to suppose that such obligations, and other more fully Good Samaritan duties as he calls them, might be supported from the Archimedean point of impartiality but would not be part of a rational *ex ante* bargain about the terms of social interaction. But I see no divergence between the two perspectives of impartiality and of agreement; both, it seems to me, support practices in which the expected benefits of adherence by others outweigh one's own expected costs. When such a practice exists, it is clearly morally unconscionable for an individual to treat a situation in which she is able to give aid to avert disaster as if it were a simple bargaining situation. Here we have an instance in which the application of minimax relative concession at the macro-level will not result in mutually advantageous practices that themselves are structured as rational bargains.

But an agreement not to treat certain situations as if they were simple bargains does not affect the way in which the initial bargaining situation is determined. There is a gap between what would be mutually advantageous, and what would involve the taking of advantage. In the absence of agreement, it would be irrational not to maximize one's expectation of utility even though agreement rationally constrains such maximization. Similarly, in the absence of a practice of mutual assistance it would be irrational not to treat any particular instance in which assistance is required as one calling for bargaining, even though a practice of mutual aid rationally constrains such bargaining.[6]

I do not think that any attempt to strengthen the proviso is likely to succeed. The real question is whether it is not already too strong. Perhaps stability can be achieved despite a weaker constraint on the initial bargaining position. In defense of the proviso, however, I argue as follows. A stable society must be perceived as advantageous to each of its members, in a way that leaves each disposed to exercise neither his exit option nor what we may call his reform/revolution option – his option to try to improve his situation by a structural alteration in the society. Now I link the latter to equal rationality – to the recognition by each agent that the existing social structure is one that everyone would accept in a fully voluntary *ex ante* bargain, so that any alteration that he might wish to bring about could not be maintained except by coercion, or as a result of some advantage extraneous to the society itself. But to be fully voluntary a bargain must be freely entered by the participants. If, holding a gun to your head, I demand that we bargain over your goods, the ensuing agreement will not be fully voluntary, even if, treating those goods as the cooperative surplus, I am scrupulously fair in dividing them between us. And similarly,

[6] Before concluding my discussion of Fishkin, I should note that his three-person dinner party does not, as he supposes, indicate a way of bypassing violations of the proviso. Although he correctly notes that C does not violate the proviso in bargaining with B,A, in forcing B to choose between bargaining with C and being tortured, worsens B's situation and violates the proviso. And of course, if A and C were to collude in exchanging opportunities to extort money from dinner guests, then both would violate the proviso.

I maintain, if what we bargain over is partly determined by prior interaction which, since it leaves me better off and you worse off than the no-interaction baseline, cannot have been voluntarily entered into by you, then the ensuing agreement itself is to that extent not fully voluntary.

Among rational persons each concerned to maximize her own utility, stable social arrangements can only be those that constitute a "cooperative venture for mutual advantage," and the proviso may then be defended as a constraint necessary to ensure mutual advantage. Having said this, I propose to turn to other matters, fully aware that the question of the conditions of stability, and their relevance to both the proviso and the principle of minimax relative concession, need further attention. Indeed, if anyone is disposed to take *Morals by Agreement* as offering an agenda for further enquiry, this is one of the core questions that I hope and believe would be addressed.

IV

(1) To this point I have said nothing about my treatment of the market. In characterizing it as a morally free zone, I have of course focused on the operation of the market, or market process, and carefully distinguished this from the conditions of the market – its initial situation as determined by the endowments of those party to market interactions. Buchanan rightly notes that in my discussion I ignore pecuniary externalities, tacitly assuming that the noncompensated harms and benefits to which they give rise need not "invoke the application of some rational morality" (*Supra*, p.91). But more importantly, he suggests that, rather than treating the market as a morally free zone, to the extent to which its operation depends on persons voluntarily refraining from force and fraud, I should rather have recognized that market relationships offer "the exemplar of rational morality" (*Supra*, p.89).

This suggests a significant conceptual revision in my account of morality. Rather than treating it as a remedy for market failure, I might rather have introduced it initially as a condition for market success. Rather than treating, if only implicitly, the coincidence of equilibrium and Pareto-optimum found within the market as the normal form of interaction, so that morality becomes a constraint enabling us to approximate to that form when it is deplorably absent, I might instead have treated the coincidence as an exceptional form made possible only by the prior acceptance of a structure of constraints identifiable with a rational morality. In effect, morality would then be seen to transcend itself, to find a way of overcoming its directly constraining character, in making possible market interaction, in which each person could straightforwardly seek to maximize his utility.

This is an attractive way of reconceptualizing my understanding of morality and its social role, and one that may, indeed, yield a stronger argument against the view expressed by Glaucon that morality is only a necessary evil. Rather than seeing morality primarily as constraining us, we may see it as making possible a state of affairs in which the genuine absence of constraint is possible. For we may suppose that morality replaces the forcibly imposed external constraints found in the natural coercive relationships that develop among human beings, by voluntarily accepted internal constraints that not only reduce the need for coercion, but open up an area, albeit limited, of genuine freedom, this area being of course the market. Buchanan's eloquent account of "the spontaneous coordination properties of the market" as "the crowning discovery of the 18th century," in that their recognition eliminates "the necessity of pervasive and overriding political direction of individual activity" (*Supra*, p.89), is one that I want to endorse. He and I can agree that it is unfortunate that so much recent thought and practice has been devoted to inventing new ways in which pervasive and overriding political direction can be alleged to be necessary after all.

(2) I turn now to Buchanan's criticisms of my argument that, given "*defined and mutually respected initial rights* . . . it becomes rational for each person to adopt a cooperative strategy" (*Supra*, p.75). Here, he raises three major concerns. The first, paralleling in part an argument previously advanced against my earlier work by Edna Ullman-Margalit,[7] turns on the "definition of the community of strategic interaction" (*Supra*, p.79). In bargaining theory, the community is given and fixed, and one shows, or tries to show, the rationality of a cooperative strategy within that community. But how do we apply this argument when there is no given community? What will constitute cooperative behavior within a particular group may become noncooperative in a larger group.

Now I am not concerned with the relevance of the type of analysis I present to the explanation of existing patterns of cooperation. It may be that to the extent to which persons identify their situation as one in which there is a potential cooperative surplus, they are motivated to adopt a cooperative mode of behavior. If this is so, then questions about the definition of community are quickly resolved, but the normative significance of the behavior may be called into question, as Buchanan indeed notes. And it is with normative significance that I am concerned.

Here I would offer three points. First, given that several persons can, by interacting, achieve a cooperative surplus, cooperative behavior has value

---

[7] See Edna Ullman-Margalit, *The Emergence of Norms* (Oxford: Clarendon Press, 1977), pp.41–45.

for them. That it may have disvalue in relation to other persons need not be worrying.

Second, David Hume correctly describes the natural development of cooperative practices, beginning by noting that "Where mutual regards and forbearance serve to no manner of purpose, they would never direct the conduct of any reasonable man. . . . as each man is here supposed to love himself alone, and to depend only on himself and his own activity for safety and happiness, he would, on every occasion, to the utmost of his power, challenge the preference above every other being, to none of which he is bound by any ties, either of nature or of interest."[8] From this solitary state of affairs, Hume says, "But suppose the conjunction of the sexes to be established in nature, a family immediately arises; and particular rules being found requisite for its subsistence, these are immediately embraced; though without comprehending the rest of mankind within their prescriptions." The next step is to the union of several families, and then to "several distinct societies maintain[ing] a kind of intercourse for mutual convenience and advantage"; at each stage "the boundaries of justice still grow larger." Hume concludes that "History, experience, reason sufficiently instruct us in this natural progress of human sentiments, and in the gradual enlargement of our regards to justice, in proportion as we become acquainted with the extensive utility of that virtue." In other words, the bounds of the community within which cooperative practices flourish are set by our perceptions of mutual advantage.

But, and this is my third point, as the bounds of community expand, cooperative behavior among the members of some group is now constrained in just the way that directly maximizing individual behavior is constrained. And this I should have said in *Morals by Agreement*. Neither rationality nor morality endorses cooperation between the prisoners in the Prisoner's Dilemma, since nonconfession leads to an unfair and rationally unacceptable division of the fruits of cooperation within the larger society to which they belong. The appropriate bounds of particular communities are thus set in relation to the overall prospect of mutual advantage in interaction among rational beings. But this need not, and I believe does not in practice, justify a strictly universalistic morality. The constraints on behavior applying among all rational beings as such may be weak or even nonexistent, if the prospects of mutually beneficial cooperation are exhausted at the level of more particular groups. But given such prospects, strong moral constraints may exist among the members of those groups.

It may well be the case that there is no unique purely rational demarcation of communities that set boundaries to cooperative practices.

[8] David Hume, *An Enquiry Concerning the Principles of Morals*, 1751, Section III, Part I.

Historical accident then partially determines the appropriate bounds of community. And it is between historically grounded communities that the revised Lockean proviso can be seen to have significant normative implications, as indeed I suggest in *Morals by Agreement*. But to embark on that theme here would take me too far afield from Buchanan's critique.

(3) The boundaries of community demarcate the scope of cooperative practices. In setting them, we must take into account not only the advantage gained from the practice, but also the cost of compliance with it. And this gives rise to Buchanan's second concern with my argument for the adoption of a cooperative strategy. As he notes, if compliance with a cooperative practice is rational for an individual only if she can expect to do better than were all to ignore the practice so that each would seek independently to maximize his utility, then as the numbers of persons involved in the practice increases, the expectation that any one person will cooperate must also increase. But such an expectation would seem "to counter common sense notions about the way persons behave" (*Supra*, p.80).

Buchanan's criticism here would be decisive, if moral practices typically involved large-number interactions in which compliance by almost everyone was necessary for the outcome to be more beneficial than each could expect in the absence of the practice. But a typical moral practice, such as promising or truth-telling, is not of this kind. And such moral dispositions as honesty or benevolence, although disadvantageous to an individual in Hume's "society of ruffians,"[9] would seem to afford each adherent net benefit, in comparison with his prospects were no one so disposed, provided he may expect the disposition to be widespread but by no means universal. If tax revenues are wisely spent in the protective and productive ways suggested in Buchanan's *The Limits of Liberty*, then each may expect to do better voluntarily paying his taxes in circumstances in which most of his fellows do the same, than in a society in which everyone pays only what is coercively extracted from him. Coase-like bargaining is not an effective replacement for voluntary compliance with cooperative strategies, in the contexts typical of morality.

(4) Buchanan's third concern is to urge the role of "the moral entrepreneur," who "acting singly, can enforce the precepts of rational morality on others" (*Supra*, p.81). If it is rational to comply voluntarily with moral practices, may it not also be rational "to behave *retributively* toward those persons who violate the contractarian precepts?" (*Supra*, p.81). And indeed, I believe that it may. I say that "we should not suppose it is rational to dispose oneself to constrained maximization, if one does not also dispose

[9] *ibid.*

oneself to exclude straightforward maximizers from the benefits realizable by co-operation." (*Morals by Agreement*, p.180.) Retribution is a form of exclusion, and perhaps Buchanan is right to complain that I do not sufficiently emphasize the difference between retribution, which I endorse, and an initial threat strategy, which I suppose would be outlawed in any well-run society.

V

(1) Since my principal philosophical concern has always been the rationality of morality, I should not want to endorse Morris's claim that the identification of morality with those constraints that rational agents will agree to and comply with "is the least important part of Gauthier's project" (*Supra*, p.120). But the most interesting research project arising out of *Morals by Agreement* seems to me to focus on the implications for practical rationality of the distinction between straightforward and constrained maximization. Edward F. McClennen's paper raises important questions for this project, by comparing constrained maximization with his own conception of resolute choice.

The idea of resolute choice is perhaps most easily understood through an example. To borrow from Jon Elster and McClennen himself, consider Ulysses and the Sirens.[10] *Ex ante*, Ulysses prefers sailing past to stopping on their island, but he knows that when he hears their song, he will prefer stopping. Also *ex ante*, he prefers binding himself to the mast to stopping, although binding himself to the mast is in itself unattractive. *Myopic* Ulysses, considering only his present preferences, resolves to sail past, but succumbs to the Sirens' song. *Sophisticated* Ulysses, aware that he will succumb if he can, binds himself to the mast. *Resolute* Ulysses resolves to sail past and does so.[11]

Now it seems that myopic Ulysses is less rational than sophisticated Ulysses. For myopic Ulysses chooses in a way that, given information available to him about how he will respond to the Sirens, requires him to expect the worst, whereas sophisticated Ulysses expects the second-best outcome – sailing past, although bound. Resolute Ulysses, however, trumps sophisticated Ulysses; *ex ante* he expects the best outcome, and as he sails

[10] See Jon Elster, *Ulysses and the Sirens* (Cambridge: Cambridge University Press, 1979), and E.F. McClennen, "Prisoner's Dilemma and Resolute Choice" in Richmond Campbell and Lanning Sowden, eds., *Paradoxes of Rationality and Cooperation* (Vancouver: University of British Columbia Press, 1985), pp.94–104.

[11] For the distinction between myopic and sophisticated choice, see Peter Hammond, "Changing Tastes and Coherent Dynamic Choice", *Review of Economic Studies*, vol. 43 (1976), pp.159–173.

past despite his desire to linger with the Sirens, he can console himself with the thought that he is doing better than if he had bound himself to the mast. In terms of his preferences both before the voyage and on hearing the Sirens, resolute Ulysses does better than sophisticated Ulysses.

In the myth, resolute choice was not an option; the power of the Sirens' song overrode any attempt at resistance. And in conventional rational choice theory, resolute choice is not an option; maximizing rationality overrides any attempt at resistance. For if when Ulysses hears the sirens he prefers to stop on their island, then stopping is his rationally required course of action.

McClennen and I are unwilling to accept this conclusion. In conventional rational choice theory, preferences are always exogenously given. McClennen rejects this. He supposes that faced with a situation similar to that of Ulysses, a rational agent is capable of determining that *plan*, or sequence "of choices to be made over time and subject to various contingencies" (*Supra*, p.112), which, given his continuing concerns over the period covered by the plan, and not just his *ex ante* preferences at the time of adopting it, affords him the greatest expectation of benefit or utility, and then shaping his *ex post* preferences so that his later maximizing actions conform to the requirements of the plan. Rational Ulysses, in McClennen's account, develops a context dependent preference for sailing past the Sirens. But, of course, Ulysses does not develop this preference in a purely arbitrary way. As McClennen says, "What is characteristic of such an agent is that his *ex post* preferences among available actions are disciplined or shaped by what he judges, from the perspective of plans taken as wholes, to be the best plan to pursue" (*Supra*, p.112). Thus, McClennen can defuse the criticism that context dependent preferences are a merely *ad hoc* device to overcome an awkward implication of the maximizing conception of rationality.

Consider now the following Prisoner's Dilemma-like situation. Next week my crops will be ready for harvesting; the following week, yours will be ready; after the harvest season, I am retiring from farming, and have no expectation of meeting you again. Each of us does better if we work together than if he harvests his crops alone. But helping the other is in itself a cost and, when the time comes to harvest your crops, I can expect no benefit to offset my costs if I help you. Now I may plausibly reason that my best plan of action is to promise to aid you a fortnight hence in return for your aid next week, and to keep my promise, even though when the time comes, I will have nothing to gain by aiding you. I may believe that I am unlikely to convince you by any insincere promise, and so unlikely thereby to gain your assistance. Doing without your help is clearly disadvantageous. And offering you some surety, or posting bond with a third party, as a guarantee that I will help you, is costlier than simply making, and keeping, a promise. On McClennen's account, then, if I am a rational, resolute chooser, I will adopt the plan of promising aid in return for yours, and I will develop an *ex post*, context dependent preference for actually assisting you, so that I will keep my promise.

McClennen's account of resolute choice is more systematically developed than my conception of constrained maximization, and it has wider applicability – to problems of individual preference change, as well as those of interaction. In embracing straightforward maximization for individual decision making, I have, as I now realize, ignored preference change, and I should want to extend the scope of constrained maximization so that rational Ulysses falls within its embrace. So extended, is there a real difference between McClennen's resolute choice model and my model of constrained maximization? And if there is a difference, which model is to be preferred?

Although McClennen generously says, "I am not so concerned with whether my argument is better seen as a reinterpretation of Gauthier's argument or as a distinct argument" (*Supra*, p.117), he does however detect a weakness in constrained maximization that, he believes, resolute choice avoids. "The problem . . . is that expected utility calculations at the *ex ante* point (point of choosing dispositions) do not appear to suffice to determine how a rational agent will actually dispose himself with respect to future choice" (*Supra*, p.105). In adopting a disposition to constrain, an agent reasons parametrically, and "one who reasons parametrically at one point in time to the conclusion that he should adopt a certain disposition, will be disposed, it would seem, to reason parametrically also at some subsequent point of choice (in a situation to which the disposition chosen is to apply), and this will lead to choice inconsistent with the disposition that the agent putatively adopted at the *ex ante* choice point" (*Supra*, p.106). To avoid this, McClennen insists that "one must restructure the argument so as to avoid the appeal to parametric reasoning. More specifically, since what is central to parametric reasoning is that antecedently definable preferences for outcomes feasible at time t are controlling for rational choice at time t, it is precisely this assumption that must be challenged" (*Supra*, p.108). And we have seen how McClennen challenges it, by relating rational choices first to the selection of a plan, and then, within its framework, to context sensitive preferences shaped by the plan. I want to discuss these two features of resolute choice – the selection of a plan, and the formation of context sensitive preferences – in the following sections.

(2) McClennen says that "if one thinks of the self as separable into discrete timeslices, then a resolute approach – a commitment to chosen

plans – recommends itself on the grounds that each of the relevant time-slices can judge himself to be better off if the plan is adopted and followed than if no such plan is put into effect" (*Supra*, pp.112–3). Now the separation of the self into discrete timeslices seems to be related to preference change, so that we might initially suppose that preference is constant in each timeslice and varies between slices.

Recall Ulysses. We noted that resolute Ulysses does better than sophisticated Ulysses, whichever of his timeslices we consider. But suppose that the effect of the Sirens on Ulysses's preferences were more complex, leading him not only to prefer stopping on their island to all else, but also to prefer being bound to the mast to sailing freely past. If Ulysses adopts the plan of sailing past, then although carrying it out would best satisfy his *ex ante* preferences, it would yield the worst outcome *ex post*. If we suppose that a resolute approach must make both timeslices of Ulysses better off than they would otherwise be, then sailing past is ruled out despite its *ex ante* appeal. In this case, Ulysses can do no better than to bind himself to the mast, as sophisticated choice would direct.

If we now review the application of resolute choice in interaction situations, we face an evident problem. Suppose that the US prefers the status quo to world domination by the USSR, and world domination to nuclear war. Suppose also that the US believes that the best plan open to it, given its preferences, is to threaten nuclear war should the USSR take certain steps that could lead it to world domination. Adoption of the plan maximizes the US's *ex ante* expectation of utility. However, the plan requires the US to be willing, under possible conditions, to initiate nuclear war and so to bring about the worst outcome. In effect, should these conditions obtain, the plan will have failed, and the US would then prefer not to have adopted it. Is it rational to act on a failed plan, given that the plan could not have been sincerely adopted unless one were prepared so to act, and sincere adoption maximized one's *ex ante* expectation of utility? And if not, can one rationally adopt a plan that includes acting on it even if it fails?

What does a resolute approach require? Here there is no preference shift, analogous to that experienced by Ulysses. But there is a time shift in the evaluation of the plan. To see this, contrast the case of deterrence with our earlier example of harvesting. If I adopt the plan of promising aid to you provided you aid me, and keeping my promise, then when the time comes to aid you, I do not consider that my plan has failed. I do not regret having committed myself to aiding you, since I suppose that had I not made the commitment, you would not have assisted me and I should be worse off overall. My evaluation of my plan is unchanged.

Since McClennen does not discuss the difference between evaluations of failed plans and of successful plans, I am not in a position to judge what he believes resolute choice requires in the case of deterrence by nuclear threat. Constrained maximization, as I have characterized it, requires making – and, if necessary, carrying out – the threat. For although a constrained maximizer can be described as choosing among plans, her basis for choice is a single *ex ante* evaluation of their expected outcomes in relation to her exogenously given preferences, and not a set of evaluations from the several perspectives that may arise in the various possible circumstances envisaged in the plan. And this differs from McClennen's account of the basis for resolute choice, when he says, "The case for the disposition to act on plans is thus to be made by reference to the interest that each and every time-defined self has in such an approach, and not simply by reference to what the *ex ante* self judges parametrically to be the superior plan" (*Supra*, p.113).

To pursue this difference here would not only require me to speculate about McClennen's views, but would also lead into some of the deepest unresolved issues in the theory of rational choice. Here I want only to acknowledge that the unease that many persons clearly express with my own work on deterrence may well be related to the fact that in my defense of constrained maximization, I have not distinguished the requirement to act on a failed plan, which is clearly incompatible with evaluating the plan as best from every perspective, from the requirement to constrain one's maximizing behavior in carrying out a plan that does recommend itself from every relevant perspective.[12] McClennen's account of resolute choice among plans may offer an alternative to the approach implicit in my conception of constrained maximization that, without further examination, I do not want to dismiss.

(3) Given a plan, one regiments one's preferences to fit. As McClennen explicitly states, this "Contextual dependency [of preferences] is here to be understood as a 'strategy' to be employed in interaction situations for securing greater benefits" (*Supra*, pp.110–11). The contextually dependent preferences one develops are not, of course, to be confused with the preferences one would have were one to face a comparable situation "*de novo*" (*Supra*, p.109). Are they preferences at all?

I think not. I offer an alternative account. A person represents her desires and beliefs to herself. In their light, she evaluates alternative plans of action; we need not decide here how this evaluation proceeds, and in particular whether it is based on a simple *ex ante* perspective, or on a set of perspectives over the duration and contingencies of the plan. All that we

---

[12] See my "Deterrence, Maximization, and Rationality," *Ethics*, vol. 94 (1984), pp.474–495.

need suppose is that her evaluation is maximizing; she selects a plan that best fulfills her desires given her beliefs.

At this point, and without abandoning or altering her desires and beliefs, she determines her reasons for action, in terms of her plan. The distinction, between a reason for action and a desire, is crucial. Desires inform the preference ordering that determines her choice among plans. Reasons follow from selected plans, and determine her subsequent choices. What tempts us to confuse them is that, in those noninteractive contexts where preference change is of no concern, and in many interactions, preferences over outcomes may be thought directly to determine reasons for acting, because the agent has no ground for departing from straightforward maximization.

McClennen notes that his model is faithful to the principle of Dynamic Consistency, which "calls upon the agent to make choices at each choice point that are consistent with the preferences he has at that point in time." But it violates "a separability principle requiring that what determines preference at any point in a sequence of decisions to be made is what would govern preference at that point, were the agent to confront that choice *de novo*" (*Supra*, p.116). Now I suppose that in choosing on the basis of preference-based plans, an agent satisfies the strongest plausible consistency principle, even though she need not maximize on the basis of her actual preferences, and so need not satisfy McClennen's Dynamic Consistency. And I suppose that separability is, or at least may be, satisfied as a condition on preference, but not on reasons for acting. An agent's reasons for acting are determined against the background of her rationally chosen plans. But her preferences are unaffected, remaining, indeed, as her basis for choosing among plans.

I want to distinguish the evaluation of outcomes that leads to plans from the evaluation of actions that follows from plans. For the former, I employ the vocabulary of desire and preference. For the latter, I employ the vocabulary of practical reason. In making this distinction, I am not denying that explanatory role of the concept of preference in choice behavior, or even that "what must shape choice now is preference now" (*Supra*, p.116). But I am claiming that the explanatory role of preference is indirect; preferences explain plans, which in turn explain choices. By distinguishing the roles of desires and reasons, I provide a richer explanatory and normative framework to accommodate the complexity of rational behavior in the face of both individual preference change and the mutual advantage of constraint. But, to paraphrase McClennen, I am not so concerned with whether my argument is better seen as a reinterpretation of his, or as distinct. For with him, "I see no conflict between what I have suggested here and the *spirit* of his argument" (*Supra*, p.117). Insofar as we differ, our differences will be settled by the further development of the theory of practical rationality that we both recognize to be one of the core issues in contemporary philosophy.

VI

(1) My remaining critics, Christopher Morris and Laurence Thomas, express concerns about the nontuistic root of the enterprise attempted in *Morals by Agreement*. Morris challenges the rationale for assuming what he calls self-interest, but should be called, to avoid misleading implications, nontuism – that each person takes no interest in the interests of those with whom he is interacting. And Thomas challenges the idea that, if one assumes nontuism, one's conclusions about rational constraints will be relevant to a morality for persons whose affective capacities extend to concerns with their fellows. If Morris is right, my argument must be restructured in ways that, he suggests, may leave it incapable of grounding minimax relative concession or the revised Lockean proviso. If Thomas is right, rational choice "ethics" must be abandoned; he would replace it by a theory that relates morality to our actual affective capacities.

Now it seems to me, on reflection, that nontuism plays two somewhat different roles in my argument. On the one hand, I want to be able to say that, even were nontuism true, moral constraints would be rationally grounded. Nontuism offers a worst-case scenario. Suppose persons take no interest in the interests of those with whom they interact; nevertheless, they are rationally required to accept constraints on the pursuit of their concerns, and these constraints are based on the interests of their fellows.

Morris challenges the idea that nontuism represents the worst case; suppose, he says, "a world of individuals who take an interest in the interests of others, albeit a particular kind of interest – for instance, envy, spite, hatred, intolerance. It is this world that threatens morality, and human welfare, more seriously than that of the self-interested amoralist" (*Supra*, p.135). Now in one sense Morris is right; in such a world there would be no morality, since persons would prefer conflict with their fellows, however destructive, to any form of mutual constraint. But human beings could not long endure in such a world. A more realistic world is one in which some persons much of the time, and almost all persons some of the time, are moved by negative, other-directed interests. One lesson of *Morals by Agreement* is that the former should be treated as enemies, lacking any moral standing, because their interests render them unfit to be participants in "a cooperative venture for mutual advantage." And a second lesson, parallel to that mentioned by Morris in note 70 to his paper, is that the rest of us will do better most of the time to curb our negative, other-directed interests, just as we do better to accept constraints on the direct satisfaction of certain of our preferences. And we will do better, even if we lack such positive other-directed interests as sympathy and love, in opposition to our envy and hatred, as long as our predominant interests are nontuistic. A world of persons whose motivation is exclusively or predominantly nontuistic provides, then, the limiting case in which moral constraint can be shown to be generally rational.

A second role for nontuism is to eliminate double-counting. If I, considering us equally fond of cake, prefer that each of us get half, not only to your having a larger share but also to my having it, and if you prefer more cake for yourself to less, whatever I get, then it seems implausible to suppose that a rational and fair division gives you three quarters of the cake and me one quarter. But this may seem an appeal to preanalytic intuitions about justice that, as I explicitly insist, can have no place in the rational choice of theory.

I agree with Morris that nontuism may seem to play other roles in a contractarian morality, which in fact it does not. Contractarianism is, or at least can be, *morally* foundational, in that it offers a justification of morality from premises that, although normative, are not themselves moral. In Morris's terminology, this is to offer a fundamental evaluation, not a foundational justification. And let me emphasize that I do not claim that the theory of rational choice, within which morality is justified, is itself normatively foundational, or indeed that we can make sense of a normatively foundational theory. What contractarianism shows is that moral norms emerge in a mutually advantageous, stable, and voluntary framework of interaction among individuals who accept norms of rationality. But this contractarian justification of morality does not depend on limiting the content of preferences to nontuistic ones. There is no suggestion that morality must be derived from nontuistic preferences because tuistic preferences would be morally loaded. To be sure, a derivation from morally loaded preferences would of course beg the question, but moral loading, at least in my view, would require a moral content to the preferences – for example, by appealing to a preference for just behavior.

The assumption of nontuism, although not necessary for a morally foundational justification, does not have the very damaging consequences that Morris suggests. Suppose, he says, that Adolf exploits Bécassine, and Charles wishes to liberate her. According to Morris, "morals by agreement will not permit him to do so" (*Supra*, p.147). For Charles's interest in Bécassine violates the nontuistic requirement, and so counts for nothing, whether he regards himself in a state of nature or in a moral relationship with respect to Adolf. But this is mistaken. In terms of his interaction with

Adolf, Charles's concern with Bécassine is nontuistic. In any interaction, concerns with the interests of a third party are nontuistic. Charles may, if he pleases, refuse to interact cooperatively with someone who, like Adolf, chooses to exploit a third party. Indeed, his preference for nonexploitation of third parties may be so strong that it would have to be recognized in the terms of any cooperation with others that would afford him minimax relative benefit. To be sure, Charles is not morally required to refuse to cooperate with an exploiter.[13] Nontuism thus does not have the implications for contractarian moral theory that the assumption that all preferences are self-interested or self-directed would have. But is nontuism necessary? It would seem not. For the basic contractarian argument, that it is advantageous for each person to comply with constraints that it would be rational for all to agree to, provided others may be expected to be generally similarly compliant, does not depend in any way on supposing that persons have nontuistic preferences. Rather, it depends only on the Prisoner's Dilemma-creating structural features of interaction. These, to be sure, do impose certain requirements on preferences. In particular, we must suppose that it is not only possible, but not infrequently actually the case, that the preference orderings of individuals over outcomes are dilemma-creating. If our preference orderings over outcomes were always identical then constraint would be unnecessary, and the utilitarian millennium would be ushered in – each, in maximizing her own preference-fulfillment, would be simultaneously maximizing everyone's preference fulfillment. But this condition is not only utopian; it is incompatible with the reflective rationality that manifests our individual autonomy.[14]

In the real world, it seems safe to assume that individuals will differ sufficiently in their preference orderings of outcomes that constraints will be needed, if mutual advantage is not to be forgone. And so the contractarian argument for morality seems firmly grounded, without further specification of the content of our preferences. It is important to show that the argument for morality is compatible with persons having strictly

[13] Those who are critical of America's relations with South Africa may think that they think that Charles is so required. If they do think this (and of course, they may not, while remaining critical of America's relations with South Africa), then, to be consistent, they must also think that America is required not to cooperate with the Soviet Union. Since virtually no one holds that America should cooperate neither with the Soviet Union nor with South Africa, virtually no one consistently thinks that Charles is morally required to refuse to cooperate with Adolf. If I were concerned to reconcile my theory with our moral intuitions, I might want to emphasize this.

[14] There are social theorists, some of whom unfortunately attain power, who endorse this unanimity requirement on preferences; each of these theorists and leaders, however, has sought a rather peculiar form of unanimity – that everyone else share his preferences.

nontuistic preferences, but to do this, we need not assume that our preferences are in fact predominantly nontuistic.

(2) What then of the second role for nontuism, the elimination of double counting? Here Morris brings a quite different objection to bear. Given my endorsement of subjective value, so that each person's good is determined strictly by her considered preferences, no discrimination based on the content of those preferences may justifiably be introduced into the contractarian argument. We may be concerned that persons with a concern for others "may be taken advantage of by moral practices. We may wish to ensure that we be not worsened or disadvantaged by our tuistic concerns" (*Supra*, p.143). And so we may wish to evaluate social institutions and practices, including morality, from the standpoint of our nontuistic preferences. This would give us a fundamental evaluation, not only of morality and society, but also of tuism. But we have no purchase for such an evaluation, given the value relativism endorsed in *Morals by Agreement*. In fundamental evaluation "the premises have an evaluative priority over the conclusion. . . . But it is not possible to hold this if one also subscribes to a subjective account of value . . . [that] denies any such . . . relations of priority amongst the preferences of an individual. No claim can be made that the . . . [tuistic] preferences of a person have an evaluative priority over her . . . [nontuistic] ones" (*Supra*, p.144).

This is a serious objection, and I can meet it only by revising the role of nontuism in my argument. As I now see it, social institutions and practices should be justified by an appeal to a hypothetical agreement based largely on the nontuistic preferences of the parties concerned, because each person expects *ex ante* to benefit if she forgoes the inclusion of her tuistic preferences in determining social arrangements provided others do the same. Double-counting will be ruled out, as, of course, will preferences directed at the frustration of other's preferences. Note that if social institutions and practices are nontuistically based, individuals are in no way prohibited from acting on their tuistic preferences, to the extent that their actions are compatible with the institutions and practices. And such actions will be compatible insofar as they are nonexploitative of the fulfillment of nontuistic preferences, so that persons can judge themselves better off, given their sociability and tuistic preferences, than were they asocial and self-regarding. Positive, but not negative, regard for others will then be furthered.

Given this revision, the exclusion of tuism from the justification of social institutions and practices and so from the public realm rests simply on an empirical fact, if, as I suppose, it is one, about the role that tuistic and nontuistic preferences play in our concerns. We may certainly imagine, or even discover, societies in which this exclusion would not be acceptable to all or a significant portion of the members. In some such cases, of course, we may expect that the public role of tuistic preferences will prove to be the result of a social indoctrination incompatible with individual autonomy, and so one that would not be endorsed in an *ex ante* agreement, or from the standpoint of Archimedean choice. But we may not assume that this must be the case.

We may further suppose, compatibly with this revision, that the exclusion of tuism from the justification of social institutions and practices is to be limited in one particular regard, in the relation between parents and children. The general rationale that I offer for an ongoing intergenerational bargain seems to me to suffice to determine appropriate savings and investment rates but, as I suggest in *Morals by Agreement*, not appropriate provision for the raising of children, given the affective demands involved. If so, then persons, aware of the social character of human reproduction and the essential role of affective bonds in this process, will surely choose *ex ante* to have its needs incorporated into their social institutions and practices in a way that will satisfy minimax relative concession provided that these needs are taken as fixed preferences shared by the members of society. I shall not, however, try to develop this matter further here.

If this general exclusion of tuistic preferences were necessary to derive the determinate results of our enquiry, in particular minimax relative concession and the revised proviso, then these would lack the level of universal applicability I have claimed for them. But I am not persuaded that these principles will fail, even though their implications for social practices and moral standards will in some social settings be significantly different than I have supposed. The acceptance of tuistic preferences, since it does not eliminate the possibility of Prisoner's Dilemma-type structures of interaction, should not undermine the basic contractarian character of my account. If, after taking tuistic concerns into consideration, persons find themselves faced with suboptimal outcomes should each straightforwardly maximize the measure of her considered preferences, then the problems resolved among nontuists by mutual rational agreement and individual constrained maximization will exist also for tuists, and will demand that same resolution.

I should like the revision in the role and status of nontuism that I have just sketched to be considered, not as a fixed alteration in my theory, but as a provisional suggestion. At the present time, it seems to me that this revision is needed to accommodate Morris's objections. But I should of course be pleased to find that a less radical change would suffice.

(3) And so I turn to the very troubling objection advanced by Thomas. "There is a way of doing moral philosophy which goes something like this: If it can be shown that it is rational for perfectly selfish people to accept the

constraints of morality, then it will follow, *a fortiori*, that it is rational for people capable of affective bonds, and thus less selfish, to do so" (*Supra*, p.154). The constraints of morality are shown to be rational for nontuists, and then made emotionally palatable by appealing to our actual affective capacities. But is this so? Thomas claims not, holding that "If there is a set of moral principles which people capable of affective capacities have reason to accept, the explanation for this cannot be that persons with nontuistic preferences would find such principles rationally acceptable" (*Supra*, p.157).

Thomas advances a number of more particular claims that are not, I believe, essential to his main point. He notes, correctly enough, that the content of morality cannot be independent of the particular affective capacities we possess, but this is no objection to my theory, since the particular moral constraints that will be rationally justified will depend on the particular preferences persons have, and these of course will be influenced by their affective capacities. My theory concerns the justificatory structure for morality, and is open with respect to determinate content.

Thomas also argues that in the absence of tuistic affections, moral constraints will be only coercively rational. I agree; indeed, I argue a parallel view at some length, in my discussion of the morals of economic man. And Thomas is of course aware of this. In itself, this observation does not seem damaging to my view. But Thomas goes on to say, "suppose that there is a set of moral principles which both nontuistic persons and persons with affective capacities would both find rational to accept. What should be clear is that these two types of individuals will not be moved to accept these principles for the same reason *cum* motivational explanation" (*Supra*, p.162). The justification of moral principles in nontuistic terms will not carry over for affective tuism, as on my theory it must. Whether tuists and nontuists will accept the same principles is not the point; the point is that whatever principles they accept, they will do so for quite different reasons, so that the demonstration that constraints can be justified to the nontuist will be no part of the rationale for tuistic acceptance of morality. The nontuist will find a ιationale for morality that involves no deep identification on her part with moral principles; they will be alien to her deep sense of self. The tuist, the person capable of being moved by affection for his fellows, will on the other hand view morality as expressive of and even constitutive of his other-directed affections. Valuing participation not only for its consequences but for its own sake, and valuing it for the ways in which it relates human beings one to another, he will value morality as the basis of such participation. And this is to relate morality to what the tuist treats as fundamental in his self-conception.

Thomas claims that on my view a person's "commitment to morality is quite explicitly contingent upon those with whom she interacts having a like commitment" (*Supra*, p.171). We should distinguish a person's unconditional readiness to enter into moral community with her fellows, from her actual acceptance of moral constraint conditional on her expectation that her fellows also accept it; treating commitment as actual acceptance of constraint, Thomas's claim is correct. But this contractarian view of moral commitment does not serve to distinguish the nontuist from the tuist. In emphasizing the essentially reciprocal character of morality, and of the moral community, it reveals what makes moral commitment instrumentally acceptable to a nontuist, and what can make it intrinsically valuable to a tuist.

That the nontuist and the tuist will view and value morality differently is evident. But does this undermine the relevance, for the tuist, of a rationale for morality that does not assume his actual tuistic preferences? I want again to insist, as I have done in *Morals by Agreement*, that such a rationale, far from being irrelevant, is actually essential to the role morality plays for the tuist. But to show this more clearly, in a way that avoids the stronger and mistaken claim that the rationale for morality must depend at bottom on nontuistic preferences, and that also avoids treating nontuistic preferences as intrinsically more basic than tuistic ones, I must return to what I take to be the distinguishing characteristic of human beings – the capacity for semantic representation.

I have claimed that in representing the contents of our beliefs and desires to ourselves, we bring them into relation one with another, and that rationality is thereby thrust upon us. We must make our beliefs and desires coherent. In so doing, we unite them into an ordered whole, and to have one's beliefs and desires so united is to have a sense of one's self. Far from being Hume's bundle of perceptions, the self is a unified set of semantically represented beliefs and desires. At one level, this involves an identification with the content of one's beliefs and desires, as providing one's particular present identity. But reflection makes one aware of this content as changing, in part through sense experience and in part through the very operation of reflection itself. These changes occur against a background set by the overall unification thrust upon us by semantic representation, and this background constitutes one's deeper sense of ongoing identity. To be sure, a change of sufficient magnitude may disrupt the background rather than being accommodated with it, but when this happens a person loses or is uncertain of her sense of self. And so it is the unifying conditions, rather than the particular beliefs and desires that they unify, which play the deep role in maintaining our sense of self, or self-identity, insofar as it can be and is maintained. Now these unifying conditions, I have supposed, must include a principle maximizing a measure defined on our considered preferences – that is, our preferences insofar as they survive the reflective moment in rationality. Utility-maximization is thus one of the core constituents in our sense of self. And this is not a contingent matter, although whether one lives in circumstances that facilitate or even permit the development of a clear sense of self is entirely contingent.

Consider now the significance of interaction for beings whose sense of self is constituted from the conditions unifying their beliefs and desires into a coherent whole, and who therefore are maximizers. Whatever particular interests they may take one in another, for our account has put no constraints on the content of those interests, it can only be a matter of accident, in relation to the sense of self that they bring to interaction, if their endeavors and evaluations are *substantively* harmonious rather than conflicting. Nevertheless, insofar as their circumstances are the Humean ones in which goods, of whatever character, are in variable supply in relation to interaction, each can recognize, in the other, a potential partner in those *formal* harmonizations that I have identified with the market and with cooperative ventures. And this makes possible, for persons with tuistic capacities, a reciprocal positive mutual evaluation, founded not on the particular contingencies of their tuistic feelings, but rather on each person's understanding of the value of partnership in interaction. However, a positive evaluation of one's partner, to become actual rather than merely possible, requires that the interaction meet the demands that one, as a rational utility-maximizer, places upon it. These demands can be jointly met if and only if interaction can be represented as resting on mutually agreed principles, and so, if my argument has been sound, on minimax relative concession. The demand for justice is thus prior to any particular tuistic concerns, in being related to that valuing, of participation and of one's fellow participators, that is most deeply linked to one's sense of self. And we may then suppose, as I do in *Morals by Agreement*, that rational persons characteristically come to develop positive affections and tuistic concerns for those whom they value as fellow participators in cooperative ventures governed by the requirements of justice. But this supposition can now be seen as grounded in an argument that gives no priority to nontuistic preferences, yet equally does not appeal to tuistic concerns, in explaining the rationale for morality.

My defense of a contractarian morality has required me to penetrate into the metaphysics of the self in a way that is at best foreshadowed in *Morals by Agreement*. I should like to think that in so doing I am deepening contractarian theory, but I am aware that I have entered a different and complex area of thought in which I have only begun to outline a position that may seem as controvertible as contractarian morality itself. Let me conclude, however, by asserting the claim implicit in advancing this position, that by reflecting on our capacity for semantic representation we shall be able to ground utility-maximization in a more general account of rationality, as what unifies the beliefs and desires that we represent to ourselves. So conceived, rationality is both supported by and supportive of a methodological individualism in our social theory and a moral individualism that demands agreement at the core of our social practices.

Philosophy, University of Pittsburgh